ST. NORBERT COLLEGE
320.01 M95p
Murphy, Joseph Samson,
3 5109 0002 8990 8

D1173836

POLITICAL THEORY
a conceptual analysis

THE DORSEY SERIES IN POLITICAL SCIENCE

EDITOR NORTON E. LONG *Brandeis University*

MACRIDIS & BROWN *The De Gaulle Republic*

MACRIDIS & BROWN (eds.) *Comparative Politics: Notes and Readings* rev. ed.

DRAGNICH *Major European Governments* rev. ed.

ROBINSON *Congress and Foreign Policy-Making: A Study in Legislative Influence and Initiative* rev. ed.

JACOBINI *International Law: A Text* rev. ed.

MANGONE *The Elements of International Law* rev. ed.

GRIPP *Patterns of Soviet Politics* rev. ed.

MINAR *Ideas and Politics: The American Experience*

MEEHAN *The Theory and Method of Political Analysis*

EDELMANN *Latin American Government and Politics*

JACOB & ATHERTON *The Dynamics of International Organization: The Making of World Order*

SPIRO *World Politics: The Global System*

BROWN & WAHLKE *The American Political System: Notes and Readings*

ROELOFS *The Language of Modern Politics: An Introduction to the Study of Government*

MEEHAN *Contemporary Political Thought: A Critical Study*

FROHOCK *The Nature of Political Inquiry*

MEEHAN *Explanation in Social Science: A System Paradigm*

LUTTBEG *Public Opinion and Public Policy: Models of Political Linkage*

MURPHY *Political Theory: A Conceptual Analysis*

POLITICAL THEORY
a conceptual analysis

JOSEPH S. MURPHY, Ph.D.

1968
THE DORSEY PRESS, HOMEWOOD, ILLINOIS
Irwin–Dorsey Limited, Nobleton, Ontario

First Printing, June, 1968

Library of Congress Catalog Card No. 68-23346

Printed in the United States of America

To
Peg, Lisa, and Susanne

Preface

THIS BOOK differs from conventional approaches to the problems of political theory in several important respects: It is not a chronological record of political thinkers and political movements; it does not suppose that the study of political theory necessarily involves or requires a parallel consideration of political events and historical institutions; it is written from the viewpoint of analytic philosophy; and it construes political theory as an activity whose purpose is the clarification and explication of political concepts.

By far the most commonplace approach to the study of political theory is chronological. Political theorists evidently suppose that the most effective introduction to their discipline is through a study of the political writings of classical figures. It is assumed that political ideas may be grasped only as far as these are seen as part of an intellectual tradition, and that apart from this tradition no good sense can be made of them. Thus, the study of Plato's political thought is said to be a prerequisite to understanding Aristotle, and the study of Aristotle, a necessary condition for understanding Hegel. This assumption seems to me to be mistaken partly on logical and partly on pedagogical grounds. It is not clear, for one thing, either what is to be meant by "understand," or that "understanding" ought to be the goal of political theory. When "understand" is construed as referring to the determination of the truth or logical adequacy of a political theory, *qua* theory, then the intellectual tradition from which the theory is considered to have emerged is irrelevant. Questions of truth and logical adequacy cannot be determined through an examination of a theory's intellectual antecedents, since such questions are, on purely logical grounds, to be decided without reference to the origin of theories. If, on the other hand, by "understanding" a political theory one means apprehending the meaning of the concepts and relations which comprise the theory, then there are no good reasons for supposing that the concepts in any one given theory are any clearer or less contingent upon its predecessors, than another. This justification of the chronological approach, it is easy to see, involves a *reductio ad infinitum* and is, therefore, inadmissible on logical grounds.

Another pedagogical procedure which political theorists have generally followed, and which the present work eschews, rests on the allegation that political theory is much too closely bound up with institutional considerations to be wholly or even partly divorced from them, and that a systematic study of political theory, if justifiable at all, is possible only after the history of the discipline and the institutional contexts in which political ideas arise have been mastered. I think that this view is false and pernicious. The task of this book is to justify the assumption that theories may be considered, studied, analyzed, and criticized independent of the political institutions which are alleged to have come about because of them, or from which they are said to have issued. Furthermore, the conventional assumption is pernicious because it presupposes what has yet to be demonstrated, viz, that there is a definable and coherent relation between political ideas, concepts, and theories on the one hand, and political, economic, and social institutions on the other. In fact, the tendency seems to be to assume something more than a relation among these, but rather to suppose, often tacitly, that the relation in question is a causal one.

The assumption then, on which this book is based, differs from the conventional treatments of the problems of political theory. I propose to analyze critically what seem to me to be the central and pervasive issues of political theory and to do so independent of historical, institutional, and personal considerations. By the latter I mean that it is wholly without relevance to the analysis of a theory that it is articulated by this or that political philosopher under such and such cultural, political, and social conditions. I am concerned with asking if a theory is true and adequate or false and deficient, and stating what my reasons are for saying so.

Admittedly there are serious questions to be raised about this approach. One reasonable counterargument to this proposal might be that theories in politics do not occur simply as intellectual products of isolated and disengaged minds. They are, rather, intellectual responses to social conditions and cannot be understood apart from them. I suspect that an objection of this sort reveals a confusion between theory and ideology.

If political theories are construed as ideologies—not an unexceptional construction in the history of the subject—then questions of truth or logical adequacy are not relevant to them, since ideologies function as rationalizations for political action, the real justification for which is based on practical considerations. Similarly, ideologies may be understood as political myths propagated to evoke emotions or generate activity on behalf of some political position or policy. Truth and logical adequacy, unless these are pragmatically interpreted, are, once again, not to the point.

Theories and ideologies, then, are two quite different sorts of things. Part of my task is to decide how they differ, what sorts of criteria may be offered in making such decisions, how such criteria may be justified, and how, in the past, the confusion between an ideology and a theory has led to problems which are easily resolvable when the distinction is made.

One of the more obviously dominant characteristics of classical political theories is the seemingly contingent relations which they have to metaphysical and ontological systems. Only rarely in classical thought does one find an admittedly major figure discussing political concepts or political systems apart from the general *Weltanshauung* to which he subscribes. Political philosophy has, in this respect, appeared to be a mere afterthought in the grand metaphysical speculations of the classical philosophers. The guilt for the alleged decline of political thinking in recent years has been laid at the doorstep of the positivists, who are thought to have destroyed political theory when they critically and, some have said, convincingly bared the metaphysical foundations of the traditional philosophical enterprise; when the deductive, rationalist edifice crumbled, the political facade came tumbling down with it. This account of the decline, if there has been a decline, of political theory is fraught with difficulties; yet leaving these aside and considering only the relation which existed, and which appears no longer to exist, between philosophical and political theorizing, there is one important question to be asked: Does political theory necessarily require (as a necessary condition) a general way of looking at the world which is itself unpolitical in character? I think that it always has required such overviews. The philosophical commitments and presuppositions made by political theorists have not always been made explicit nor have political speculations and their philosophical assumptions always been consistent with each other. What has changed is the way in which philosophy proceeds and what it takes to be its task. With the rise of analytic philosophy, particularly during the past 50 years of Anglo-American philosophy, new and fruitful ways of looking at old problems have emerged. These new techniques and newly devised instruments of analysis have had, and are now having, considerable effect in other disciplines. The influence of the now absorbed and defunct school of logical positivists, for example, has been felt in all the social sciences, both in the method and substance of their disciplines. As the logical apparatus of analytic philosophy is made more refined and as it becomes more self-critical, the sophistication of these instruments of analysis will provide more fruitful ways of looking at old problems in political theory. If philosophy can no longer provide a metaphysical foundation from which political prescriptions can be deduced, it does at least provide the political theorist with a critical framework for analyzing central concepts in political thinking.

The locution "analytic philosophy" is systematically ambiguous; a multitude of different sorts of techniques and procedures with rather different histories and purposes fly her banner. These different kinds of analyses are more interesting to academic philosophers than they are to political theorists. I have characterized my interpretation of analysis as "therapeutic," not because I wish to distinguish it from this or that style of doing philosophy, but because the goal shared by all forms of analysis seems to be to "set things right again." The use of an analytic tool requires, so far as I am concerned, no further justification than the fact that it does the job it is intended to do, viz, it sets things right again. It is germane to ask "what things?" The possibilities are two: either our ways of thinking about political problems are altered, the institutional occasion for the problem vanishes, and we simply recognize it as a problem no longer; or analysis provides us with procedures for changing the institutions or policies themselves. The latter task has long been considered by political theorists as a genuine objective of political theorizing. The former alternative has been interpreted in two ways. Perplexing issues may be overcome through rational inquiry where the issue in question is thought to rest on a logical or linguistic muddle, an intellectual confusion, a mistaken judgment about what the facts are, or some combination of these; or a political problem may be treated as a psychological (rather than intellectual) aberration which calls for treatment similar to that given anyone suffering from compulsive or obsessive behavior. It is this second possibility which has given substance to the charge that the therapeutic dimension of analytic philosophy leads to nihilism when applied to problems in political theory. But if the inquiry adheres to national principles and criteria, and if the analysis is directed towards discovering and correcting conceptional muddles or examining the ways in which different theoretical enterprises are confounded, the charge does not apply.

What is the relation between political theory as generally conceived and the inquiry in which I am here proposing to engage? Political theory has been variously interpreted (not always explicitly) as a descriptive enterprise; or as having a prescriptive function; or as a persuasive or programmatic procedure urging people to support or eschew a policy or program; or as metaphysical, viz, as consisting of a set of propositions about political goals or political behavior which are believed true though no empirical data could in principle be offered in support of them. By conceiving of political theory as therapeutic, I do not intend to be taken as recommending an alternative which excludes conventional possibilities. On the contrary, by therapeutic I mean that the theory purports to be critical, a metatheory as it were, which stands outside the array of procedures which belong to the widely dissimilar enterprises collectively characterized as political theory. Its function is to examine these procedures according to criteria which are logical or methodological rather than political in character.

The criteria used in any given analysis depend on the ends seen as proper within the structure of specific theories. Once a theory is revealed to be essentially descriptive, the methodological apparatus governing the use of empirical political facts will apply. It will, in this context, make good sense to ask whether or not the theory is true. If it is true when evaluated in accordance with conventional, generally accepted criteria of empirical adequacy, it is to be retained, and if not, then not. If a theory is intended, on the other hand, not as a description, but as ideology or a rationalization, then other criteria apply. And once the character of a theory is revealed, it is to be examined and analyzed according to the purposes which occasioned it and the assumptions and presuppositions on which it is based.

My fundamental assumption is the simple proposition that it is pedagogically sound to teach students of political theory to *do* political theory rather than simply train students of classical political literature.

I am indebted to my many friends and colleagues at Brandeis University, and among them especially Herbert Marcuse, John Roche, Norton Long, Eugene Meehan, and Henry Aiken. It is, I think, safe to say that in characteristic fashion, all will be ardently critical of the contents of this book. Of all, however, I am deeply indebted to Harold Weisberg for a decade of friendship, support, advice, and unfailing *menschlichkeit*. Others from whom I have learned much include John J. Sullivan and Frank Manuel of New York University, David Kettler of Ohio State, E. V. Walter of Boston University, Felix Oppenheim of the University of Massachusetts, John Passmore of Australian National University, Israel Scheffler of Harvard, and William Gorham and John Gardner of the Department of Health, Education, and Welfare.

Washington, D.C. JOSEPH S. MURPHY
May, 1968

Table of Contents

1

What is political theory?

A RANDOM SAMPLING of the *apologia* which preface the works of modern political theorists offers us some measure of security—all are agreed that whatever else might be involved in writing and thinking *about* politics, the precise character of the discipline cannot be described or defined in a neat or elegant way. One author claims, "As a general rule it is a mistake to attempt a precise definition of a subject before starting on the investigation of it. What the investigator can do is to give a provisional indication of the general direction in which he is going to start, while reserving to himself the right to extend, restrict, or modify his field of study as the argument seems to require."[1]

Professor Thomas Cook argues that the character of a discipline reflects the character of the data with which that discipline must deal. Therefore: "There is neither neatness nor simplicity to the human relations of political association. Equally, thus far there has not been neatness and simplicity in political theory nor agreement among theorists on a generalized description or explanation of the relationships in which political society consists. Indeed, much of the interest and stimulation to be discovered in the study of political theory derives from the extreme complexity and intractability of the data with which the political theorist deals."[2]

The implication of this previous statement seems to be that clarity and

---

[1] G. C. Field, *Political Theory* (London: Methuen & Co., Ltd., 1956), p. xi.

[2] Thomas Cook, *The Study of Political Theory* (New York: Random House, 1955), p. 1.

distinctness in political theory is at least theoretically possible. Professor Sheldon Wolin suggests that the very nature of the discipline is such that no definition of political philosophy, in the conventional senses of definition, is intended or, for logical reasons, possible.

Political philosophy, he says, is not an essence with an eternal nature. "It is . . . a complex activity which is best *understood* by analyzing the many ways that the acknowledged masters have practiced it. No single philosopher and no one single historical age can be said to have defined it conclusively, any more than any one painter or school of painting has practiced all that we mean by painting."[3]

It ought to be clear that *understanding* what is involved in the meaning of a concept does not exhaust what is meant by *definition*. There are many different kinds of definition. Wolin is saying that one sort of definition which we ought not to be looking for, which is, as it were, inappropriate for the concept in question, consists of specifying the essential properties which the activity called "political theory" must possess for it to be called political theory, such that no other activity exhibits those properties.

In other words, understanding what a thing or activity is may be possible despite the fact that we cannot offer a definition of the sort that requires the specification of the essence of the thing or state of affairs denoted by the concept. Every child *knows* what a horse is, at least in the sense that he can point to one and he knows a fair number of linguistic contexts in which the word may be appropriately used. We would want to say that he knows or *understands* all this without requiring that he be able to define the word—a task which is, in fact, quite difficult.[4]

But the history of political theory is replete with efforts directed toward discovering *essences* denoted by critical concepts, or toward discovering the eternal and immutable meanings of political concepts. This enterprise is doomed from the start because it mistakes the logic which governs the use of such concepts. It is simply wrong to suppose that words have meanings

> . . . in the same sort of sense as that in which children have parents. Thus, if little Willie was deposited in a telephone booth at an early age, nobody may

---

[3] Sheldon Wolin, *Politics and Vision—Continuity and Innovation in Western Political Thought* (Boston: Little, Brown & Co., 1960), p. 1–2. My italics.

[4] According to Webster: "A large, solid-hoofed, herbivorous mammal (*Equus caballus*) . . ."

know who his parents are, but it is certain that he had parents, and it is possible to start an enquiry with a view to discovering their identity. This may be wholly or partially unsuccessful. The evidence may be lost or the detectives may not be clever enough to discover it or to see the relevance of it. Nevertheless this is the kind of enquiry we know well enough how to conduct, and so it is reasonable to suppose that, if words and especially nouns always have meanings, we should, if we are pertinacious and fairly clever, usually be able to unearth those meanings.[5]

But it is clear that words do not have meanings in the sense indicated. The meaning of the concept "political theory" and the meaning of the concepts which are considered to be part of political theory ("justice," "obligation," "state") are uncovered not by seeking some eternal and immutable essence which the expression denotes, but, rather, by examining some of the ways in which the expression is used. Presumably the collection or sum of such usages exhaust the meaning of the concept in question. It is easy to see that a concept like "political theory" is not easily exhausted in terms of its possible usages; but by the same token its meaning is not so easily decided, and we must not be too concerned at this point if we discover considerable ambiguity in its use in our language. It may well be that ambiguity may be evidence of the rich variety of tasks which the concept performs in our language, though, of course, we must not rest content merely with having said so.

What does political theory mean to those who are engaged in the activity generally denoted by that name? That is to ask, what are the properties of the activity called "political theorizing"?

POLITICAL THEORY AS METAPHYSICS

We are obliged, by virtue of custom and utility, to begin our inquiry with Plato. We are not here interested in Plato's political theory as such, but rather in what he takes political theory to be. For although it cannot be said that Plato draws a fine distinction between questions which are moral in character and those which are political[6] (and, in fact, between

---

[5] T. D. Weldon, *Vocabulary of Politics* (London: Penguin Books, Ltd., 1953), p. 18.

[6] No good will come from attempting a definition of "political" or "politics." Even working definitions tend either to include factors which one would not ordinarily want to call "political" or they exclude qualities which we ordinarily

issues which are neither moral, nor political, but metaphysical), he is after all concerned with the political dimension of social life so far as political relations are part of the fabric of all human relations.

The words "political theory" as such do not appear in the Platonic text. For Plato, politics is the art of ruling, the royal art, and thought about the activity or the principles which govern the activity are logically on a par with the principles which govern any human enterprise, from medicine to horsemanship. The principles which govern the successful pursuit of any art consist in *knowing that* something is the case, or ought to be the case, and *knowing how* that particular state of affairs is to be brought about. Therefore, our first question concerns what Plato thinks is the character of knowledge, for that will be our path to discovering what he takes political knowledge to be.

The objects of knowledge, whether political, moral, or metaphysical, are, according to Plato, eternal and immutable. "To know," in this special sense, is to know an unchanging reality, to know, that is, universals rather than particular things. Now this is neither a strange nor a difficult notion. Consider what might be involved in trying to answer the question: "What sorts of things can I properly be said to know." For the most part one would be tempted to reply that he knows how to do a great many things—tie his shoes, drive a car, speak French, hold his liquor. But it is clear that these answers will not satisfy the sense of the question. What is called for here is an answer to a question about "knowing that" rather than about "knowing how."[7] If it is to be said (by me or others) that I *know* something, in the sense of *knowing that* something

---

think of as "political." Consider Wolin's attempt at specifying what he takes "politics" to include: "(*a*) a form of activity centering around the quest for competitive advantage between groups, individuals, or societies; (*b*) a form of activity conditioned by the fact that it occurs within a situation of change and relative scarcity." To this point of Wolin's definition a college football game would have to be considered a political activity. The third ingredient is: "a form of activity in which the pursuit of advantage produces consequences of such a magnitude that they affect in a significant way the whole society or a substantial part of it." Resisting the temptation to say that the annual Rose Bowl competition is compatible with this requirement, it is enough to point out that it is well nigh impossible to know what "affect in a significant way" is supposed to mean, unless we are supplied with further, somewhat more precise criteria of what is to be counted as being "significant." Cf. Wolin, *op. cit.*, p. 10.

[7] For an extensive analysis of this important distinction see Gilbert Ryle, *The Concept of Mind* (New York: Barnes & Noble, Inc., n.d.), chap. ii, pp. 25–61.

is the case, it must be that I could not be mistaken about the state of affairs in question. When one says that he *knows* that something is the case he, presumably, wants to be clear about the claim that he has made. He knows rather than thinks, suspects, supposes, or whatever weaker word indicating a weaker sense of "know" one might use. To know, it is argued in this sense, is to know with certainty.[8] Since all the judgments made about the empirical, everyday world are as contingent as that world itself, no statement which is a description of the empirical world can be established with the certainty which is required for a proposition to be necessarily true. The everyday world is after all a contingent one, and what may be said truthfully about that world today will not necessarily be true a short time from now. Nor, of course, is it *necessarily* true now, for anything in nature could be other than it is without involving a contradiction. It follows then that the occasion on which one may legitimately claim that he *knows* that something is the case occurs when the proposition known is a formal or analytic statement whose truth is necessary; that is, its denial is self-contradictory and it is independent of experience in the sense that its truth does not depend upon experience.

Now the propositions which may be considered proper objects of knowledge for Plato are analytic. That is to say, they are as certain and irrefutable as the truths of mathematics and logic. In fact, a good portion of what can count as objects of knowledge are mathematical and logical propositions. But they are not *all* of that order, and what else is to be counted as a proper object of knowledge we will examine below. The first property then of knowledge in general and, derivatively, of political knowledge is that whatever is claimed to be true is claimed to be necessarily true.

The second property of knowledge is that it is of universals. This property is related to the first. To say that "I know that *p* is red," is to

[8] It is sometimes observed that this analysis of the logic of the word "know" is compatible with ordinary usage because of our ordinary disposition to revise a judgment in which we claimed to know that something is the case, but where we were in fact mistaken. For example: one says "I know that *x* is true." After examination it is demonstrated that *x* is not true. We are generally inclined to say: "I *thought* I knew that *x* was the case"; we do not ordinarily say: "I know that *x* was the case, but I was mistaken." A philosophical skeptic is inclined to go further: he might allege that all statements which are not analytical are contingent statements and therefore not in the class of statements about which one may claim knowledge.

assert a contingent statement about a particular thing. For Plato the predicate or quality attributed either essentially or accidentally to the particular thing in question constitutes a higher order of existence than the particular thing itself. This is so, it appears, because the knowledge of *redness* is of a universal quality which "exists" independent of whether there are examples of particular shades of red in the world or not. This view is not an especially strange one if we consider that it is not unreasonable to suppose that we know what a quality like *red* or *triangular* is independent of experience. For example, we all know precisely what a triangle *is,* though we have never seen an object which is precisely a triangle. By the same token, we all know what red is, in some sense or other, though the extent of our experience is with shades of red. For Plato what can be known with certainty (and, therefore, said to be known in the only acceptable sense of the word) must be universal and independent of empirical contingencies.

Thirdly, man's knowledge of ultimate reality (of the universals, or essences, or archetypes) encompasses a class of proposition in which certain conventional distinctions do not occur. Plato does not separate ethical, moral, political, logical, aesthetic, and metaphysical truths. The Platonic heaven contains them all as well as the relations which obtain among them; it is, as it were, a promiscuous heaven.

We may then say that a proposition functions as an object of knowledge, for Plato, if it is certain, immutable, and universal, and that if it possesses those properties its precise character (normative, prescriptive, and so on) is irrelevant.

The next step in trying to determine what Plato takes political theory to be consists of trying to determine how knowledge and political knowledge come about. That is to say, though we now may say that we know something about the properties of those propositions for which we may claim knowledge, we must go one step further to ask the question: How do we know what we know?

In our naïve moments we have few doubts about the sorts of things that we encounter in our everyday world. Only children, madmen, and philosophers may doubt the evidence of their senses with impunity. There is generally no question in one's mind about whether the table on which they are writing or the chair in which they are sitting is there. But when I say, if I am called upon to do so, that I know that I am sitting in this chair right now or that I know that there are fish in the sea, do I know something in Plato's sense of "know"? Obviously not; the propositions for which I claim knowledge are contingent, rather than necessarily certain, and they are particular, or generalized on the basis of particulars, rather than universal. In short, what I know about myself and about the world in which I live, the everyday world of people and things, are not, according to Plato, real and proper objects of knowledge. Whatever else might be required as a condition of knowledge, empirical observations and statements which are based on such experience will not do. For Plato, only truths which are deduced from axioms and postulates are the essential ingredients, the bare furniture, as it were, of our minds. The truth is discovered not by investigating the tangential and fragmentary illusions of the everyday world, but by explicating what is already part of our consciousness, by rendering explicit the truths implicit in the innermost recesses of our intellect.

Are all men equally capable of knowing the truth according to Plato? The answer to this question is not so clear as superficial readers of Plato sometimes pretend. What is clear is that there is a discrepancy among men with respect to quantity and character of their knowledge. We learn that very few of the best of men do, in fact, begin to approach the pinnacle or apex of human knowledge. The fact of life which seems to have impressed itself upon Plato is that men differ among themselves with respect to temperament and character and that these differences are reflected in the extent to which different men utilize or exploit the rational or intellectual dimensions of their lives. It follows then that there are some who are preeminent in knowledge and virtue; that there are men who know what there is to know, men whose character and intelligence exceed by far that of the common run of the species. Such men are the natural rulers of society–Plato named them philosopher kings. When we come to examine what they know and how they know what they know we see why it is easy to justify the political elitism that Plato proposes as the best and most rational form of government.

The philosopher king knows a set of propositions which are true, necessary, and immutable. He knows the nature of ultimate reality, or, at any rate, he knows more of it than any other man. Among these propositions are normative judgments as well, for as we have seen Plato does not distinguish between analytical statements and statements of value.

The Good and the Just are as much objects of knowledge for the philosopher king as Being itself. Thus, the philosopher knows both how the world really *is* and how it *ought* to be; and, since part of what is involved in knowing what ought to be done, is *doing* what ought to be done, the philosopher king knows and does what is best.[9]

To the extent that others are fitted, by character or intelligence, to perform other tasks, to that degree can their preeminence in the performance of certain tasks establish their position in the society. Plato's point is that a man is obliged to live out his life within the narrow range of possibilities dictated by nature. We are not, in the course of this discussion, concerned with the content or value of Plato's demonstration of political elitism as such. For the proof of political elitism is a valid one provided that we agree to accept Plato's basic premises. Thus we can see that the following argument depends upon certain assumptions which are far from self-evident, but are nonetheless perfectly rational presuppositions:

1. To know that something is the case is to *know* with certainty.
2. Knowledge (of this immutable sort) is available only to some—and *ultimate* knowledge to some *one* or other.
3. Propositions about *what is* and propositions about *what ought to be* are not logically heterogeneous statements.
4. The objects of knowledge, properly speaking, are eternal and immutable forms, idealizations of what there *is* in the universe.
5. The ideal political system is knowable (just as the best medicine for a given disease is knowable) though it may not be in fact known.
6. To discover the best (most appropriate) medicine for a given disease, one consults the man who knows the most about such things—knows, that is, general principles about diseases. By the same token, to find out what sort of political system is best, we

[9] The Platonic aphorism "knowledge is virtue" can be interpreted in one of several ways. The statement could be treated as a straightforward empirical description, that is, as a behavioral maxim based on systematic observations of human behavior. If it is seen in this way, and if it is taken to mean that men do invariably what they know they ought to do, then it is clearly false. On the other hand, if the statement is taken as a linguistic recommendation, as an appeal to use the word "know" only in contexts where one does actually do what one knows one ought to do, then it is true, in the way in which any analytic statement is true.

ought to rely on the expertise of those who have the requisite character and knowledge.

7. A further analogy that illuminates the relationship between ruling and other tasks is the captaincy of ships. Just as the passengers of a ship put their lives and destinies in the hands of the captain whose knowledge of navigation is, by virtue of the fact that he is captain, greater than that of anyone else, so similarly are we warranted in recognizing the essential rightness of obeying the commands of the captain of the ship of state.

Now, these assumptions and arguments are faulty. They display a variety of logical and analytic mistakes. But it is not our purpose here to expose these. The question with which we began is: What is political theory? How have we answered this question?

We have used Plato as an example of one of the very important ways of answering the question. For Plato, political theory is a deductive, metaphysical, and ethical inquiry, the purpose of which is to discover the ideal state, the ultimate and most important of human institutions in its most appropriate and immutable form. Political theory is a theoretical enterprise, carried on independently of empirical considerations, and requires the precise specification of the rules which ought ideally to govern human behavior and the forms of institutional life most appropriate to the sort of characteristics men have by nature. The division of the soul into three parts, a division political philosophers have interpreted as being nothing more than a fitting ideology justifying the fragmentation of society into parts based on a convenient division of labor, is the most revealing aspect of what is involved in Plato's method.

The critical questions for the political theorist are: What is the real, essential nature of human life? What are the basic and irreducible properties and characteristics of the human personality? In short, what are men really like? Once it becomes possible to establish the categories into which the specie falls, then it is possible to ask the further question: What sort of creature have we decided men are? Given this set of truths about the nature of the world (among which are creatures called "human beings") what can we deduce about the conditions under which this species can best flourish?

This is Plato's problem and, more importantly, his procedure. Political theory is essentially metaphysics. We are asked to look at the world and discover the general and eternally valid principles which govern the world. Among the totality of true propositions are those which concern themselves with the way in which men ought to lead their lives. Once the true character of man is established we need only consider what sort of institutions would be most appropriate for that sort of creature, and we are in that way, involved in that part of metaphysics which we call "political theory."

This is our first and perhaps most influential answer to the question: What is political theory?

POLITICAL THEORY AS SCIENCE OF BEHAVIOR

The temptation in a construction of this sort is to exaggerate the differences between Plato and Aristotle. Yet their views on many important issues are similar, their approach to and conception of the nature of political inquiry are instructively different. Plato's transcendental concept of knowledge led him to suppose that whatever else might be involved in political inquiry, political theory, as with any intellectual endeavor whose object is knowledge, must eschew the merely temporal and empirical. Political knowledge must be concerned with the eternally enduring principles of political life and bears no important relationship to the actual institutions and activities of everyday life. Such views led Plato away from any sort of serious analysis of existing political realities and away from the historical antecedents of those realities contemporaneous to his own life. Political thought was essentially intellectual rather than empirical. It is easy to see that if science is thought of as an activity at least partly empirical and in some sense descriptive of the everyday world, then Plato has no room in his system for scientific inquiry, and that whatever other virtues his view of political inquiry might exhibit, it cannot be described as scientific.

Plato, we noted, is entirely unhistorical. He is altogether unconcerned with the political experience of the peoples in his own past or present world. If political philosophy is the construction of the perfect state according to ideal categories, then the empirical world has nothing to teach us, for idealizations are not to be found in experience. Just as the figures of the geometrician are purely formal and are only approximated in the empirical world, so are political idealities products of the philosopher king's intellect; and these products are only poorly represented in the world of natural objects. When we alter the epistemological assumptions attributed to Plato and consider a theory which allows for the possibility of contingent knowledge, we see immediately how one's view of political theory is, in turn, altered.[10]

Aristotle provides us with the first systematic effort to establish political theory as an empirical enterprise. What are the conditions for establishing political theory as a science? First, it is necessary, one assumes, to draw a rigorous distinction between statements of fact and statements of value. Second, the character of political knowledge must be seen as contingent upon the facts of political life. Third, general assertions or universal statements must be buttressed by hard empirical data rather than issue from purely speculative premises. And finally, there must be an area of human life or institutional forms in human society which can be, at least theoretically, isolated and treated as essentially *political* in character. Aristotle seeks to establish a discipline in which these conditions are fulfilled. On the difference between Plato's approach on the one hand and Aristotle's on the other, consider Pollock's observation: "A balloon is a very fine thing if you are not anxious to go anywhere in particular; a road is common, and the travelling on it may be tedious, but you come to the journey's end. Plato is a man in a balloon who hovers over a new land, and now and then catches a commanding view of its

---

[10] Changing assumptions about the character of political knowledge alters one's view of substantive political issues as well as being reflected in a different conception of political theory itself. For example, if the paradigm of knowledge is mathematical, then the undemocratic concept of a philosopher king makes perfectly good sense. Democratic procedures are hardly appropriate in trying to discover who is better of two mathematicians. There are, presumably, objective criteria or, at least, generally accepted canons of professional competence and the decision about performance is made by peers who, if not equally knowledgeable, are at least approximately so. What is more, certain undemocratic practices are entirely reasonable in a society where the truth can be (and apparently is) actually known to the ruler and when the ruler, by virtue of possessing true knowledge, acts in accordance with it. It makes no sense to discuss, examine, analyze, compromise and try, in general, to reach a consensus as in democratic societies, if the truth is known and where action is based on true propositions. Freedom of thought and discussion are appropriate procedures, perhaps necessary rights, only if it is supposed that there are no eternal and immutable truths (or if there are, they have yet to be discovered) and where every person's private interest is as clear (or unclear) a guide to public policy as every other person's.

contours through the mist. Aristotle is the working colonist who goes there and makes the roads."[11]

Or, put somewhat more extensively:

> . . . the materials Aristotle starts with are the materials he finds at hand, the materials of Greek culture and civilization. This is obvious in the *Politics,* where he starts from a slave economy, from the Greek form of the family, from the Greek status of women, from the Greek city-state, political organization. But it is equally true in the *Ethics,* where he begins with the norms, standards, and ideals of Greek culture and Greek tradition. . . .
>
> The very core of the Aristotelian attitude toward the conduct of man's life is this insistence that we must start with what we find at hand, and perfect the tendencies that are actually there. We must set out with our own particular cultural heritage. In comparison with Plato . . . this gives us the impression of a much more limited horizon. There is in Aristotle none of the free play of the imagination to be found in the *Republic,* there is no talk of "remolding human nature" in the light of a more perfect model than that used by God in creating man. There is a sense of the limits imposed by the encountered facts of experience, and of a bondage to them.[12]

It would be an error, however, if Aristotle were made out to be a conscious advocate of an extreme and uncritical empiricism. If his techniques of analysis and classification required empirical commitments, he was prepared to make them, but it was analysis to which he was wedded. Yet, his preoccupation was with the facts of everyday political life, with the forms of political organization which he encountered as ingredients of his own political experience, with the practical and empirical dimension of political reality, and with the subtle distinctions between fact and value, between the practical and the theoretical. All this serves to make Aristotle the first political *scientist.* Political theory must therefore be seen as doing the job that *theory* performs in any scientific enterprise. It constitutes that class of propositions which state in systematic fashion the universal facts of political life and political institutions. Aristotle does not take the task of political theory to consist of recommendations for the radical remolding of political life. Thus we find him, in the *Ethics* claiming that "It is proper to state the accepted views on the subject, and

---

[11] Sir Frederick Pollock, *An Introduction to the History of the Science of Politics* (London: Macmillan & Co., Ltd., 1935), p. 16.

[12] John Herman Randall, *Aristotle* (New York: Columbia University Press, 1960), pp. 247–48.

after thoroughly discussing them, to establish the truth of all, or at least the most important of the popular opinions."[13] For Aristotle, the proper method of the political scientist consists in the systematic observations of political events and the systematic classification of beliefs about political life and institutions. Whatever else might be involved in doing political science, in being engaged in political inquiry, changing the world is not a part of it.

In the preceding pages we have used the methods of Plato and Aristotle to prepare the way for a somewhat more elaborate analysis of two major traditions juxtaposed. What we have not done, except perhaps indirectly, is to contrast the political theories of Plato and Aristotle. Such a task would exceed our concerns here. We are interested only in seeing each as representing in some important respects vastly different views of what is involved in *doing* political theory, and in recognizing that such differences are reflections of profoundly different ways of looking at the world.[14]

POLITICAL THEORY AND SUBSTANTIVE POLITICAL ISSUES

There exists both historically and contemporaneously a considerable body of responsible opinion to the effect that theory in politics consists of the methods and techniques of political manipulation, or that it is essentially an ideological expression of deeper and more influential social processes. The latter of these alternatives we shall consider later and the former we shall turn to by introducing the most formidable exponent of that point of view, Machiavelli. At first glance it would seem reasonable to think of Machiavelli's theory of politics as an extension of the empirical and inductive methods of Aristotle. For the burden of Machiavelli's work in *The Prince* and *The Discourses* appears to be that of an advisor who draws upon a vast collection of universalized behavioral

---

[13] *Nicomachian Ethics VII,* chap. 1: 1145b, 3–6.

[14] Though we have used Aristotle as our prototype of a view of politics which follows from the admission that political life is practical and political knowledge is contingent, it is easy to see that other theorists who differ from Aristotle in many other respects may, nonetheless, be considered as legitimate inheritors of Aristotle's view of politics. John Stuart Mill is perhaps the best example of an empiricist philosopher who tries to work out the political implications of his basic epistemology. The relationship between his philosophy and politics is reasonably clear.

maxims in order to guide the statesman in the exercise of his craft. So far as the maxims are derived from Machiavelli's observation of human behavior in general, and political behavior in particular, to that degree his procedure appears to be inductive and empirical.[15] We turn now to Machiavelli's science of statecraft and consider what is involved in his novel vision of politics.

In *The Prince,* Machiavelli expresses what has been described as the *principle of imitation:*

> Nobody must be surprised if in my discussion of new principalities . . . I make reference to very imposing examples; for as men nearly always follow the path traced by others and proceed in their actions by imitation—though they cannot quite keep to the path or reach the full merits of those whom they imitate—a prudent man ought always to walk in the path traced out by great men and imitate those who are most excellent, so that if he does not attain their prowess, he may at least achieve something of the flavor of it.[16]

Thus he is able to write in the Dedication of *The Prince,* ". . . I have been unable to find among my possessions anything which I hold so dear or esteem so highly as that knowledge of the deeds of great men which I have acquired through a long experience of modern events and a constant study of the past."

The force of the past and its value to us can be established only if we are prepared to grant a further assumption of considerable importance, namely, that the future is a duplication or replica of the past. This assumption is the second of Machiavelli's theses. Consider the following passage from *The Discourses:*

> Whoever considers things present and things past will easily understand how the same appetites and humours are and always have been incident to all states and people, so that by diligently examining the course of former ages it is an easy matter for men to forsee what is going to happen in any commonwealth, and not only to provide such remedies against future evils as their predecessors did, but (if there be no precedent) to strike out new ones on the basis of the existing analogies. But since considerations of this kind are too often neglected or little understood, or are beyond the knowledge of those

---

[15] He recommends and persuades, not as a priest, but as a physician. He prescribes as a doctor would: "If you desire x, then do y." And this is so because when men in the past have done x, y has come about.

[16] Quoted in Herbert Butterfield, *The Statecraft of Machiavelli* (New York: Macmillan Co., 1956), p. 29.

men who govern states, it comes to pass that the same evils and inconveniences take place in all ages of history.[17]

And once again the same thesis restated even more sharply: "Wise men say (and perhaps not unjustly) that in order to form an impression of what is yet to come, we ought to consider what is already passed; for there is nothing in this world at present, or at any other time, but has and will have its counterpart in antiquity; which happens because these things are operated by human beings who, having same passions in all ages, must necessarily behave uniformly in similar situations."[18]

Forgetting for a moment the dubious validity of the inference that similar personality structure implies (necessarily) uniform political behavior, consider the apparently unambiguous empirical assumptions and procedures. He argues that politics, like other sciences, may proceed if there exists some uniformity in nature and in human institutions; if, that is, we may validly assume that the future will be like the past and that therefore our inductive procedures will work. These assumptions, taken together with his objectivity and the seemingly value-free character of his method, and his refusal to take conventional morality into account, all suggest that Machiavelli represents a paradigm for the scientific political theorist. And yet, at the critical moment and in a crucial respect he falls short of the mark. As Sir Frederick Pollock observes: ". . . Machiavelli, full as he is of observation and practical wisdom, is only on the threshold of political science. His doctrine is a theory of the preservation of States rather than a theory of the State."[19]

Why is this so? It is so because Machiavelli's method is the method of the engineer or the physician rather than of the scientist. He thinks of history, of the raw data of politics, not as an undifferentiated mass from which general principles of political life and institutions are to be derived, but rather as the source of practical precepts and rules of political action, as though history were a book of rules which, when one encounters a given practical issue, one consults to discover the clear and unambiguous solution. Or history is comparable to a book of remedies which one consults when one falls ill. As Butterfield observes:

[17] *Discourses* I, 39.

[18] *Discourses* III, 43.

[19] Sir Frederick Pollock, *op. cit.*, p. 47.

His [Machiavelli's] doctrine of imitation does in fact mean the imitation of definite specimens of successful policy, with a particular stress on the actions of great men and on the examples of antiquity. Speaking roughly and stating the case perhaps at its crudest, we may say that the position he takes up rests on the view that if a certain expedient has proven successful in some conjuncture in the past, the trick ought not to be forgotten in a world in which historical situations are being constantly repeated. Studying history in examples, Machiavelli draws lessons from striking incidents, and catches the very tones of the school teacher who rounds off the story with a moral, saying perpetually: "From this short narrative we may observe. . . ."; "It behoves all princes, therefore," . . . and then will follow some political maxim.[20]

The mere fact that history exhibits uniqueness is not in itself sufficient to show that Machiavelli has gone astray. For despite the unique character of historical events, general principles are nonetheless derivable. But such derivation is possible and valuable only if history is not restricted to a succession of object lessons. Machiavelli fails because he does not offer us the principles and procedures for analyzing political institutions, but merely a handbook of recipes the object of which is merely the baking of a political pie.

Thus a political thinker to be a political theorist must go beyond the immediate, concrete and particular phenomenon to the abstract, general, and theoretical propositions in terms of which political life may be understood.

POLITICAL THEORY AS IDEOLOGY

The classical analysis of the concept of ideology is the work of the German sociologist, Karl Mannheim. According to Mannheim there are two distinctly different meanings of the term "ideology," the *particular* and the total. The *particular* conception of ideology is implied: ". . . when the term denotes that we are skeptical of the ideas and representations advanced by our opponent. They are regarded as more or less conscious disguises of the real nature of a situation, the true recognition of which would not be in accord with his interests. These distortions range all the way from conscious lies to half-conscious and unwitting disguises; from calculated attempts to dupe others to self-deception. . . ." The total conception of ideology refers to the "ideology of an age or of a concrete historico-social group, e.g., of a class, when we are concerned

[20] Butterfield, *op. cit.*, p. 38.

with the characteristics and composition of the total structure of the mind of this epoch or of this group."[21]

It is the second of these meanings which interests us here.[22] Our problem is to determine what would be the character of a political theory which is thought of as an exercise in ideology. That is to say, what sort of activity is theorizing about political things when such theorizing is the product of forces which are themselves not to be understood as political and of which the theorist may in fact be unaware.

It is generally recognized that the latter interpretation of political theory belongs to Karl Marx. For it is Marx who sees political phenomena as possessing only a contingent status, resting on, as it were, and dependent upon, a substructure which determines its character and content. For political thought is integrally bound up with social life: "It is not the consciousness of men that determines their existence but, on the contrary, their social existence which determines their consciousness."[23] For according to Marx, the content of political thought, the kinds of political ideas which men have in any given era, is a product of economic forces. Indeed, the criteria in terms of which conflicting political views are resolved, or according to which each is proclaimed as superior to the other, are themselves functions of forces which produce them.

In a more general way, it would be correct to say that the intellectual productions of a culture are merely expressions of material forces of production. The way men produce goods, i.e., control nature, constitutes the "real basis" of society. Political thought is an ideological form and the chief difficulty for the scientific investigation of political institutions and their intellectual justification (or rationalization) is the failure to take

---

[21] Karl Mannheim, *Ideology and Utopia, An Introduction to the Sociology of Knowledge* (New York: Harcourt, Brace & Co., 1952), pp. 49–50.

[22] The first meaning is no different than sheer political manipulation. No doubt there are those who conceive of the task of political theory as the production of myths, lies, distortions, and so on, whose purpose is to bring about some end thought to be desirable. But we generally use the word "propaganda" to characterize this sort of activity and although it is possible that a political theory might sanction or even, perhaps, attempt to justify such procedures, the political theory is not to be confused with propaganda. Plato's theory of the ideal state is not exhausted or even profoundly affected by the fact that he appeared to sanction the use of falsehoods as acceptable practice in the affairs of state.

[23] Karl Marx, *A Contribution to the Critique of Political Economy,* trans. N. I. Stone (Chicago, 1913), pp. 11–12. Cf. Mannheim, *op. cit.,* p. 112.

into account that political ideas are not true or false, adequate or inadequate, prudent or imprudent, *in themselves,* but can be evaluated only within the context of the stage of economic development achieved by the culture under investigation. What all this comes to is that political thinking as, indeed, styles of thought and social relationships in general, are subject to a complete transformation as a consequence of a corresponding change in the economic foundations of the society. "In considering such transformations," writes Marx, "the distinction should always be made between the material transformation of the economic conditions of production which can be determined with the precision of natural science, and the legal, political, religious, aesthetic or philosophical—in short ideological—forms in which men become conscious of this conflict and fight it out."[24]

The concept of ideology has undergone a variety of changes in the uses to which it has been put in the specialized languages of the social sciences. In addition to the use attributed to Marx which we have examined, the word has been used to denote political ideas which are simply false, that is, a deliberately misleading system of political ideas.

A third construction is to characterize political notions as ideological if they have practical consequences. In this connection, Daniel Bell writes:

> Ideology is the conversion of ideas into social levers. Without irony, Max Lerner once entitled a book *Ideas Are Weapons.* This is the language of ideology. It is more. It is the commitment to the consequences of ideas. . . . What gives ideology its force is its passion. Abstract philosophical inquiry has always sought to eliminate passion, and the person, to rationalize all ideas. For the ideologue, truth arises in action, and meaning is given to experience by the "transforming moment." He comes alive not in contemplation, but in "the deed." One might, in fact, say that the most important, latent, function of ideology is to tap emotion. Other than religion (and war and nationalism), there have been few forms of channelizing emotional energy. Religion symbolized, drained away, dispersed emotional energy from the world onto the litany, the liturgy, the sacraments, the edifices, the arts. Ideology fuses these energies and channels them into politics.[25]

---

[24] Marx, *op. cit.,* preface. Cf. T. B. Bottomore and Maximilian Rubel (eds.), *Karl Marx, Selected Writings in Sociology and Social Philosophy* (London: Watts & Co., 1956), p. 52.

[25] Daniel Bell, *The End of Ideology—On the Exhaustion of Political Ideas in the Fifties* (New York: Collier Books, 1961), p. 394–95.

Leaving aside for the moment certain pejorative uses of the word "ideology," those uses, that is, where the word merely expresses disapproval of a rival political view, what is there to be discovered as to Marx's common notion on the one hand and Bell's usage on the other?

In both cases a theory or set of ideas described as ideological are rendered immune from conventional judgments about their truth or falsity. The clarity and precision of political thought is no guarantee that anything about the nature of society is actually discovered or understood. In fact, according to Marx, just the reverse is true! "*Political* thought is really *political* thought in the sense that the thinking takes place within the framework of politics. The clearer and more vigorous political thought is, the less it is able to grasp the nature of social evils."[26]

Secondly, on both views, political thought is either the product of forces which are beyond merely political understanding or political thought consisting of rationalizations for actions which occur or are brought about for nonpolitical reasons. In the section of this chapter which allows for a critical discussion of these views, we shall consider what sort of relationship can be established between a theory and an ideology and consider the hypothesis that to construe political theories as ideologies is to effectively destroy the meaning of political theory.

Thus far we have examined four different answers to the question, "What is political theory?" We have tried to answer the question not by canvassing political theorists to tell us what they thought they were doing, but rather by offering descriptions of what we think they are actually doing. Also, we have restricted our discussion to classical political philosophers.[27] We turn now to some modern and contemporary thinkers with a view to examining their answers to the question: "What is political theory?" It goes without saying that those of our contempo-

---

[26] Karl Marx, "Kritische Randglossen zu dem Artikel: Der Konig von Preussen und die Sozialreform Von einem Preussen," in *Vorwarts,* August 7, 1844. Bottomore and Rubel, *op. cit.,* p. 217.

The reason he gives for this curious assertion is that the principle of politics is the will of the legislator. "The more partial and perfected *political* thought becomes, the more it believes in the omnipotence of the will, the less it is able to see the *natural* and mental *limitations* on the will, the less capable it is of discovering the source of social evils." The source, being of course, essentially historical and economic.

[27] Bell being an exception, of course.

raries who have addressed themselves to this and related questions are part of a continuous tradition and that their answers and attitudes will reflect the degree to which each has been influenced by their predecessors.

SOME RECENT VIEWS

According to Professor Leo Strauss "political theory" is all too frequently understood in its modern acceptation as a discipline which consists of "comprehensive reflections on the political situation which lead up to the suggestion of a broad policy."[28] He prefers, therefore, to think of his enterprise as "political philosophy" and in his essay "What is Political Philosophy?" he sets down the goals and procedures for systematic thought about things political:

> Political philosophy will then be the attempt to replace opinion about the nature of political things by knowledge of the nature of things political. Political things are by their nature subject to approval and disapproval, to choice and rejection, to praise and blame. It is of their essence not to be neutral but to raise a claim to men's obedience, allegiance, decision or judgment. One does not understand them as what they are, as political things, if one does not take seriously their explicit or implicit claim to be judged in terms of goodness or badness, of justice or injustice, i.e., if one does not measure them by some standard of goodness or justice. To *judge* soundly one must know the *true standards*. If political philosophy wishes *to do justice* to its subject matter, it must strive for *genuine knowledge* of these standards. Political philosophy is the attempt truly to know both the nature of political things and the right, or the good, political order.[29]

Strauss supposes, with Plato, that there are *true standards,* that these standards provide us with an image of the "right" or the "good" political order, that these standards of right and good in politics are proper objects of knowledge—that is, they are removed from the realm of opinion and are known to be true and immutable, and that the political philosopher must judge "political things" in the light of these standards. "The umpire *par excellence* is the political philosopher."[30]

---

[28] Leo Strauss, *What is Political Philosophy? and Other Studies* (Glencoe, Ill.: Free Press, 1959), p. 13.

[29] *Ibid.*, p. 11–12 (italics added).

[30] *Ibid.*, p. 81.

But Strauss means to go beyond a mere latter-day platonism. He sees classical political philosophy as a unique phenomenon, as the moment genesis or conception of the discipline.

Classical political philosophy is non-traditional, because it belongs to the fertile moment when all political traditions were shaken, and there was not yet in existence a tradition or political philosophy. In all later epochs, the philosopher's study of political things was mediated by a tradition of political philosophy which acted like a screen between the philosopher and political things, regardless of whether the individual philosopher cherished or rejected that tradition. From this it follows that the classical philosophers see the political things with a freshness and directness which have never been equalled. They look at political things in the perspective of the enlightened citizen or statesman. They see things clearly, or do not see at all.[31]

According to Strauss, modern political philosophy is abstracted and divorced from political realities; it cannot recapture the face to face relation which obtained between its classical counterpart and "political things." The classical conceptions were agreed in supposing that there existed a single, unifying goal of political life, viz, virtue. If modern political philosophies have anything at all in common it is the rejection of that principle. How then is it possible, if indeed it is, to reestablish modern political philosophy, assuming, of course, that Strauss is correct in his descriptions of classical political thinking and of modern political philosophy. There are two ways to seek to answer the question: either we examine what Strauss says modern political philosophers ought to do, or we assume that Strauss belongs to the class of modern political philosophers who follow his own prescriptions and examine Strauss' procedures. If we follow the second alternative, we discover that Strauss is a student of philosophical literature rather than a judge who adjudicates among conflicting political claims or between disputants about political principles. The first alternative explains this peculiar inconsistency and clarifies for us what Strauss takes to be the task of political philosophy. Consider, in this context, how the past is to be used in the clarification of modern political concepts:

A social science that cannot speak of tyranny with the same confidence with which medicine speaks, for example, of cancer, cannot understand social

[31] *Ibid.*, p. 27.

phenomena as what they are. It is, therefore, not scientific. Present day social science finds itself in this condition. If it is true that present day social science is the inevitable result of modern social science and of modern philosophy, one is forced to think of the restoration of classical social science. Once we have learned again from the classics what tyranny is, we shall be enabled and compelled to diagnose as tyrannies a number of contemporary regimes which appear in the guise of dictatorships. This diagnosis can only be the first step toward an exact analysis of present day tyranny, for present day tyranny is fundamentally different from the tyranny analyzed by the classics.[32]

What Strauss has in mind appears to be the following: The paradigm of political thinking is the classical political philosophy of the Greeks, particularly Plato and Aristotle. Modern political philosophy can never recapture the pristine purity of ancient political thought. This is so because too much water passed under the bridge. The Greeks did not need or rely on the political texts of the past. Firstly because these were sparse and inadequate to their needs and secondly because historical political texts were unnecessary in view of the direct and immediate confrontation of the classical political philosopher with the intricacies of political life. The modern political philosopher who, though he cannot hope to duplicate the "noble simplicity and quiet grandeur" of the Greek model, can nonetheless learn from the classical treatment and analysis of political concepts. What can he learn? For one thing he can avoid the intellectual plague of modern philosophical thought which Strauss thinks is the refusal to make judgments of value and the restricting of the discipline to merely descriptive and analytic tasks. The difficulty with the doctrine of "ethical neutrality" is that rather than imply the classical attitudes of objective, unbiased, and disinterested *judgment,* one which avoids "radical partisanship,"[33] it encourages and approves total irresponsibility with respect to questions of value.[34] Modern political philosophy Strauss thinks, must redirect its attention to the content and method of classical political thought; to, that is, reacquainting itself with the classical goal of seeking the conditions of political virtues.

---

[32] *Ibid.*, p. 95.

[33] *Ibid.*, p. 81.

[34] Strauss also contends that "value-neutrality" is not merely perverse, but removes the possibility of understanding social phenomena much of which is contingent upon value-oriented goals. To refuse to recognize value, Strauss argues, is comparable to refusing to recognize part of the phenomenon which the scientist is allegedly describing.

Professor A. J. Ayer describes a position developed by the Vienna Circle wing of the philosophical movement known as *logical positivism* or logical empiricism. According to the analysis of propositions offered by Ayer and the positivists no statement is meaningful unless it is either a description which may be verified by empirical procedures or a formal statement which may be confirmed according to logical criteria. No other statement may serve as a proposition, that is, may be described, as true or false. Moral philosophy, therefore, so far as it contains statements which prescribe how one ought to act, or so far as it ascribes value to persons or things or states of affairs, to that extent it contains statements which are neither descriptive nor formal. Such statements are not, properly speaking, propositions at all and may not, therefore, function as acceptable objects of knowledge.

Now the thrust of T. D. Weldon's critique is to show that most "ideological" disagreements (he prefers to call these "disagreements about foundations") are of the same order as moral disagreements and are, therefore, not resolvable in the same fashion as genuine disagreements. Consider the following:

> Suppose we are looking at the dog of our hostess. I say "Fluffy is a Peke," and you reply, "No, he is an Aberdeen." We know what we are disagreeing about and how to settle the issue. If I say "The Athens of Pericles was a democracy," and you reply, "No, it was an oligarchy," the matter is rather more complicated because of the vague and conflicting *uses* of "democracy" and "oligarchy." But if we agree on usages and find out enough about Periclean Athens there is no room for argument.[35]

But disagreements about the value of ideological positions are not of this order, for there are no criteria or canons commonly agreed upon to which one can turn in deciding between conflicting claims. Weldon claims that reasons in support of one ideology over another cannot be given, but rather that the sorts of arguments which *have* been offered in the past are generally misleading or merely false. It is his position that: ". . . the theoretical foundations of political thinking which are claimed by Democracy, Hegelian Idealism, and Marxism are all equally worthless. They do not support the superstructures which are supposed to support and could not conceivably do so."[36]

---

[35] Weldon, *op. cit.*, p. 85.

[36] *Ibid.*, p. 14.

Weldon's point is an important one. Strauss, we recall, took the position that if one were not prepared to accept objective standards of right and wrong, good and evil, then logically one would be compelled to assume a position of utter indifference in which no judgment whatever could be made concerning the character of certain political arrangements. To exclude moral statements or to deny such judgments any cognitive status, Strauss insisted, was to render the so-called *science,* unscientific. Concentration camps, the causing of unnecessary pain, exploitation, all these are in no uncertain terms evil, and to refuse to call them evil, to be unable to perceive them as contrary to eternal principles and standards of essential humanity, is itself evidence for the corruption of character brought about by the positivist notion of science.

Strauss, in other words, sees two alternatives: either there are eternal and immutable moral standards or there are not. If there are, then and only then can an adequate picture of political life develop from the bits and pieces of scientific description. To deny the existence of values, to suppose that statements which attribute value are either meaningless or are merely reports of the psychological state of the person expressing a sentiment, is to embrace value subjectivism and to perceive the value-laden world in a distorted, myopic fashion.

Weldon's position consists of denying the allegedly mutually exclusive character of the two alternatives perceived by Strauss. He denies that there are such universally valid standards of right conduct and denies that the only alternative available is pure subjectivism. His conclusions about the nature of political thought do not involve "cynicism, skepticism, or the rejection of moral or political evaluations. All that is discarded is some metaphysical lumber."[37] When we examine the discarded lumber we discover that in large part it consists of those concepts and assumptions about meaning and value subscribed to by Strauss. Once these are gone, how can Weldon prevent being driven to a complete subjectivism in which any political judgment is to be considered an expression of taste and is as fit a subject of debate as are matters of taste? To this question Weldon replies:

Precisely what is meant by describing a view about politics or morals as "subjectivist" or as "involving subjectivism" is usually far from clear, but what

[37] *Ibid.,* p. 15.

is vaguely asserted by those who use this language is something like this. Unless we can produce some valid deductive argument in favour of one variety of political . . . institution, we shall be reduced to saying "Well, we do things in this way here and now, but people do them differently at other places and times. It is now all a matter of personal preference and you may please yourself." After all, we do not usually criticize the Russians for liking vodka though most of us do not think it is very nice, so why should we criticize them for liking concentration camps, direction of labour, one party government, and state ownership of all important property? We like to have a good deal of personal liberty, they care very little about it, but that is entirely their affair and it is impertinent to criticize them for it.[38]

Though this is not a stupid view, it is not likely that it will be maintained for long by those whose ox is being gored. When alien views about race or property are translated into action we are quick enough to judge those views as offensive and unacceptable. And when we do so, we are not intending merely to offer a description of our own psychological state or to offer an autobiographical sketch of our feelings, but we are intending rather to show that the views in question are themselves, in themselves, evil and that they lead to evil actions. Now Weldon faces the problem of showing how such judgments (or, as he prefers to call them, "appraisals") can be justified such that they are neither merely emotive responses to subjective states nor do they require objective, eternal, and immutable standards of Good and Evil. Such appraisals, to be justified, require that we understand rightly what can reasonably be expected of them. It is an error, and an old one (17th century science is at the root of things here) to suppose that only propositions which ascribe properties or qualities which are not subject to metrical tests are subject. The notion of objective and subjective and the abyss which is alleged to exist between them, comes about because of a principle in 16th and 17th century science which insisted that properties that are measurable in a precise fashion, length, width, impenetrability, height, weight, motion, are the real constituents of the objects in the external world. Properties like color, heat, odor, sound are immeasurable, and therefore exist, not as ingredients of real things, but rather as modifications of our minds, as phenomenal objects, and are, therefore, subjective. This curious view, this vestigial remain from the physical philosophies of

---

[38] *Ibid.*, p. 147.

classical mechanistic physics, leads to peculiar analysis of statements. To say that Harry is six feet tall, is to assert an objective statement since Harry may be measured, and we are all satisfied that he is measured by a ruler which we all agree is more or less accurate. "Harry has red hair" is presumably less objective since what passes for red in your experience may not be what passes for red in mine, and the statement is therefore more subject to controversy than the first. "Harry is a good worker," it is easy to see, is alleged now to be altogether subjective for each man may agree or disagree as he chooses and neither ruler nor individual perceptions will serve to settle our disagreement. But all this comes about because we expect, and are disappointed when we do not find, the same precision in appraisal judgments as we find in judgments made about the primary qualities of physical objects. The difficulty however lies not in the objects or in the judgments, but rather in our unreasonable expectations. The logic of appraisal language is simply not to be equated with the logic of a descriptive language. Failure to recognize this distinction leads to the unreasonable demand that all propositions in our language are to be characterized as objective or subjective according to the degree to which they approach propositions which ascribe measurable properties to things.

If, however, we come to realize that not all propositions may have their truth established by referring to some one single criteria, then the objective-subjective distinction becomes somewhat less impressive. Consider for a moment that we are impressed by the simple precision of "Harry is six feet tall" because there is but one standard according to which this statement is true—a metrical rule. But aren't there also standards in terms of which "Harry is a good worker" may be shown to be true or false, such that most of us, under a given set of circumstances in some context or other would be inclined to agree that Harry is, or is not, a good worker? For "good worker" does not attempt to ascribe one single property to Harry, comparable to being six feet tall and redheaded. The statement intends, rather, to sum up many things which can be said of Harry. Harry arrives on time, he is efficient, he is productive, and so forth. We are all well aware of how to go about assuring ourselves that Harry is (or is not) a good worker. Though there may be greater room for error in judgments of this sort, judgments which are about the propensities of people to behave in certain ways, than there is in cases of simple judgments about height and weight, nevertheless we would not want to say that such appraisals are "subjective" in the sense that no reasons, other than psychological or autobiographical responses about feelings, can be given. For reasons *can* be given and they often are convincing reasons on the basis of which rational men may sometimes alter their views. Thus, appraisals are "objective" in the sense of being about what they are intended to be about, viz, the real, external world, and though their truth cannot be determined according to some one fixed rule, it may nonetheless be determined given an analysis of all the statements which are subsumed under the general term in the judgment. Now it is, of course, necessary to show how what we have said about appraisals in general applies to strictly political appraisals.

How, after this lengthy analysis, have we answered the question, "What is political theory?" In a sense we have answered the question by showing how Weldon proceeds in offering an analysis of what he takes to be the status of judgments made about political things and what he sees as mysterious and puzzling in the way in which others interpret the status of political judgments. It is Weldon's view that political theory ought to be understood as consisting principally of the analysis of political concepts and of the assumptions made on the basis of these concepts. To put the case somewhat more radically than Weldon might care for, we might say that it is his object to perform a bit of therapy. Therapy, which is understood generally as an activity whose aim is the elimination of defects which allows one to proceed successfully, may here be understood as meaning the clarification of political problems which puzzle political theorists, not as a result of the character of political institutions or processes (which are after all empirical matters, and the difficulties they engender are to be overcome through the use of improved empirical procedures), but rather because of the logical or procedural defects in the posing of the problems themselves. The entire discussion about the status of political appraisals in which we have been engaged is a case in point. Weldon's reasoning has been used to show that Strauss perceives a mutually exclusive alternative between platonism on the one hand and complete subjectivism on the other, only because he does not fully understand the morphology of the concept of subjectivism. Once that concept has been clarified and a third alternative justified, Strauss' dilemma of a false theory on the one hand and an absurd one on the other is overcome. Weldon, of course, offers the analysis in order to show that the level and quality of conventional disagreement about different ideological foundations, such as communism on the one hand and democracy on the other, is the product of a misunderstanding. The misunderstanding comes about when each protagonist refuses to recognize that much more than the simple, reductive standards which are the backbone of such disagreements are involved. Whatever else such ideological disputes might rest on, it is important to see that neither can be justified by vacuous and uninformed references to natural law and the rights of man, on one side, or by historical materialism on the other. It is the task of the political theorist, according to Weldon, to show that much of what men say about political institutions, at the level of theory, is misleading, muddled, and sometimes merely false: That much of what has passed for genuine disagreement and real differences are based on misunderstanding. The political theorist must clarify and analyze political concepts with a view to putting things aright, with a view to distinguishing between real problems and illusory ones. The task so described is not so far from Socrates' analogy in the *Theatetus* between the philosopher and the mid-wife. The disanalogy, Socrates pointed out, consists in the fact that it is the philosopher's job to distinguish between a real and a phantom birth. This, according to Weldon, is the job of the theorist in the realm of political ideas.

We have considered political theory as metaphysics, as ideology, and then as analysis. Now we turn to considering political theory as a scientific enterprise. The classical instance of scientific procedures applied to political phenomena is Aristotelian. Yet it is natural that modern views of science will influence scientific interpretations of political things. What precisely is the relationship between political science and political theory or, at any rate, what ought that relationship consist in? Before this question can be answered it must be seen as arising as part of a greater context. Political inquiry is but one branch of social inquiry, and although it is undoubtedly the oldest of the social sciences, it is perhaps partly for this reason, among the last to adapt or to attempt to utilize the methods of science. It ought to be clear to us that the notion of "using the methods of science" is itself not clear. Are we to suppose that by science we mean that activity of which physics is the paradigm model? Or are we saying a neutral thing and alleging that any inquiry which utilizes certain procedures which permit, on the basis of observed and observable data, predictions which may be affirmed (or disaffirmed) is scientific? If we are saying the first, then we are narrowing the range of possibilities much too severely—physics is thought to be the paradigm because of its greater mathematical precision compared with, say, biology or geomorphology—but the fact that some aspects of nature are more amenable to mathematical measurement than others tells us more about nature than it does about what is a reasonable conception of precision. The emphasis placed on measurability is a legacy we are left by the philosophies of science of the 16th and 17th centuries. Descartes, Galileo, and Locke were all more or less under the impression that what was real was measurable. But of course this view is seriously defective for a variety of reasons noted earlier. What is important is that many thinkers suppose that to make politics scientific implies that it must be made as precise an inquiry as physics and that a true science, like physics, is thought to be so because its language is mathematics. Once this assumption is made (and it is surely an erroneous one) the debate becomes irrelevant, for it turns then not on the assumption concerning the criteria of measurability for scientific inquiry, but rather on whether it is possible to mathematize and thus categorize human behavior. It is at this point that those of Strauss' persuasion argue that social science, so construed, is heartless, inhuman and, "unscientific" in some greater and more vital sense of that word. Yet the issue need not come to this, for it is simply not necessary to operate on the assumption that mathematical precision is a necessary criterion of scientific inquiry. Thus if we deny the proposition that physics is the paradigm for scientific inquiry, we may maintain that the method and content of a science may be conditioned by the subject matter which characterizes it, and our expectations ought not to exceed what may be reasonably hoped for in the way of conclusions and general principles.

The irony of this latter day attempt at introducing scientific procedures into the study of politics arises from the curious fact that it comes at a time when the appropriateness of strictly scientific procedures are being brought into serious question in other disciplines of social science. As David Easton puts the point:

Our own epoch has . . . increasingly turned away from confidence in the usefulness of a rational outlook to help solve the problems of the world. In the more limited area of the social sciences this mood is reflected in a declining conviction about the ability of reason to help us understand social life in the way it has aided us with the physical world. Although in the past the claims of social science had never been wholly accepted without challenge, today the doubts are increasing in scope and intensity. Even social scientists themselves have begun to respond so faithfully to the new temper of the times that they too show an increasing willingness to admit the presence of hitherto unadmitted kinds of limitations without scientific method.[39]

Forgetting for a moment the obvious problem in Easton's reasoning as to whether one can interpret the current arguments about the limitations of scientific method as a rejection of reason (why not an affirmation of reason—for it is reason which is required to detect the flaws in a system which had been thought, as a matter of faith, to have no flaws), we shall examine an issue too long taken for granted, viz, that we know what we mean when we say that scientific procedures are, or ought to be, applied to problems of political theory.

First, we must ask the general question: how does a *theory* function in science? A science, any science, must at the very least provide rules which define its subject matter and which indicate in some fashion its procedures. The subject matter is a parochial issue, each discipline offering working hypotheses about what it supposes falls within the area of its own proper concern.[40] But the procedures which the discipline follows must fall within the general category of what will pass as scientific. Among the more notorious misconceptions concerning the manner in which a science is alleged to proceed revolves around the question of facts. Consider, for example, the following sentiment quoted by Easton from an important and influential political scientist, James Bryce:

The Fact is the first thing. Make sure of it. Get it perfectly clear. Polish it till it shines and sparkles like a gem. Then connect it with other facts. Examine it in its relation to them, for in that lies its worth and its significance. . . . To

---

[39] David Easton, *The Political System* (New York: Alfred A. Knopf, 1959), p. 5.

[40] It is rare, if it is possible at all, for a science to clearly and unambiguously indicate what falls within its purview and what does not. That the boundary lines are muddled is best witnessed by the proliferation of hyphenized sciences whose subject matter seems to straddle the boundaries of the more mature and established sciences: biochemistry, biophysics, social psychology, and so forth.

counsel you to stick to facts is not to dissuade you from philosophical generalizations, but only to remind you . . . that the generalizations must spring out of the facts, and without the facts are worthless.[41]

This paean to facts supposes that though there may be some difficulty in discovering them, there is no problem in recognizing them for what they are. But of course it is easy to see that what will count as being a fact depends upon decisions which may not themselves be made directly on the basis of facts. There must be some way of deciding what sort of data will be relevant to the task at hand. Now *relevance* may be established in a variety of different ways and not all of these ways will be compatible with scientific procedure. The criterion of relevance invoked in deciding what sort of facts will be mentioned in a Sears, Roebuck catalog is simply that these are the names and prices and descriptions of the items sold by Sears, Roebuck. Now this catalog is a complete collection of all the relevant facts, and criteria of relevance is clearly and firmly established. But one would not want to confuse such a catalog with a scientific treatise. Obviously a scientific treatise is something more than a rule of relevance and a collection of facts. What makes it different is the *sort* of rule of relevance involved here. Whether an occurrence will count as a relevant fact will depend upon its relation to a set of general statements (varying in relative generality from hypothesis to law). A fact is relevant if it confirms or disconfirms a general statement, i.e., a hypothesis, theory, or law. If an occurrence does not support such general statements or the negation of such general statements, it is not a fact at all. What is more, not *any* general statement will do. The general statement (hypothesis, theory, law) must be a device which enables one to predict that future occurrences, recognized as facts (that is, as relevant to this law or hypothesis) will be of such and such a sort and occur under such and such conditions, and have a specifiable character. The entire effort of a science is therefore directed at providing us with instruments which enable us to make statements about the future which will prove to be true with greater frequency than any other set of instruments. Naturally, on any given occasion when a theory does not seem to have held, that is, when an occurrence appears, on the face of it, to be incompatible with theoretical expectations, if it is possible to *explain* the

[41] Easton, *op. cit.*

deviation between what occurs and what was on the basis of theory expected, the theory may nonetheless be true.

Now there are those who believe that political theory is nothing other than the theories formulated by political scientists for the purpose of ordering, selecting, and generalizing about the facts of political experience. Political *theory,* then, means the *theory* of international relations, or the *theory* of political parties. Presumably the classical meaning of political theory, though it may be compatible with philosophy or theology, is fundamentally different from the sort of thing scientific political scientists have in mind when they speak of theory.

Why are we barred from the same expectations of general agreement among those who are engaged in political theorizing with regard to what constitutes the method and matter of inquiry? It is after all not difficult to find consensus with respect to what constitutes a natural science. Disputes about proper method and procedure may preoccupy philosophers of science, but these are largely irrelevant to the physicist, for example, and rarely do physical scientists disagree about the subject matter of their discipline. This has, perhaps, not always been true, for natural scientists have had to face issues in the past which called for speculation concerning the character of their subject. What has saved them from becoming enmeshed in philosophical disputes about matter and method is the unambiguous commitment to formulating general laws and to criteria of empirical adequacy which requires that it be possible to verify descriptive and predictive statements about physical phenomena. Rival interpretations of the scope and method of physics are not likely to enlist the support of rational men unless their claims can be justified within the context of the existing scientific apparatus. *Confirmation, verification, proof* are public and objective procedures and the very standard of what constitutes a rational man is one who believes no propositions or statements to be *true* which are neither empirically verifiable or logically demonstratable.

The question "What is political theory?" is not like the question "What is physics?" It is more like the question "What is philosophy?" or "What is literature?" Why is there less agreement about such questions? Why do these issues continue to perplex us, to gnaw at our consciousness, to demand our attention and thought? The answer lies in the absence of generally accepted and agreed upon criteria of logical and empirical adequacy. Describing and predicting single instances or events subsumed under general laws does not exhaust what has in the past been meant by "political theory," just as they are, for the most part, irrelevant to literary studies. The physical scientist operates with a relatively unambiguous and generally accepted theory of meaning, and as a consequence the area of inquiry and methods appropriate to it are equally clear and unambiguous. For political theory, no generally convincing criteria of meaning exists and the consequences are that neither the content nor the procedures of the enterprise can be clearly defined. The distinction between the physical and natural sciences has been expressed in a variety of different, if not always consistent, ways. A traditional way of distinguishing between the two consists of characterizing the physical sciences as *nomothetic,* and social, cultural, and historical inquiries as *idiographic.* By *nomothetic,* the 19th century social philosophers Wilhelm Windelband and Heinrich Richert who first used these terms meant to refer to that characteristic in the method of the physical sciences which eschews the unique, particular, and concrete nature of things and events and limit its area of concern to the abstract, universal, generalized properties of classes of things and events. The term *idiographic* refers, on the other hand, to those disciplines which are principally concerned with the unique, particular, and concrete aspects of historical and social events with a view to representing and describing these within the framework of a context which does full justice to the properties, qualities, and relations, accidental as well as essential, which are part of the thing or event in question. Within the context of this distinction, it should be obvious that political science and *a fortiori* political theory fall within the category of *idiographic* sciences. Though there are serious questions to be raised about the validity of this distinction, if one accepts it then there are good grounds for concluding that political theory is, at least in part, like history or literature in the sense that subjective, intuitive, and personal assessments made according to criteria which are neither public, objective, or demonstrable are acceptable so far as they contribute to a coherent and more or less convincing and likely reconstruction of particular and concrete historical phenomena. This is not to say, of course, that there are no objective and generally accepted canons of evidence and rules of interpretation that must be adhered to and in terms of which the reconstruction in question may be evaluated, but rather to point up the subjective character of the procedures involved in reconstructing political and historical events.

2

Natural law

HISTORICAL CONCEPTS OF NATURAL LAW

The concept of natural law is among the most baffling and tenacious in political theory. It is a baffling concept because it means, and has historically meant, a variety of different things to a wide array of different political thinkers. Among its adherents are men who have virtually nothing else in common intellectually: Heraclitus and Cicero; Aquinas and Locke; Sophocles and Rousseau; Plato and the authors of the Constitution of the United States. It is a tenacious concept because it is thought to be the answer to an extraordinarily important set of fundamental political questions. For despite the obscure origins of the theory of natural law and the many different meanings and theoretical tasks which have been assigned to it, the single central burden of the natural law theory is the justification of social and political compulsion and social and political relationships. That is to say, the job that the theory has been called upon to do, whether it is formulated by a pre-Socratic or by a contemporary political scientist, is to frame a standard against which existing laws and institutions may be evaluated and judged. Were there no natural law, it is sometimes argued, there would exist no grounds for judging a given law or state to be better or worse than any other law or state, and the absence of such standards of judgment and the subsequent impossibility of such judgments themselves would be morally and politically intolerable. We turn now to an examination of this view.

Plato's concept

No small part of Plato's energies were given over to the task of destroying the irreverent skepticism of the Sophists. The Sophists' position, according to its principal expositor, Protagoras, is expressed by the aphorism that man is the measure of all things. That is to say that men collectively are the ultimate arbiters of truth and justice and that such conventional truths as men may agree upon are relative to the time and place in which and for which they are established. This revolutionary view which strikes at the heart of the hitherto accepted and respected doctrine that laws are sanctioned by their divine origin, renders laws and constitutions subject only to pragmatic criteria. It makes no sense to the Sophist to describe a law as morally good or morally offensive except so far as the law or constitution promotes some tentatively agreed upon good or retards a tentatively agreed upon evil. For Plato, however, law by convention is but one sort of law, one which belongs to a lesser order of things. To argue that what is just at one time and in one place is unjust in another time and another place is to make a mockery of the concept of justice. Men, the view goes, are essentially rational creatures, and the kinds of institutions which they establish for themselves and according to which they regulate their lives cannot be wholly arbitrary. So far as they remain men, so far that is that they retain their essential rationality, to that degree all institutions and legal systems must exhibit some central features in common. If, indeed, it is their rationality which distinguishes them from other sorts of creatures, then to that extent those social and political systems which best enable them to live their lives in accordance with reason are those which are most natural. Natural, in the sense that men are by nature, it is thought, rational creatures. Now it is an obvious fact that legal and social systems differ from one society to another. But *facts* are only the ingredients of the way the world *is*—and not constituents of the way the world ought to be. Social and political realities may at best only approximate the ideal patterns of society. For Plato, existing social and political organizations are not to be judged willy-nilly according to pragmatic or utilitarian criteria—not, that is, to be evaluated simply by observing that each set of institutions or legal rules satisfies some immediate need or other at some particular point in time and space. Laws and institutions are, to be sure, conventions—social productions—

but they are to be judged as praiseworthy or blameworthy and ultimately as comparatively good or evil with respect to the degree that they approach an ideal, absolute, irrevocable, and immutable paradigm—the ideal *Republic*.

Plato's contrast between the customary laws and traditional institutions of a given society and the single, eternal archetype of all societies is but one instance of the classical Greek distinction between nature and convention. Engaged in the study of the physical world, of the ordered and unambiguously natural world, the classical Greek perceived that in nature there are fundamental principles which are universal. As Ernest Barker put this point: ". . . while the study of physics had worked toward the conception of a single underlying substratum of all matter, the anthropological study of the human world worked toward the conception of an infinite diversity of institutions."[1]

Plato's resolution of the conflict is eminently clear: There are absolute moral laws and ultimate models of social and political institutions which are altogether comparable to those of physics. The task is to articulate these and to provide operational procedures which enable men to reconstruct existing societies so that they more closely approach the ideal. To discover universal moral and political principles we must look for the universal qualities and properties common to all men which underly the superficial differences reflected in the vastly different customs and conventions of different societies. What, in other words, are the *natural* constituents of the human character, the essential, unalterable characteristics of all men everywhere. The institutions and laws of the ideal state must ultimately be embodiments or reflections of this "natural human character." The variety of institutions and laws of the ideal society will reflect the essentially different kinds of personalities which men may possess. When institutions are accurate expressions of these fundamental human qualities, then that society is natural, for it conforms to human nature and, consequently, to nature itself. The natural and, therefore, ideal state is the natural human character "writ large."

A second and equally important aspect of Plato's theory, is the view that nature is not morally and ethically neutral. The highest dimension of human character is reason, and reason enables a man to live in

[1] Sir Ernest Barker, *Political Thought of Plato and Aristotle* (New York: Dover Press, 1959), p. 29.

accordance with nature. To live a life in accordance with nature is to live the life of a just man. Thus Plato writes:

> And in truth, justice . . . does not concern a man's management of his own external affairs, but his internal management of his soul, his truest self and his truest possessions. The just man does not allow the different principles within him to do other work than their own, nor the distinct classes in his soul to interfere with one another; but in the truest sense he sets his house in order, gaining the mastery over himself; and becoming on good terms with himself through discipline he joins in harmony those different elements, like three terms in a musical scale—lowest, and highest and intermediate and any others that may lie between those—and binding together all these elements he moulds the many within him into one, temperate and harmonious. In this spirit he lives; whether he is money-making or attending to the wants of his body, whether he is engaged in politics, or on business transactions of his own, throughout he considers and calls just and beautiful all conduct which pursues and helps to create this attitude of mind. The knowledge which superintends these actions is for him wisdom, while any conduct which tends to destroy this attitude is for him unjust, and the belief which inspires it, ignorance.[2]

We have dwelled at some length on Plato's conception of natural law despite the conventional view of many political thinkers that the theory of natural law has its origin in the Greek and Roman stoics and that the theory is first articulated in a systematic fashion by Cicero. The point of this discussion will be clearer when we recognize that in a general way Plato's analysis provides the essential ingredients of subsequent theories of natural law. The first is the idea that it is necessary to contrast the ideal pattern of society expressed by the law of nature and the positive legal institutions which we discover in our confrontation with human relationships. And, secondly, that the natural law is not without a moral and ethical content—that the law of nature is, in fact, a moral law which prescribes patterns of behavior and demands moral and political obedience.

Aristotle's concept

The answers provided by the earliest Greek philosophers to the question "what are the ultimate constituents of the world?" strike us

[2] Plato, *Republic,* Bk. IV, paragraph 443.

today as quaint and even frivolous. The notion that the underlying substratum to which the diverse objects of our experience may be reduced could be understood in terms of fire, water, air, or earth seems to be little more than an historic curiosity of interest principally to antiquarians. Yet the speculations about the physical world of Thales, Anaxamander, Anaxemines, Heraclitus, and their colleagues, are motivated by rational and reasonable motives. The question which these ancients raised, "what is the single universal principle in terms of which all temporal and spacial phenomena may be explained and understood?" is as critical for scientists today as it was serious in the fifth century B.C. The question, it should be noted, is not *whether* there are such universal principles, but rather, what these universal principles might be. The question is not, moreover, restricted to the nature of physical world. If, in the physical sense, the world appears on the one hand as a "buzzing confusion" and on the other, when seen through the eyes of the philosopher, ordered, regulated, and rational, so in the political sense there are two different frames of reference. On the one hand are the laws of this and that community and, on the other, the eternal and immutable laws of nature. Just as the physical philosopher draws a distinction between false propositions which apply to experiences of common objects in the everyday world, and the propositions which, by virtue of their reference to universal principles are valid, so does the moral and political philosopher distinguish between just and unjust actions. According to Aristotle, there are two kinds of law and each provides criteria for a complete classification of just and unjust actions.

By the two kinds of law I mean particular law and universal law. Particular law is that which each community lays down and applies to its own members: this is partly written and partly unwritten. Universal law is the law of nature. For there really is, as everyone to some extent divines, a natural justice and injustice that is binding on all men, even on those who have no association or covenant with each other.[3]

If the written law tells against our case, clearly we must appeal to the universal law, and insist on its greater equity and justice. . . . We must urge that the principles of equity are permanent and changeless, and that the universal law does not change either, for it is the law of nature, whereas written laws often do change. . . . We shall argue that justice indeed is true

[3] Aristotle, *Rhet.*, Bk. I, chap. 13.

and profitable, but that sham justice is not, and that consequently the written law is not, because it does not fulfill the true purpose of law.[4]

Justice then is possible when men obey the written law, the particular law, only when it is consonant with the meaning and spirit of the eternal law—". . . the better a man is, the more he will follow and abide by the unwritten law in preference to the written."[5]

The universal, eternal law of Aristotle is the natural law as well. It is natural law because it demands of men that they live according to rules which are in conformity with the highest and noblest properties of his character. "He who bids the law rule, may be deemed to bid God and Reason alone rule, but he who bids man rule adds an element of the beast; for desire is a wild beast, and passion perverts the minds of rulers, even when they are the best of men. *The law is reason unaffected by desire.*"[6] And since, for Aristotle, a life lived according to reason is a life lived in accordance with what is most distinctive in man's nature, the ultimate rules which govern that life and which establish and guide the institutions which made such a life possible are natural.

As men's natures differ among themselves, the institutions of the society will differ. Since for Aristotle it is a fact that some men are more capable by nature of living the rational life and others are not, the institutional expression of these differences will result in a stratified social structure. A man may be a slave by nature—capable of obeying the commands of others more rational than he, but incapable of living an independent life of his own. To make a slave of a man who is by nature able to live the life of a truly rational being is a violation of the natural law. Thus, the institution of slavery is justified so far as it is an expression of and accommodation to real, natural differences among men.

The role of universality

The political and legal speculations of both Plato and Aristotle are rife with assumptions many of which are rarely made explicit. The notion of universality which plays an important role in their thought about political matters was hedged with qualifications. The concept of universality implies that there are no exceptions to the application of the rule which

[4] Aristotle, *Rhet.*, Bk. I, chap. 15.

[5] *Ibid.*

[6] Aristotle, *Politics*, Bk. IV, chap. 8.

is described as being universal. But the Platonic and Aristotelian conception of man implies a somewhat more restricted notion than the general concept we have become familiar with. For to be a man is to be a member of a political organization, to belong to a state: ". . . the state is a creation of nature and . . . man is by nature a political animal. And he who by nature and not by mere accident is without a state, is either above humanity, or below it; he is the 'tribeless, lawless, heartless one,' whom Homer denounces–the outcast who is a lover of war; he may be compared to an unprotected piece in the game of draughts."[7] A stateless creature is something less than fully human. But what sort of entity does Aristotle have in mind when he speaks of the "state"? Clearly he means the Greek city-state–the polis–and that political organization of a less structured and sophisticated character are little more than lawless bands of barbarians who do not answer to the name "man." If the state is a creation of nature, and if man is by nature a political animal, then the laws of nature apply only to political animals and the claim to the universality of the natural law is restricted to political animals.

THE RELATION OF NATURAL LAW TO THE LAW OF MEN

Despite the differences among those who subscribe to a theory of natural law, there are a variety of common conceptions about what the natural law is, and how it is related to the law of men:

1. Natural law is an ideal pattern which positive law, when it is equitable, expresses. There may indeed occur instances where the natural law is silent, and on those occasions the positive law may be other than it is and adequate all the same.
2. The natural law is universal. Men, on a given occasion may not know what it is, none the less may discover what it is. It is discoverable by all men through the exercise of reason–and reason, it is alleged, is equally distributed among all men; or, at least, men are by nature *capable* of exercising reason.
3. It is not merely descriptive in the sense that all men act in accordance with it (though they may, of course, so act) but prescriptive as well.
4. The natural law, as an ideal pattern of perfection, is unchanging, true and eternal.

[7] Aristotle, *Politics,* Bk. I, chap. 2.

5. States whose positive laws are compatible with natural law are just and equitable and their institutions provide the conditions under which men achieve their natural ends—self-realization in some Aristotelian sense. Such laws are educative. Such a state creates moral men as well as good citizens.
6. The natural law does not confer rights as such, but provides rather the limits and proper functions of positive law.

Natural rights

The 17th and 18th centuries' notion of natural law, though they have many aspects in common with earlier formulations, are appreciably different in several important respects. First, the emphasis is placed on natural rights rather than natural law.[8]

Hobbes is the first to recognize that natural law and natural rights are not identical concepts: ". . . though they that speak of this subject use to confound *ius* and *lex, right* and *law:* yet they ought to be distinguished; because *Right* consisteth in liberty to do, or to forbear: whereas Law determineth, and bindeth to one of them: so that law and right differ as much, as obligation and liberty."[9]

Hobbes' example:

> The Right of Nature, which writers commonly call *Jus Naturale,* is the Liberty each man hath, to use his own power, as he will himselfe, for the preservation of his own Nature; that is to say, of his own Life; and consequently of doing any thing, which in his own judgment and Reason, he shall conceive to be the aptest means thereunto.
>
> A Law of Nature (Lex Naturalis) is a Precept, or general Rule, found out by Reason, by which a man is forbidden to do that which is destructive of his life, or taketh away the means of preserving the same; and to omit, that, by which he thinketh it may be best preserved.[10]

Strauss interprets this as follows: "According to Hobbes, the basis of morals and politicals is not the 'law of nature,' i.e. natural obligation, but the 'right of nature.' The 'law of nature' owes all its dignity simply to the

[8] Following Leo Strauss' interpretations on this point: Strauss in his *The Political Philosophy of Hobbes: Its Basis and Its Genesis* credits Hobbes with fathering modern political theory by placing crucial emphasis on the "right of nature" as opposed to the Greek and Roman conception of the "law of nature."

[9] *Leviathan,* p. 1, chap. 14.

[10] *Leviathan,* chap. 14.

circumstance that it is the necessary consequence of the 'right of nature.' It is from this standpoint that we can best recognize the antithesis between Hobbes on the one hand, and the whole tradition founded by Plato and Aristotle on the other. . . ."[11]

Some support for this view is expressed by E. Barker who says: "While modern thought starts from the rights of the individual and conceives the state as existing to secure the conditions of his development, Greek thought starts from the right of the State."[12]

The right of the state should be understood as expressed in the law: "Freely as the spirit of Socrates ranged, he acknowledged himself the slave of the law. And what is true of Socrates is true of the Athenian people. They might appear, as they stood assembled . . . sovereign under heaven. But they too recognized the sovereignty of the laws."[13]

Still, there is some controversy about the intention of 17th and 19th century authors concerning the logical priority of natural law and natural right. Are the natural rights of men to be deduced from a prior natural law or are the rights themselves prior? Hobbes' position seems clear on this point, and Strauss marks Hobbes' distinction between *jus* and *lex* as the origin of modern political thought. d'Entreves claims that Locke would not have subscribed to the distinction if it implies (as Hobbes means it to) that natural law is fundamental and that rights are derived from or contingent on the natural law. As evidence d'Entreves cites Locke's remark to the effect that the "natural freedom of man is nothing else than his knowledge of the law of nature, in the same way that the freedom of an Englishman consists in his 'liberty to dispose of his actions and possessions' according to the laws of England."[14] We shall closely examine Locke's view on the subject shortly; suffice it to say that the distinction between law and right is a critical one.

The meaning of "nature"

A second respect in which the modern view of natural law diverges from the classical conception revolves around the concept of nature. The

---

[11] Strauss, *op. cit.*, p. 155.

[12] Ernest Barker, *Greek Political Theory: Plato and His Predecessors,* rev. ed. (New York: Barnes & Noble, Inc., 1947), p. 27.

[13] *Ibid.*, p. 38.

[14] A. P. d'Entreves, *Natural Law: An Historical Survey* (London, 1951), p. 60.

word *nature* is, quite obviously, systematically ambiguous. In place of providing at this point an abstract analysis of the ways in which the word "nature" has been used, we shall, rather, examine two different concepts denoted by the term and contrast the classical and modern concepts in the light of that distinction. Aristotle's notion of a rational man required, both as a condition and as a prerequisite, for his essential humanity, that he "participate in the political life of a society. With the state, considered even in a broad sense, construed that is as civil society, man becomes the most unholy gluttony."[15] Man's natural place in the world is within the confines of a state—a political entity whose institutions create the conditions under which he can fulfill his true nature as a human being. The state is a natural expression of man's natural character; man is, after all, a *political animal*. The same point is made, albeit in an idealized sense, by Plato.

The modern point of view of nature and man's relation to it is articulated in its most extreme and uncompromising aspect by Rousseau. In his *Discourse on the Origin of Inequality Among Men* (1754) Rousseau condemns civil society which he perceives as the agency responsible for contributing to the degeneration of natural human character. In nature, conceived here as a pre-civil, nonpolitical condition anterior to political and social organization, man may be, in Aristotle's words, a savage, but he is, at any rate, a *noble savage*. The state (civil society) which Aristotle sees as a natural condition of human life, becomes for Rousseau, the agency which perverts his natural condition. "Man is born free, yet everywhere he is in chains." In his *Discourse* we find confirmation of this view: ". . . our souls have been corrupted in the proportion in which our sciences and arts have advanced to perfection." Yet, the important issue here is not how Rousseau views the perversity of civilized life, but rather the conception of nature which he espouses.[16] Whatever else may be *natural* to man, the state is not. And this view contrasts sharply with Aristotle's classical view. It is, of course, not surprising that Rousseau is a vociferous critic of natural law theory. But if we abstract his view of

---

[15] Aristotle, *Politics*, Bk. I, II, sections 15, 16.

[16] It should be observed that this interpretation of Rousseau is at odds with that expressed by David Ritchie in his *Natural Rights* (George Allen & Unwin, Ltd., 1894), p. 48 f.; and also with those of C. W. Vaughan in his edition of *J. J. Rousseau: The Political Writings* (Oxford: Basil Blackwell, 1915), 2 vols. See particularly vol. I, "Introduction," p. 16 ff.

nature and couple it with a belief in natural law theory, we discover Locke, to whom we now turn.

The theory of natural law according to Locke is closely linked to his theory of the social contract. In nature all men are equal, but in society some men are rulers and others are ruled. How this difference is to be explained is another subject to be discussed elsewhere.[17] Natural equality of men is based on the availability to all men of the dictate of reason—the source of natural law. The law of nature "teaches all mankind, who will but consult it, that being all equal and independent, no one ought to harm another in his life, health, liberty, or possessions." The natural law prescribes natural rights, among these are man's right to his own person, to property (to be understood in a special way), and to liberty. These rights are bequeathed to men by nature itself. They are part of whatever may be involved in being a man. They are natural to men and belong to men before the state ever comes into existence. Indeed, no state may abrogate these rights whatever the circumstances on pain of being destroyed.

CONTEMPORARY VIEWS OF NATURAL LAW

Some contemporary political theorists subscribe to a theory of natural law. Not surprisingly their formulations are more or less extentions and elaborations of views which we have stated and which belong for the most part either to classical or modern theories of natural law. Some, however, have provided some interesting innovations to the earlier theories and it is these which we now consider.

1. Consider Margaret Mead's definition of the natural law: " 'Natural law' might thus be defined as those rules of behavior which had developed from a species-specific capacity to ethicalize as a feature of those examples of such ethicalizing that appear in all known societies."[18] Among the examples which Mead gives are: ". . . rules concerning the sacredness of life (under some circumstances), rules concerning the prohibition of incest in the pri-

[17] *Infra,* chap. 6.

[18] Margaret Mead, "Some Anthropological Considerations Concerning Natural Law," *Natural Law Forum,* Vol. 6 (University of Notre Dame Law School, 1961), p. 54.

mary familial relationships in most circumstances and rules governing an individual's rights over some differentiated physical or cultural items. . . ."

2. Another modern argument (or, perhaps better, recent restatement of a classical conception) is expressed by Leo Strauss. Strauss contends that the denial of the natural law thesis: "necessarily leads to nihilism or to the view that every preference, however evil, base, or insane, has to be judged before the tribunal of reason to be as legitimate as any other preference."[19]
3. The natural law may be expressed as denoting moral and ethical truths which are self-evident and which cannot (psychologically) be denied or doubted. This seems to be the meaning of E. F. Carritt's statement that: "I know the reality of obligations and goodness with as much self-evidence as I know logical, geometrical, or causal necessitation. . . . I cannot doubt the obligation to keep promises or to spare unnecessary pain; I cannot doubt that the man who, believing he has a duty, tries to fulfill it to his own hindrance does a good act."[20]
4. The Roman Catholic philosopher, Jacques Maritain, speaks of the natural law as follows: "Natural law is the ensemble of things to do and not to do which follow therefrom in *necessary* fashion, and *from the simple act that man is man* nothing else being taken into account."[21]
5. A. P. d'Entreves in his admirable little book, *Natural Law,* quotes with apparent approval, the German philosophy of Wilhelm Dilthey as saying that: "In order to understand the dominance of natural law we must interpret it psychologically, and therefore relate it to the forces that operated through its medium."[22]

d'Entreves goes on to remark that what he finds interesting about the theory of natural law is the "part that the doctrine has played in the course of our history." "But for natural law the petty laws of a small peasant community of peninsular Italy would never have become the universal law of an international civilization. But for natural law the

[19] Leo Strauss, *Natural Right and History* (Chicago, 1952), p. 52.

[20] E. F. Carritt, *Ethical and Political Thinking* (Oxford, 1947), p. 43.

[21] Jacques Maritain, *The Rights of Man and Natural Law* (New York, 1943), pp. 58–64.

[22] d'Entreves, *op. cit.,* p. 12.

great medieval synthesis of godly and of worldly wisdom would not have been possible. But for natural law there would probably have been no American and no French revolution, nor could the great ideals of freedom and equality have found their way into the law-books after having found it into the hearts of man."[23]

MODELS OF NATURAL LAW

It is abundantly clear that "natural law" means many different things to many different people. We shall try, in this discussion, to construct models of representative theories of natural law and we shall do so without reference to the particular formulations of particular theorists. Such a topology will stress certain distinctive features of what has variously been characterized as natural law—and our efforts will be directed to making clear the plethora of constructions which we have gathered in a random-like fashion in the first section.

A word about "model-building" is in order. A model, as it is construed in this context, is an idealization based on the synthesis of certain features abstracted from a multiplicity of particular instances. The features which we decide to abstract are chosen according to pragmatic criteria. That is to say, the business of structuring models is to establish a basis for analyzing and clarifying key concepts, and the criteria which determine the features which are to be emphasized are nonhistorical. The best idealized structures are those which enable us to clarify, explain, and understand social phenomena, independent of the particular meaning a given theory may have had for a given political theorist at some point or other in the past. We shall, therefore, discuss the problem of natural law where natural law is construed variously as (1) moral law;[24] (2) theological law; (3) science; (4) ideology; (5) reason; and (6) natural law as the essence of man.

Natural law as moral law

The natural law is an imperative which exhorts all men to act in accordance with certain moral principles. These principles are taken to

---

[23] *Ibid.*, p. 13.

[24] Cf. Felix Oppenheim: "Natural Law Thesis: Affirmation or Denial?" *American Political Science Review,* March, 1957, pp. 41 f.

be indisputably and demonstrably true. There are, on this view: "normative statements in the area of law and politics which are demonstrably true or false . . . certain kinds of political behavior which can be proven to be morally right or wrong . . . [and] political institutions which are objectively just or unjust."[25] Natural law is not, therefore, merely a formal or structural concept; it has a moral content as well. As Grotius declares: ". . . the law of nature is a dictate of right reason which points out that an act . . . has in it a quality of *moral baseness* or *moral necessity*."[26] But the law of nature does more than simply *point out* the moral status of an act, it *exhorts* us to behave in certain definable ways: it *prescribes* what constitutes moral conduct in a given case.[27]

Interpreted this way, it becomes possible to evaluate a given legal system or political institution as "good" or "bad"; to say, for example, that "only good laws are laws" and to reject laws and constitutions which are seen as incompatible with the natural law (an external, immutable moral command which may never, under any circumstances, be abrogated). Let us consider an example of how the natural law (as moral law) might be used in a moral-legal argument.

A conscientious objector might, on purely moral grounds, refuse to recognize an obligation to obey a positive law which requires him to bear arms in "defense" of the nation of which he is a citizen. He takes the position that it is the law of nature that human life is inviolate, that this value is universal, and that there are no conditions where it does not apply. A civil law, this argument might continue, which recognizes conditions under which a man is not merely justified in depriving another of his life, but which obliges him to do so, is an evil law.

The ultimate test of a good law is that it is compatible with the natural (moral) law. The view, expressed by Blackstone that natural law is the "ultimate measure of obligation by which all legal precepts must be tried and from which they derive their whole force and authority,"[28] is the

---

[25] *Ibid.*, p. 42.

[26] *De Iure Belli ac Pacis,* I, i, 10 (my italics). Cf. d'Entreves, *op. cit.*, p. 81.

[27] Following R. M. Hare [*The Language of Morals* (Oxford, 1952), pp. 163–79] and Oppenheim (*op. cit.*, p. 43n), a value-judgment is used in an evaluative way only when it implies an imperative. Thus, the judgment "to do *x* is just" implies the imperative, "do *x!*"

[28] Roscoe Pound, *Law and Morals* (Chapel Hill, 1924), pp. 1–2.

outcome of an ancient conviction: "That the purpose of law is not only to make men obedient, but to help them to be virtuous."[29]

Natural law as theological law

Though pre-Reformation Christian theologians were careful to distinguish between theological or divine law on the one hand, and the law of nature on the other, statements by post-Reformation theologians seem to imply that God is the guarantor of natural law. Whereas, Aquinas, for example, believed that there would be a natural law even if God did not exist; Emil Brunner argues that the natural law is to be found in the will of the living God.[30] In the recent revival of the natural law thesis the view has been repeatedly advanced by Christian theologians that natural law and natural rights rest wholly on certain theological principles which, if denied, imply the denial of the natural law. Generally the theological principle in question is the belief in a God who has ordained the natural law as a characteristic property of human life. It appears, moreover, that not all conceptions of God would be equally compatible with this view. A God who endows men with inalienable rights, who issues commands, and legislates laws for settling the disputes which divide men, is a special sort of divinity, an essentially anthropomorphic God who must be supposed to speak to all men and whose words may convincingly be referred to in the adjudication of disputes.

Natural law as science

In this category fall those concepts of natural law which attempt to demonstrate the universal and natural character of those cultural properties or folkways which can be discovered in all peoples of whatever level of community and social life they may have achieved. Anthropological evidence is generally thought to lend strong support to this particular conception of the natural law. Anthropologists (like Mead) have observed that there seem to be certain rules of conduct which no observed societies, no matter how primitive, are lacking.

---

[29] d'Entreves, *op. cit.*, p. 83.

[30] Emil Brunner, *Justice and the Social Order* (New York, 1945), p. 8.

Laws governing property, laws protecting life (under certain circumstances) and laws prohibiting certain sexual practices (e.g. incest) are found, apparently, in every known culture. That this is so cannot be explained, it is thought, by referring to local conditions such as climate or political organization or economic and social relationship. For though these may all vary from one culture to another, the formal prohibitions against certain practices do not vary accordingly. Thus, it is reasonable to believe that there exists universal modes of conduct peculiar to human beings in general, moral imperatives whose objective force is demonstrated by the fact that no one, anywhere, can for long doubt their validity. From the fact that these values are universally recognized by men, it is supposed that they ought to be practiced by them. To discover, then, the content of the natural law, it is necessary only to study the history and structure of cultures in order to discover those cultural properties which are invariably found among them.

Natural law as ideology

Another dimension of the theory of natural law treats the doctrine as though questions concerning the truth or validity of the theory were irrelevant. What is significant about the theory of natural law, according to this view, is the effects which the theory has had on the affairs of men. This seems to be what d'Entreves has in mind when he says that without the theory of natural law, the great ideals of freedom and equality would never have become codified in the statutes of living societies. In this context, natural law is not being construed as a theory at all, but rather as a belief or attitude which has served desirable or, perhaps (depending on one's point of view) undesirable ends. It is a convenient instrument and even if it were not a true society, it must nonetheless be made "an inviolable precept in every society, before it can be civilized or made free."[31]

Historically and logically the theory of natural law seems to be politically neutral. That is to say, logically the theory, so far as its formal structure is concerned, does not imply or exclude any particular political organization. Accordingly, historically, "the doctrine of natural law is at times conservative, at times reformatory or revolutionary in character. It

[31] *Works of John Adams* (1851), p. 9.

either justifies positive law by proclaiming its agreement with the natural . . . or it puts in question the validity of positive law by claiming that it is in contradiction to one of the presupposed absolutes. The revolutionary doctrine of natural law, like the conservative, is concerned not with the cognition of positive law, of legal reality, but with its *defense* or *attack,* with a political not with a scientific task."[32]

Others who treat the doctrine of natural law as an ideology tend to view it as expression of certain specific interests. The fact that the right to own property is often thought to be guaranteed by natural law has suggested to some theorists that natural law is an ideological justification invented by property owning classes in order to perpetuate and advance their own private interests.

Evaluating the models

Natural law as moral law. We turn now to a critical examination of the theory of natural law. The natural law, when it is construed as moral law, must suppose as a corollary that there exist eternal and immutable moral truths. A major counterargument to this view of the natural law consists in denying that it is possible to verify the truth of ethical propositions, and therefore ethical statements, or statements of value are logically different from those statements which appear in scientific or descriptive languages. According to this view,[33] the meaning of a proposition is contingent upon the manner in which it can be verified. Since ethical statements cannot be verified or confirmed by referring to some experience or other, and since they are not purely formal statements (e.g. $7 + 5 = 12$) then they are not, in a technical sense, meaningful.[34] Furthermore, when we say that an action or a person is "good" or "just," we are not, on this view, asserting anything about the person or action.

[32] Hans Kelson, *General Theory of Law and State* (New York: Russell & Russell, 1961), p. 11 (my italics).

[33] See Alfred J. Ayer, *Language, Truth and Logic* (New York: Dover Publications, Inc., 1946), pp. 102–19. Also Vernon Van Dyke, *Political Science: A Philosophical Analysis* (Stanford: Stanford University Press, 1960), pp. 8–13; and A. R. M. Murray, *An Introduction to Political Philosophy* (London: Cohen & West, 1953), pp. 1–23. Also Quentin Gibson, *The Logic of Social Enquiry* (London: Routledge & Kegan Paul, 1960), pp. 59–69.

[34] For an explanation of this view see, *infra.,* Chapter 1.

"Good" and "just," it is argued, are not properties or qualities of things in the same way in which "red" or "hard" may be a property of something. There are, therefore, no intrinsically or essentially "good" or "just" actions or persons, and there exist no eternal or immutable ethical values with regard to which a specific action may be judged.

This counterargument is sometimes called a "noncognitivist"[35] theory of value and stands in juxtaposition to the theory we have been examining which might be termed a "cognitivist" approach to value. The dispute is one about the status of our knowledge of matters of value. The natural law theorist, who sees the natural law as moral law, must suppose that values can be known with the same (or a greater) degree of certainty as facts are known. The "noncognitivist" counterargument insists that they cannot be known with equal certainty if, indeed, they can be known at all. The proponents of this latter argument may themselves not propose an alternative theory of value, except in this negative sense. To deny the objectivity of values is not to be interpreted as necessarily implying a specific theory of value. The denial of the concept of eternal values is compatible with a variety of views about morality which are not themselves compatible with each other. It is important to see that "value noncognitivism" does not necessarily imply that there are no values whatever, or even, that values are purely subjective preferences, raw appetite, or desire.[36]

A second difficulty with the view that there are eternal and immutable moral laws comes about when we consider that contrary commands may issue from the same natural law. How do we resolve, for example, two incompatible demands upon us, each justified by natural law? The natural law, for example, is thought to assert that men are free and that men are equal. Freedom and equality are not always compatible with each other. How does the natural law provide the criteria necessary for resolving a dispute where the two are in conflict? A theorist who takes the position that men are by nature free and equal must resolve the conflict when it arises in terms of a norm which does not itself have its

---

[35] Following, inter alia, Felix Oppenheim, "Natural Law Thesis: Affirmation or Denial," *American Political Science Review,* Vol. LI, No. 1 (March, 1957).

[36] John Wild, *Plato's Modern Enemies and the Theory of Natural Law* (Chicago: University of Chicago, 1953), p. 215.

justification ordained by the natural law. Consider a case where two disputants take the following positions:

A. "It is only just that the wealth of a community be equitably distributed among all men, for it is so ordained by the natural law that all men be treated equally."

B. "To deprive me of my property in the name of equality is to do me an injustice for the natural law assures me that I am free and part of what is involved in being free is to be free to dispose of my property as I see fit."

Both appeal to the natural law; to equality on the one hand, to freedom on the other. Yet the issue cannot be resolved by referring to still another natural law. For the natural law does not provide a means for adjudicating between conflicting laws, nor can it provide such means since to do so would be tantamount to granting to a higher authority a status which it claims for itself. Disputes about conflicting natural laws are generally settled, if they are settled at all, by introducing other criteria: a theory of utility for example, or tradition, custom, and precedence.

Another apparent difficulty issues from the disparate character of questions concerning morality on the one hand and legality on the other. There are, obviously, a good many issues which are properly the concern of morality which are not necessarily mirrored in civil law. Whether or not to support one's aged mother where one is able to do so and where a *bonafide* need exists is a moral question. Most people in our culture would be inclined to agree that to refuse such support is immoral. Yet, there are no civil laws which require that one be coerced to do so on pain of suffering civil sanctions. There are many such cases where morality commands and the law is silent: "Tell the truth" (not a legal matter except under conditions when it is specified as such); "Honor thy mother and father," "Love thy neighbor," "Keep your promises," "to thine ownself be true," and so on. On the other hand, a considerable segment of positive law has no moral content whatever. A law which requires two witnesses to a will, or the renewal of a permit to drive an automobile every other year, or laws of enablement, are not fit subjects of moral concern.

Now these latter cases where the law has no moral content are recognized by natural law theorists to be nonmoral rules of conduct established by convention and custom. Cicero called them *jus civile* and Aquinas thought of them as *human laws*. The law of a community may be whatever it is so long as it is appropriate to the circumstances which occasioned it and so far as it is about issues where the natural law does not apply. But the former case, where a moral imperative may not be reflected in existing legal codes, creates difficulties which we cited to point this disparity out have several features in common. There are no formal sanctions against the breaking of a moral law. One may well suffer the expression of disapprobation by the community, but one cannot be put in prison for violating a moral law. Secondly, the law can coerce a person to behave in certain ways, but it cannot make him moral. If the law requires that one support one's indigent mother and the requisite conduct is forthcoming but against one's will, we would hardly call such a person moral. Can one be said to behave morally if the behavior in question is the result of threats of punishment?

Whatever else the natural law may be said to be, it does not appear reasonable to interpret it as moral law. As one natural law theorist in the neo-Kantian tradition put the point:

> The juridical criterion differs from the moral . . . by its logical position. . . . The logical function of law exerts its influence where a collision between the acts of two or more agents or an antithesis between two or more wills is possible, and tends to promote objective coordination among them. The moral criterion, on the other hand, supposes an antithesis between two or more possible acts of the same agent and tends to settle internal strife, that is, to establish a subjective ethical order.[37]

In short, as one critic says, "the essential function of law is to make life in society possible. Law presupposes society. Morals do not. Moral experience is essentially a matter for the individual. Legal experience is tied to the notion of a community."[38]

Natural law as theological law. The view is advanced by some natural law theorists that natural law and natural rights rest wholly on certain theological premises, which, if denied, imply the denial of the

[37] Giorgio Del Vecchio, *The Formal Basis of Law* (New York: Macmillan Co., 1921), pp. 63–64.

[38] d'Entreves, *op. cit.*, p. 85.

theory of natural law; a theory of natural law is defensible only if it is construed as an extension or derivation of theological principles. The view might be expressed in a solemn and impressive quote from T. D. Weldon:

> Praise the Lord! for he hath spoken,
> Worlds his mighty voice obeyed.
> Laws which never shall be broken
> For their guidance he hath made.[39]

We have seen this theme and variations of it expressed by several thinkers cited in the last section of this chapter. We must, however, be careful to distinguish between those who see the natural law as an independent phenomena which may exist with or without the support of the deity and those theorists who hold to the view being considered here, for whom the natural law is literally God's command. An instance of the latter view is St. Paul's dictum that every man in his heart knows "the law of God, which forbids man to sin, and commands him to do what is right."

Two more or less obvious difficulties with this conception of natural law immediately come to mind. First, the logic of the words "sin" and "doing right" is such that it seems redundant to say that sin is forbidden. To inform someone that a given act is sinful is comparable to saying that it ought not to be done. That is not to deny that there are situations where one may say: "I know it is sinful to do *x*, but let's do it anyway." For nothing is more apparent in human behavior than that we often do what we desire rather than what we ought to do. But such situations merely emphasize the fact that when conduct is characterized as sinful we are expressing, perhaps, among other things, that we ought not to engage in that sort of conduct. It would seem, therefore, that according to Paul's dictum, God is doing little more than legislating a rule governing the use of the concept "sin" such that part of the meaning of "sinful" is "that which one ought not to do."

The second fairly obvious objection to this interpretation of natural law rests on the presumption that natural law is compelling because it is God's command. Belief in natural law, therefore, presupposes belief in

---

[39] T. D. Weldon, *The Vocabulary of Politics* (London: Penguin Books Ltd., 1953), p. 62.

God. Thus the universality of the natural law is limited to those who, on independent grounds, have affirmed a belief in God. Further, since not all conceptions of God are compatible with natural law doctrine, a belief in God is not in itself a sufficient condition for a belief in natural law. It is a curious fact that of those who have set themselves the task of demonstrating the existence of a Divinity, none has attempted to prove that all these demonstrations prove the existence of the same sort of entity. By no means are all conceptions of God equally amenable to the notion of natural law. Thus, this view of the natural law can hardly claim to be valid universally.

Another difficulty comes about when we consider the sources of knowledge for the *dicta* of natural law. If natural law is the word of God, then there must exist procedures for deciding what His word is and how it is to be discovered. Differences of opinion about the authenticity of one piece of revealed knowledge over another will be reflected in differences of opinion concerning what the natural law is. It would appear then, that what one takes the natural law to be depends upon which books or parts of books one thinks are authoritative. Since there cannot be objective criteria for deciding which piece of allegedly revealed knowledge is in fact revealed knowledge, there cannot be, by the same token, objective criteria for determining what the natural law happens to be.

A theory of natural law based on revelation seems to present a special sort of problem: the distinction between a law and a command. T. D. Weldon states the problem in the following way:

> God has issued a number of commands or fiats which have to be obeyed by physical and biological creation. These are the Laws of Nature. Rivers do not choose to run downhill. They cannot help it. There is a law which shall never be broken except occasionally and by what is called a miracle, in accordance with which their behavior is eternally and inexorably determined. The difference between these Laws of Nature and moral and political laws is that the latter can be broken since men, unlike rivers and plants, are capable of being disobedient and wicked. But still the law is there. And just as it is the function of natural philosophy to discover and tell us about natural laws so it is the function of the moral philosopher of law to tell us about the true, real, or ideal laws of commonwealths.[40]

[40] *Ibid.*, p. 62.

It is Weldon's point that "law" and "command" are not equivalent concepts and that they differ in at least one important respect. To say: "Put out that cigarette," is not to assert a proposition at all for it cannot sensibly be said that the utterance is true or false. If, on the other hand, one says, "Smoking on this train is prohibited," the utterance is a proposition since its truth or falsity may be decided by the simple expedient of looking up the rules of the railroad company. Not merely is the rule to be discovered there, but it would make perfectly good sense to ask why it is there in the first place, what adverse conditions it was intended to meet, and what, if any, the circumstances are under which it would be sensible to change the rule. The rule must be justified to us, and we must, collectively and in the long run, agree that it is a sensible rule to make and to obey. A command, however, need not fulfill any of these conditions. God's commands may not be questioned in this fashion, it is argued, because as the arbiter of what is reasonable we cannot in turn ask whether He is Himself subject to reason as a criteria of legitimacy. A law is like the rule of the railroad company; a command is of a logically different order.

Natural law as science. In an earlier discussion Margaret Mead was cited as an instance of one who defended the doctrine of natural law on scientific grounds. To her we attributed the view that natural law consists of rules of behavior which appear in all known societies. Among the examples of such rules she offered the following: "rules concerning the sacredness of life (under certain circumstances), rules concerning the prohibition of incest in the primary familial relationships in most circumstances, and rules governing an individual's rights over some differential physical or cultural items."[41]

The plausibility of this view of the natural law rests partly on the possible connection between statements of fact on the one hand and ethical statements on the other. The obvious argument against Mead's view consists in demonstrating (1) that science contains no ethical statements, (2) that both inductive and deductive arguments cannot yield conclusions which contain terms which do not appear in the premises, and that therefore (3) no scientific judgment may be made about ethical questions. Applying this argument to Mead's examples, it

---

[41] Mead, *op. cit.*, p. 53.

would appear that from the fact that every observed culture exhibits certain practices or recognizes certain values or rights, it cannot logically follow that such cultures ought to do so, or that such practices are intrinsically valuable. Presumably only statements of fact may be inferred from factual premises. If Mead's observations were expressed as constituents of a piece of inductive inference, they might be expressed as follows:

Premise: Cultures X, Y, and Z prohibit incest.
Conclusion: In view of these facts, it is more probable that all cultures prohibit incest.

We cannot validly conclude that cultures *ought* to prohibit incest.

This argument is certainly a commonplace one, and the reader has no doubt often encountered it; it is generally stated in a shorthand way by saying that facts and values are two quite different sorts of things, and that it is not logically possible to derive one from the other. If this is so, then the scientific view of natural law cannot be a valid one and Mead must be interpreted as using the concept natural law in a rather unusual way. Her attempt to establish the existence of certain natural laws parallels the procedures involved in various sciences to establish certain so-called laws of nature. The natural law as a legal or political or moral concept is clearly quite different in character from the scientific conception of the law of nature. Laws of nature refer, after all, to statistical uniformities in the physical world. Though cultural uniformities may be discovered it would be a mistake to suppose that these shed significant light on the natural law. For natural law must mean more than the simple fact that some cultural practices appear to be universal, or it bears little resemblance to the ways in which the concept "natural law" has been used by others. If there can be said to be one strand of thought common to all theories of natural law, it is the prescriptive character of the concept. But Mead's notion of the natural law, as we have seen, does not admit, on logical grounds, to prescription.

Suppose, however, that we challenge the logical presumption that science does not contain statements of value. One might argue that the presumption in question depends upon what one means by "statements of value." If one means to say that a statement of value is a statement about what is desirable and that what is desirable is that which is in fact desired by someone, then it is apparent that observation can confirm whether an action or policy is held to be desirable by someone or other. This interpretation of ethical statements renders them indistinguishable from statements of fact and makes ethics and morality a subdivision of science. There may be serious difficulties with this view, but some distinguished philosophers and political thinkers have subscribed to it—among them J. S. Mill.[42] However, if this view may be made to hold in a convincing fashion, have we reestablished Mead's concept of natural law as an adequate one? The answer seems to be that we are still left with some questions about Mead's analysis and these questions have to do with the nature of the empirical findings themselves.

It may be true that all observed societies exhibit certain general practices which we are inclined to describe as ethical; so far as these observations are contingent, their universal character may be upset by the next society examined. In other words, the ethical beliefs which are alleged to be universal are not established by deducing that these must be so because, for example, they are essential properties of all human beings, but rather because they have been observed to hold in all those societies which have been examined. Were their universality established in another fashion, by intuition or deduction, they would not count as scientific conclusions. For these to be arrived at on scientific grounds, it is required that it be possible for us to imagine a society that does *not* conduct its affairs according to these ethical principles. That is to say, we must be able to describe those conditions or occurrences which would, if observed, disconfirm or disverify the hypothesis in question. Now according to Mead, the right to property is construed in such as fashion that it does not appear to be a conclusion arrived at scientifically. All societies, she alleges, prescribe certain property rights, but she does not say precisely what will count as "property" except to say that at the very least each person in all societies has a name which is singularly his and his alone. Now this is indeed, as she grants, a bizarre sense of the word "property." We must conclude that to understand the word "property" in this way is to virtually eliminate the possibility of discovering a dis-

---

[42] Cf. *infra,* chap. 3

confirming instance, in any practical sense, of the allegation or hypothesis that all societies place some value on private property. Mead appears to be saying more about the use of the word "property," and in particular, how *she* proposes to use it, than she is saying something about the sorts of ethical practices or values observed in cultures. There is a vast difference between linguistic legislation and scientific conclusions, and it is a serious matter when the two are muddled.

Natural law as ideology. The concept of ideology has often driven those who concern themselves with such matters to distraction. Some have solved the problem by the simple expediency of using the concept in whatever context their literary ear finds appropriate. In an earlier discussion the ideological interpretation of natural law is stated as claiming that arguments about the truth or falsity of natural law are fundamentally irrelevant and that the chief importance of a theory is to be sought in the manner in which it has been used to justify or condemn political institutions, political movements, or agencies of political power. "Ideology" in this sense, is used principally to denote statements whose logical and empirical truth play, at best, a secondary role to their political efficacy. This interpretation is not to be confused with, though it appears similar to, the concept of the therapeutic lie or the notion of the political myth. The latter notions are postanalytic in the sense that a decision has been made as to their truth-functional character, namely, that they allege what is in fact false, but that they are important so far as they contribute to certain political beliefs which are thought to be desirable. Theories of racial superiority are of this sort. The belief that Aryans are racially superior to Jews or that Englishmen are racially superior to Irishmen are myths, rather than ideologies, for they are known to be false, but may be affirmed because they induce in those who believe them patterns of behavior desired by the creators and perpetuators of the myth. An ideology, on the other hand, is preanalytic, in the sense that its truth or falsity has yet to be determined, if it can be determined at all (for some ideologies, like those of Marx, claim that the very concepts of truth and falsity are ideological in character). An ideology may become myth, but myths do not become ideologies.

We have seen that there are those who defend natural law theories on the grounds that great and important historical movements have been possible because of them (d'Entreves); or that if there were no natural laws, then "every preference, however evil, base, or insane, has to be judged before the tribunal of reason to be as legitimate as any other preference."[43]

Now to say that the truth of the theory of natural law is irrelevant in view of the part which the doctrine has played in the course of history[44] is, in effect, to urge an ideological interpretation of the doctrine. This view appears to rest on the assumption that there is in history some special or unique or particular role which may be assigned to the theory of natural law. If this construction of the natural law were merely a plea that the theory must be taken seriously if we are to understand basic political principles in historical perspective, surely no one would quarrel with this view. But if we are to suppose that the theory, true or false, is to be credited with bringing about desirable political institutions and discouraging other undesirable political possibilities, then it becomes necessary to discuss, on other grounds having nothing to do with natural law, what is desirable in political terms and what is not. It appears that this interpretation of natural law is wholly misguided, for it is self-defeating. It is to the natural law that one must appeal in order to discover what is good and what is bad in political life, according to the traditional meaning of natural law. If one takes the position that natural law is ideologically correct because it advances the welfare of mankind, then it seems that natural law has an instrumental function which leaves us groping for criteria governing what is to be taken as the public good—a task traditionally assigned to the natural law theory itself.

The other ground for this interpretation of the natural law, put forward by Leo Strauss, argues that nihilism is the deplorable consequence of denying natural law: the view that there can be no criteria for deciding between conflicting political principles. This view assumes that nihilism and natural law are mutually exclusive alternatives and that since the former is unacceptable on moral grounds, we have no choice but to subscribe to the latter, whether or not it can be established as a correct theory. But is it the case that there are no alternatives to nihilism on the one hand and natural law theory on the other? Surely we are in a bind if there are no such alternatives, else we must hold as true a theory

[43] Strauss, *op. cit.,* p. 42.
[44] d'Entreves, *op. cit.,* p. 13.

which has not been demonstrated to be true, a sad state of affairs for those who respect reason.

Reason, nature, and natural law

It is obvious that a prominent theme in theories of natural law is reason.[45] That reason is involved in the discovery and articulation of the natural law is a point of agreement among many theorists whose notion of the natural law may, in other respects, be quite widely divergent. Consider Cicero's observation that "there is . . . a true law, namely *right reason*—which is in accordance with *nature,* applies to all men and is unchangeable and eternal;" or Grotius' dictum that the *law of nature* is a dictate of *right reason.* Are we confident that we know what is meant by "reason" or by "nature" or by "right" in these contexts? What follows are some arguments intended to shatter whatever confidence we might have had in the clarity and distinctness of these concepts.

One difficulty lies in the peculiar status given to reason in theories of natural law. Reason, it is thought, is that property or characteristic which serves to distinguish man from lower animals. Aristotle thought that reason is the *essence* of being human, a necessary condition of humanity. To express the point in an older rhetoric: Reason is that without which man could neither be nor be conceived. Since reason is man's defining characteristic, it is the foundation too, it is thought, of his natural rights as a human being; and this is thought to be so because it is this characteristic property which enables man to engage in his most characteristic activity, viz, living in society according to rules which he enables for himself in accordance with reason.

Now if reason is to be understood in a narrow sense as the ability to abstract and generalize by the use of symbols in speech and writing, then it is clear that reasoning is an activity beyond the capacity of nonhuman animals. But it is equally clear that the use of symbols by men is as variable a capacity among them as sight and hearing. Do the rights of man vary as men's ability to symbolize varies?

Reason in its common acceptance is used in a broader sense and often

---

[45] This discussion is heavily influenced by Margaret McDonald, "Natural Rights," *Philosophy, Politics and Society,* ed. Peter Laslett (Oxford: Basil Blackwell, 1956).

includes nonverbal expressions of intelligence. In fact, the most characteristic of human activities do not depend upon abstractions or the use of symbols; for example, cooking, driving, sewing, carpentry. In these intelligent activities, men are joined by other creatures who perform with skill and adaptability. They use tools, exploit each other, wage war, and live a highly organized social life. Reason understood in this latter sense, as "knowing how" as well as "knowing that" can no longer serve as an exclusive attribute of human beings.

But what must be granted here, is the fact that a certain level of intellectual development must be attained before it occurs to men to abstract their own interests and rights from those of others in society. At some levels of social development men may simply leave unquestioned that which custom prescribes. With greater sophistication, greater rationality, as it were, men may come to claim rights as individuals independent of society. To this extent the ability to claim natural rights depends upon reason. But we cannot conclude from this fact that reason alone constitutes the essential nature of man or that the intrinsic worth of a human being is predicated on his intelligence. Reason is one, but not the only, human excellence.[46]

Reason may be thought to play a somewhat different role. Consider the hypothesis that there are certain political and social propositions which all of us take to be firmly established as being true though not as being clearly demonstrable. Such truths might be said to be self-evident. These propositions are known to all of us to be true because the nature or structure of our minds and characters are such that we cannot doubt them. The truth of these statements is, apparently, a truth of reason. As E. F. Carritt says: "I know the reality of obligations and goodness with as much self-evidence as I know logical, geometrical, or causal necessitation. . . . I cannot doubt the obligation to keep promises or spare unnecessary pain."[47]

But what is the force of the *cannot* in these statements? A statement is self-evident in one of two ways; it is either psychologically or logically self-evident. That is to say, either (1) One cannot imagine or conceive that the denial of the statement could be true (psychologically self-

---

[46] McDonald, *op. cit.,* p. 43 ff.

[47] Carritt, *op. cit.,* p. 43.

evident) or (2) The denial of the statement is self-contradictory (logically self-evident). It is fairly clear that one's obligation to keep promises is not psychologically self-evident for not only is it possible to imagine cases where one does not keep one's promises, but it is an easy matter to imagine cases where it would be irrational to do so.[48] Statements of the second sort—those which are allegedly self-evident on logical grounds may indeed be as certain as mathematical and geometrical truths. Yet this claim, rather than having the desired effect of convincing one that such propositions are informative and compelling, trivializes and renders innocuous the propositions in question. For if natural law commands are logically necessary statements, they are little more than shorthand agreements or conventions governing the use of words in our language, or in some sort of specialized language. Mathematical statements, which are after all paradigm examples of logical truths, can tell us only what we already know and about which we have already agreed. So when Maritain, for example, defines natural law as "the essence of things to do and not to do which follow therefrom in a necessary fashion, and from the simple fact that man is man, nothing else being taken into account,"[49] we can only reply that no command, no description, no observation, no sensible statement can follow from the simple tautology that "man is man."

What Maritain and others have in mind here seems to be the empirical observation that beneath the accidental or conventional predicates which attach in one way or another to all of us, there exists an essential humanity or ultimate essence and part of that essence is awareness that each man has certain natural rights, that he has these by virtue of a natural law, and that there is an end or purpose to his life which is somehow bound up with the sort of creature he is by nature.

It is true, to quote M. McDonald, that a person is "accidentally a native of England, France, America; a Red Indian, Negro, or Jew. His social environment is determined by accident of birth. He may change his family by adoption and his citizenship by naturalization. And he is accidentally, or conventionally, a doctor, soldier, employer, etc. . . . He

---

[48] The most famous discussion of the issue of keeping one's promises is to be found in Plato's *Republic,* Bk. I, in the discussion between Socrates and Polemarchus.

[49] Maritain, *op. cit.,* p. 36.

is not accidentally human. Humanity is his essence, or nature."[50] But how does the nature of man determine his natural rights? Or further, how does his nature determine that these are *necessarily* his rights? The key, of course, is *necessarily*. If it is necessary, i.e., it could not be otherwise, then it is so because Maritain and those who take the position in question have defined man's essence as having such and such properties. They proceed to deduce a necessary conclusion about the nature of man, which states only what has been said about the nature of man in the premises of the argument. Such arguments, as we have seen, are indeed true, but they are also, unfortunately, trivial.

Still, we have not examined the concept "essential humanity" or the allegation that part of what is involved in "being human" is a person's "ability to determine his ends, to put himself in tune with the ends necessarily demanded by his nature."[51] The notion that there exists a fixed and immutable nature and that there is a purpose or goal which corresponds to that nature is one which we owe principally to Aristotle. It is a notion which dies hard. Consider McDonald's analysis of this view:

> Human beings are not like exactly similar bottles of whiskey each marked "for export only" or some device indicating a common destination or end. Men do not share a fixed nature, nor, therefore, are there any ends which they must necessarily pursue in fulfilment of such nature. There is no definition of "man." There is a more or less vague set of properties which characterize in varying degrees and proportions those creatures which are called "human." These determine for each individual human being what he *can* do but not what he *must* do. If he has an I.Q. of 85, his intellectual activities will be limited; if he is physically weak, he cannot become a heavyweight boxer. If a woman has neither good looks nor acting ability, she is unlikely to succeed as a film star. But what people may do with their capacities is extremely varied, and there is no one thing which they must do in order to be human. It would be nonsense to say: "I am not going to be an actress, school teacher, a postman, a soldier, a taxpayer, but simply a human being." For what is the alternative? A man may choose whether he will become a civil servant or a schoolmaster; a conservative or a socialist, but he cannot choose whether he will be a man or a dog. There is certainly a sense in which it is often said that in the air-raid shelter or in the battle people forgot that they were officers or

---

[50] McDonald, *op. cit.,* p. 41.

[51] Maritain, *op. cit.,* p. 35.

privates, assistant secretaries or typists, rich or poor, and remembered only that they were all human beings, i.e., all liable to die without regard to status. But that is always true. . . . And . . . when the "all-clear" sounded, each returned to pursue his or her own end, not the purpose of the human race. Certainly, many human beings may cooperate in a joint enterprise to achieve a particular end which each chooses. But that cannot be generalized into the spectacle of all human beings pursuing one end. There is no end set for the human race by an abstraction called "human nature." There are only ends which individuals choose, or are forced by circumstances to accept. There are none, which they *must* accept. Men are not created for a purpose as a piano is built to produce certain sounds. Or if they are we have no idea of the purpose."[52]

For McDonald's part, it is useless metaphysical speculation to talk about a special human essence whether it be called reason or sentiment or whatever, and certainly misleading to deduce from man's allegedly defining characteristic the imputation that all men have some special end or goal common to the entire species toward which end it is the moral responsibility of man to strive.

Perhaps "human essence" refers not to reason or ends but rather to a natural human sentiment, a feeling as it were, of what is proper or fair in human affairs. In this view justice is the expression of an innate and universal moral sense which is understood as an unanalytical inclination or disinclination to accept or reject certain classes of actions. The following vignette helps make this point:

I know a man who was the first Christian missionary to live among the Dyak people in the interior of the island of Borneo. He and a British civil servant were the only white men there among tribes who only recently had advanced beyond the stage of head hunters. Another quaint custom, still practiced, was sexual hospitality; and so these two men—the missionary and the civil servant—as they made their rounds from village to village were made welcome by the chief of each village by the offer of one of his wives for the night. The civil servant accepted the gesture, and more than the gesture; my friend did not. I mention this fact to call attention not to the noble example of the virtues of Western man with centuries of the positive law and religious instruction behind him; but rather to what then began to happen behind the brow of the native chieftain. For, lo, a greater man than Solomon was there! He corrected the inequality in that state of affairs by ceasing to offer his women to the British civil servant; where upon, as is usual, the missionary was

[52] McDonald, *op. cit.*, pp. 44–45.

called in and given a lecture on the harm he was doing by contributing to the rapid disintegration of native *mores,* and told to mend his ways. What stirred in the mind of the chief, however darkly, was the sense that the unequal better be set straight, Indeed, in this noble savage there was the mind of a Rousseau with its insight that the law, to be true law, must be general in essence and in application as well as . . . general in its source; and that the wise ruler or legislator will see to it that "the conditions are the same for all."[53]

Paul Ramsey, who reports this curious tale, concludes that what has "stirred in the mind of the chief" is the recognition "that males should not extend hospitality to other males *by means of* their wives . . . or that generality of application is needed with regard to males and females alike so that no one will be tempted to make social conditions or practices more burdensome for others than he is willing to have rebound upon himself."[54] Ramsey's point seems to be that every human being, whatever the cultural and social circumstances, seems to have a *sense* of fairness of what is *just* or *fitting*.

Ramsey supposes that the chieftain perceives the fundamental inequality involved in using one of his women in a way which he, the chieftain, would apparently not wish himself to be used. The chief, Ramsey thinks, is inclined to feel some discomfort at his neglect of the golden rule so far as he is responsible for the exploitation of another person without regard to that person's wishes or best interests.

But, even if Ramsey were correct in supposing that the chief's motive in acting as he does is to set an inequality aright, it is not clear which of several possible inequalities the chief has in mind. To the disinterested observer, and in the absence of additional information about what has gone on in the chief's mind, we would be quite justified in supposing that the chief is simply not content with extending hospitality to British civil servants who do not reciprocate in like manner.

If the point which Ramsey and others wish to make is that men have a sense of right and wrong, a sense of what is fitting and what is not, independent of the cultural and social circumstances that decide which of various possible alternatives happens to be right or wrong, then no one can dispute the issue that obviously men suppose some sorts of conduct

---

[53] Ramsey, pp. 210–11.

[54] *Ibid.*, p. 211.

to be acceptable and others to be unacceptable. This is a plain fact. What is not so plain is that men, by nature or by instinct, can agree that some particular mode of conduct is invariably just and another invariably evil.

We have seen that the concept of natural law and the concept of *nature* are closely intertwined. Historically the classical conception of nature was of an "active creative force, so that the nature of a thing became an innate tendency toward the realization of a certain ideal of the thing."[55] Anything which contributes to those conditions under which an entity might best achieve the ideal is good or valuable. But it is mistaken to believe that what is good, or of value, is somehow built into the nature of things. Nature itself does not and cannot provide us with standards or ideals. Everything that exists in nature is on logical all-fours with everything else.

> There are not, by nature, prize roses, works of art, oppressed or unoppressed citizens. Standards are determined by human choice, not set by nature independently of men. Natural events cannot tell us what we ought to do until we have made certain decisions, when knowledge of natural fact will enable the most efficient means to be chosen to carry out those decisions. Natural events themselves have no value, and human beings as natural existents have no value either, whether on account of possessing intelligence or having two feet.[56]

With the conclusion of our critical analysis of some selected models of the theory of natural law, we turn now to a consideration of the alternatives to natural law.

ALTERNATIVES TO NATURAL LAW

We have discovered that of the various theories of natural law examined here, none are wholly without serious logical or empirical defects. We have seen that these defects may not themselves constitute sufficient conditions for rejecting the theories in question since it is obvious that there are occasions when the doctrine is treated less as a theory than as an ideology, though such treatment entails problems of its

---

[55] Edward S. Corwin, *The "Higher Law" Background of American Constitutional Law* (Ithaca: Cornell University Press, Great Seal Books), 1955, p. 10, n. 23.

[56] McDonald, *op. cit.*, p. 45.

own. We began our discussion of natural law with the observation that one rarely encounters a theory in any area of human inquiry which compels enduring interest and concern despite the difficulties involved in stating and defending its structure and content in a convincing fashion. One would suppose that some attempt ought to be made to explain this curious intellectual phenomena.

Historically the theory of natural law has not been without its critics. Yet, with only eccentric exceptions criticisms of the theory of natural law have been offered by those who propose alternative theories. Perhaps when we consider the alternatives to the theory of natural law for providing control, we shall better understand the tenacity with which theorists have clung to the theory of natural law.

Hobbes' attack on natural law was carried on under the guise of a supporter of the law and natural rights, for though he supported the theory rhetorically, his view of natural law and natural rights was altogether contrary to the traditional principles which have carried the banner of natural law. For when the conventional theories of natural law and natural rights set limits to what may be considered to be proper areas of human authority, and though Hobbes' laws do the same, they do so at a level so basic and on grounds so unlike the conventional theories that they, in effect, constitute a denial of what the traditional doctrine was meant to assert. Consider Plamenatz's analysis of Hobbes' position:

> Hobbes had taken this notion of natural law and had quite emasculated it; or rather, had taken the phrase and given it a new meaning. His law of nature is not properly a moral law; it consists only of rules which experience teaches men it would be to their advantage to follow if they could be sure that other men would follow them too. The laws of nature, as regards their contents, are only maxims of prudence whose general observance would put an end to the war of all against all. Merely as maxims they are not obligatory, but are so only as divine commands; and they are obligatory in a peculiar sense which does not make them what most people call moral laws. They are the commands of an omnipotent God, whom men, when they see that they are powerless before Him, cannot choose but obey. Hobbes' natural laws do not serve to limit the authority of government. It is usually not safe (and therefore not obligatory) to obey them until there is a sovereign to enforce them; and where there is a sovereign they are contained entirely in his actual commands. There is no appeal to them to show that what the sovereign commands is, in some higher sense, illegal. Hobbes' method is to take a time-

honored phrase, put a new meaning into it, and incorporate it in a theory whose purpose is to deny precisely what the traditional doctrine of natural law was meant to assert. Hobbes' method is subversive. It uses the letter of an old doctrine to destroy the spirit. It does not reject but undermines; and to that extent is of necessity ambiguous.[57]

David Hume had no intention of denying the rights and duties established on natural law grounds, but questioned the validity of the grounds themselves. According to Hume no action is intrinsically right or wrong. An action is right or wrong by virtue of some attitude toward it. For Hobbes right is the result of superior power—might makes right; Hume maintains that it is the general approval or disapproval of an action which determines whether it is right or wrong. Quoting Plamenatz:

To explain how it is that there are rules of behavior among men, both Hobbes and Hume begin by considering what it would be like if there were no such rules. If men were unrestrained in their attempts to satisfy their natural desires, they would repeatedly come into conflict with one another. But conflict is painful and men naturally seek to avoid pain. Reason teaches them, not what is inherently right and inherently wrong, but how they must behave to avoid the conflict. About these rules, as reason discovers them, there is nothing either moral or legal. For reason could as easily discover the means of exacerbating conflict. What gives to the rules which reason discovers the character of law is, Hobbes tells us, that there is someone with the will and the power to compel obedience to them. And Hume tells us that the rules are moral only because men feel as they do about them.[58] In neither case are the rules obligatory because they are rational. The office of reason is not to lay obligations upon us but to discover how we can get what we want. "Reason is and ought to be the slave of the passions."[59]

Hume supposes that this account of the role of reason constitutes a more satisfactory explanation of how rules and laws come about and a general reason for obeying them. Whatever the virtues of this alternative to natural law theory, it becomes apparent that the question as to why men feel as they do calls for a social or psychological answer.

A third sort of alternative is due to Jeremy Bentham, the English

---

[57] John Plamenatz, *Man and Society*, Vol. I (London: Longmans, 1963), pp. 300–301.

[58] But why do they feel as they do?

[59] Plamenatz, *op. cit.*, p. 302.

Utilitarian. According to Bentham, the foundation of moral and legal right is the principle of utility. "Nature has placed mankind under the governance of two sovereign masters, *pain* and *pleasure*. It is for them alone to point out what we ought to do."[60] The utilitarian ethic, though appearing to parallel Locke and the 18th century contract theorists who subscribed to Locke's psychology, actually substitutes the principle of the greatest happiness for the greatest number for natural rights and thereby effectively bankrupts the theory of natural law and natural rights. "For if morality and social institutions are justified merely by their utility, rights must be so too, and in consequence any claim to a natural right is either nonsense or merely a confused way of saying that the right really does conduce to the greatest happiness."[61] Bentham's attack on natural law was a conscious attempt to extend Hume's argument against that theory. If the two criticisms seem to be all of a piece, it is because on general principles Bentham and Hume are in agreement, but so far as Hume was unable or unwilling to provide a reasonable and sensible explanation for the rules and laws that men actually adopt (claiming that rules of property for example are chosen in a random way, that there are no good reasons for the rules or laws in question, the only requirement being that such rules exist), to that extent Bentham's analysis goes beyond Hume's. Bentham cannot permit rules to be arbitrary and correctly insists that some account must be given as to why people adopt this set rather than that set of rules. For Bentham the reasons are, of course, utilitarian. Also, Bentham launched a sustained, if not vituperative, attack on natural law and natural rights. He claimed, among other things, that to say that human laws must not be permitted to contradict natural laws, is tantamount to offering arms to every fanatic opposed to established government. Consider Bentham's argument for the futility of natural law and natural rights:

The primitive sense of the word *law*, and the ordinary meaning of the word, is—the will or command of a legislator. The *law of nature* is a figurative expression, in which nature is represented as a being; and such and such a disposition is attributed to her, which is figuratively called a law. In this sense,

---

[60] Bentham, *Introduction to the Principles of Morals and Legislation*, chap. 1, sec. 1.

[61] George H. Sabine, *History of Political Theory*, 3d ed. (New York: Henry Holt & Co., 1961), pp. 566–67.

all the general inclinations of men, all those which appear to exist independently of human societies, and from which must proceed the establishment of political and civil law, are called *laws of nature*. This is the true sense of the phrase.

But this is not the way in which it is understood. Authors have taken it in a direct sense; as if there had been a real code of natural laws. They appeal to these laws; they cite them and they oppose them, clause by clause, to the enactments of legislators. They do not see that these natural laws are laws of their own invention; that they are all at odds among themselves as to the contents of this pretended code; that they affirm without proof; that systems are as numerous as authors; and that, in reasoning in this manner, it is necessary to be always beginning anew, because everyone can advance what he pleases touching laws which are only imaginary, and so keep on disputing forever.

What is natural to man is sentiments of pleasure or pain, what are called inclinations. But to call these sentiments and these inclinations *laws*, is to introduce a false and dangerous idea. It is to set language in opposition to itself; for it is necessary to make laws precisely for the purpose of restraining these inclinations. Instead of regarding them as laws, they must be submitted to laws. It is against the strongest natural inclinations that it is necessary to have laws the most repressive. If there were a law of nature which directed all men towards their common good, laws would be useless; it would be employing a creeper to uphold an oak; it would be kindling a torch to add light to the sun.[62]

Bentham and those who join him in subscribing to the theory of utility argue that it is superior to the older theories in two important respects—it explains the same facts and it does so in a simpler fashion referring to dispositions and sentiments which may be described and understood on empirical grounds without reference to obscure metaphysical essences or ideolized conceptions of nature. What can it not do? For one thing, the utilitarian does not seem to be able to provide grounds comparable to those offered by natural law theorists for judging positive law according to the dictates of the higher law. Does that mean then, that the utilitarian has no criteria whatever for deciding right principles of legislation? The reply, of course, is that the principles of utilitarianism are themselves criteria for moral and political rules. To attack utilitarianism, the logical and pragmatic adequacy of the theory must be attacked, but

[62] Jeremy Bentham, *The Theory of Legislation* (London: Kegan Paul, Treach, Trubner & Co. Ltd., 1931), Bk. I, chap. 16.

it cannot be voided on the grounds that it does not intend to provide such ultimate criteria.

The final alternative to be considered is the real will theory. The real will theory is complex. It is associated historically with Rousseau and Hegel, though there are no doubt others who subscribe in broad outline to what may be called real will theories. Since this theory will be considered at great length in Chapter 6, we shall briefly indicate the general direction of the theory and how it may be said to be an alternative to the natural law.

Rather than grounding the ultimate criteria of right and wrong, good and bad, legal and illegal, moral and immoral, in nature, reason, or utility, the real will theorist argues that the ultimate moral arbiter is the state itself. According to this theory, the state or society has an existence and essence over and above the collectivity of individuals who comprise it. The state expresses and represents a system of values which cannot be measured or judged through references to transcendental legal or moral systems—to, that is, natural law or natural rights. For any individual person, morality may be determined by discovering what is permitted or encouraged by the state. Morality and legality are one and the same. All this depends very much on the concept of the state which this theory accepts. We shall examine the theory and its defects below.

CONCLUSION

How far have we come in this discussion? We have stated various theories of natural law and natural rights, we have examined abstracted models of the theory and found them to be logically or empirically defective, we have shown that alternatives to the theory exist which, if not established as being more adequate, have nonetheless not yet been as thoroughly discredited as the theory of natural law. Yet we have neglected to explain this curious phenomena—this tenacity which we attribute to the theory.

The search for natural law is the quest for a primary moral postulate. We seek a proposition, or a set of propositions, which we believe to be true quite apart from whether their truth can be established in the conventional and accepted manner of scientific or logical truths. To refuse to affirm the essential validity of a moral rule (as, for example, that no one ought ever to cause another unnecessary pain) on the grounds that it cannot be demonstrated in a fashion comparable to scientific statements, is nothing less than silly. Yet, if we assert our belief in the truth or validity of such statements, the belief must be seen as irrational. For whatever else we might want to include in the meaning of the word reason, at the very least "to the rational" must mean the disposition to accept or reject beliefs on the basis of evidence which may be brought to bear in support of that belief. Normally we should be inclined to withhold characterizing someone as reasonable if he affirms a belief in statements which either cannot be confirmed or which have been clearly demonstrated to be false. Yet the propositions of natural law are not in the least subject to demonstration. We cannot affirm or disconfirm their validity. It is this property which makes them natural laws.

We are faced with a paradox. If we affirm our belief in moral rules, we believe something to be true which we cannot demonstrate to be true. If we refuse to affirm a belief in moral rules, then there are no moral principles at all to guide our political and personal lives. The answer, if there is an answer, must lie in some third possibility.

3

The concept of the state, I

In an earlier chapter, we cited Isaiah Berlin as asserting the view that "wherever concepts grow firm and clear and acquire universal acceptance, a new science, natural or formal comes into being."[1] One of the surest indications that a scientific inquiry is not yet appropriate or even possible comes about when we are faced with concepts which raise questions for which there are no set procedures or automatic techniques allowing for solutions. Perhaps the best case of a concept in politics which cannot be treated with the sort of confidence required by scientific methods, is the concept of the *state*. Few concepts in political language are as ambiguous and misleading as this. Yet, the *state* is after all what politics is all about. Our first task is to clarify the differences between the concept of the *state* and a host of other concepts with which it is often confused: as a social whole, as a social association, as nation-state, as city-state, as society, as community, etc. Secondly, we shall consider the state as it is construed by political theorists: Aristotle's conception of the state as a natural entity, a creation of nature; Augustine's view of the state as an expression of original sin; Thrasymachus or Machiavelli regarding the state simply as the rule of the stronger; Burke's notion that the state is a partnership between those who are living, those who are dead, and those yet unborn; Marx's theory of the state as an instrument of repression of one class by another and ultimately doomed to disappear; Hegel's con-

[1] Isaiah Berlin, "Does Political Theory Still Exist," *Philosophy, Politics and Society*, ed. Peter Laslett (Oxford: Basil Blackwell, 1956), p. 3.

cept of the state as God's mind revealing itself in time. Thirdly, we shall contrast two theories of the state—holistic[2] and individualistic[3]—and show how each of those general theories have functioned as foundations for different political ideologies. Finally, we must be careful to show that the entire discussion in political theory concerning states takes place at two utterly different levels of discourse—the state as it actually exists historically, and the state as an idealized entity embodying some eternal moral principle.

THE STATE AS AN ASSOCIATION

Let us begin with a discussion about the character of associations generally. The kind of association in a political context which comes easily to mind is *society*. It is commonplace in our ordinary discourse to say that men live in society, that they "owe" something to society, that they are "socially conditioned," that society permits or prohibits certain kinds of behavior, and so on. It is easy to see, on reflection, that being in society is not a matter of being spacially in some specific place or other. Consider Peters and Benn on this point:

> If an ornithologist says that woodpeckers live in trees there is little to puzzle us. For trees and birds are easily picked out; they have definite contours; they move about; they have parts which mutually influence one another so as to make them both recognizable wholes. But when a social theorist tells us that men live in society, the matter is more puzzling. We are not inclined to dispute what he says, but it is not quite clear what he is saying. For though men are recognizable wholes like birds, societies are not wholes of the same order at all. The way in which a man lives in a society is quite different from the way in which a woodpecker lives in a tree. For membership of a society does not necessarily imply residence in some larger spacial whole.[4]

The first and most obvious fact is that whatever else we mean when we say that men live in society, we do not intend to be saying something about spacial location; nor does the word expressing the relation "in" suggest such a meaning. We often say things like "He is in trouble," or

---

[2] The locution "holistic" is used in the following discussions as synonymous with "organismic."

[3] The locution "individualistic" is used as synonymous with "atomistic."

[4] S. I. Benn and R. S. Peters, *Social Principles and the Democratic State* (London: George Allen & Unwin Ltd, 1959), p. 13.

"He is in dire straits" without intending to mean "in" in the same way that we mean it when we say that "He is in Chicago." Society, then, is not a place, in the sense of being a thing, or a part of a thing, or even a collection of things. The most obvious characteristic of a thing is that it is spacially extended with recognizable contours, a requirment which society cannot meet. Secondly, it should be fairly clear that there is no such thing as Society, but rather a collection of various groupings such that any one person is a member of many different societies. What is important in this discussion is that society is no single agreed-upon entity which is denoted by that word, in the way that this chair is denoted by the word "chair."

Consider the example of Karl Marx's use of the concept "class." Marx's concept of social class:

> . . . presupposed a highly sophisticated theory about relation of people to the means of production. The proletariat class, for example, were those who sold their labor but owned none of the means of production. Yet others, who did not share Marx's theory about the significance for social life of people's relationship to the means of production, held that it was more fruitful to define a social class in terms, perhaps, of people's education or occupation. The point is that such ways of grouping people together presuppose all sorts of assumptions which are highly disputable.[5]

And, one may add disputable in a way in which decisions about particular concrete objects are not. Groupings are after all arbitrary; there is no universally recognizable and binding type of ordering denoted by any of those concepts which groups peoples in this or that way.

Thirdly, it may be asked what can a social whole, or group, or society be, if it is neither a place, nor an entity in the sense of being a thing, nor even a universally agreed upon group of individuals such as a social class, or economic class. The answer is that an association's identity and its character are to be found in its rules. Let us consider some examples: We say that "The New York Yankees played well against the White Sox" or "The Senate passed the civil rights bill." In each case we are not saying that every Yankee player did well, but rather that the team as a whole did. Similarly, we do not mean to imply that every Senator voted

---

[5] *Ibid.*, p. 14.

for the civil rights bill, but only that a majority did. When we attribute action to an association we refer generally to some in the association who are acting for the whole. What sets the limits on how some in authority may act in representing the whole, are the rules or laws (or under less sophisticated circumstances, customs) to which all have agreed (or have not considered the matter) to abide by. The Yankees cannot play more than nine men at a time, and the U.S. Senate is governed by a law which says that a bill supported by a majority of senators is, if other conditions set by law obtain, to be considered the law of the land. To understand the association would be, then, to understand its rules and orderly procedures. But it is easy to see that this alone leaves many things out which appear to be important aspects of organization. The rules say nothing about the New York Yankees as an "institution" in the romantic sense. Clearly, the Yankees are the Yankees whether Ruth and Gehrig or Mantle and Berra are on the team. They are the Yankees when they win four straight World Series games as well as when they lose four Series games (though some would deny this allegation, the denial would be poetic, not factual). The loyalty, devotion, and patriotic sentiments which are associated with this particular institution are not to be discovered by an examination or analysis of the rules of baseball, or even of the customs of the team. They are to be found in the mental attitude which people have toward the institution and we shall see that though these contribute to the character of institutions in general, and to the *state* in particular, they are not in themselves subjects of logical analysis. (The sentiments do, however, play an important role in discussions concerning the sense of obligation which persons feel toward various institutions and must therefore be taken into any account of the concept of obligation.)

The state therefore, is not a "thing," but consists, at least in part, of rules, procedures, roles played by individuals, and certain goals, ends, and functions.[6] To this degree, the state is no different from any other sort of association, a workingmen's fraternal order, or a baseball team. To put the point bluntly, though it might be misleading to say that the state has an essential mode of operation, there is at least one respect in which it

---

[6] *Ibid.*, p. 253.

operates differently from other associations of whatever character, that is, in the exercise of coercive sanctions. ". . . [T]he state is distinguishable from other political systems only to the extent that it successfully upholds its claim to the exclusive right to determine the conditions under which certain kinds of severe penalties, those involving physical coercion, may be legitimately employed."[7] This is not to suggest that this is the only way in which the state functions. To be sure its policing activity in the protection of life and property is among its most obvious responsibilities. Yet, from this central role have developed many other operations which are clearly noncoercive: the role of the state in education, economic planning, scientific research and development, and social service. Traditionally, among classical liberal theoreticians there existed a desire to limit the functions of the state to its protective and coercive powers. (John Locke ought to come immediately to mind.) This desire issues in the efforts to draw distinctions between state on the one hand and society on the other—the point being that whatever requires the regulation of areas of life which does not in some obvious way involve coercion by legal sanction, ought to be left to other social institutions. The picture thus conjured up, is one of the state as another social institution having no special prerogatives which distinguish it from any other institution; the church, the economy, education, the family and so on. It is simply the institution whose functions are limited to the political dimension of social life which is interpreted as meaning little more than what Hobbes meant when he said that the sole aim of government is the protection of life and maintenance of security with respect to the life and property of its citizens. But if this is the function which classical liberals (and perhaps modern conservatives) wish to assign to the state, it is not to be achieved by defining the state in such a way that it has only those functions which a given group want it to have, and no others. Obviously, the way to change the world is to change it—not define it in such a way that one no longer recognizes what one does not wish to recognize.

We have noted that associations in general (the state being no different in this regard) require rules and procedures which define their character. The rules of the state are called "laws." Among the most

[7] Robert A. Dahl, *Modern Political Analysis* (Englewood Cliffs, N.J.: Prentice-Hall, 1963), p. 50–51.

perplexing questions raised in political theory is the issue of the primacy of law versus the supremacy of the state. The past five centuries have witnessed the increase, at least in one sense, of the sphere of influence and authority of the state. For gradually, as family, kinship, guild, and parish have lost in scope and influence, relatively large associations, like the state, have come to supplant them. The issue of law, historically, was more or less determined by the fact that it proceeded either from God and/or nature and could therefore, not be altered by the deliberations of men.

In the feudal world the primary concept was not the state but law—a law not made by politicians but part of a universal and eternal order, to be discovered by a study of custom and precedent. Kings, councils, and judges found and formulated it, but could not make it; for to create new law would be to impose a new obligation by an act of will, and only God could do that. Political authorities—i.e. those exercising legal authority backed by coercive power—were regarded as being as much under law as any other corporate institution; for law was not thought of as the creation of the political order, nor as linked to it any more intimately than to any other. Law was thought of as the eternal and objectively valid normative system within which all associations were contained, and from which all roles drew appropriate rights and duties.[8]

Curiously, with the development of modern concepts of natural law, the law of custom or of civil society could be judged in accordance with the quasi-moral standards of the natural law. In fact, the local law could be renounced as having no validity if it did not prove to be compatible with the natural law (the law of reason, as Locke put the point). Once it is possible to judge local laws, to evaluate the law of custom and civil society against some other standard, then it is clear that law can be created, changed, or altered to suit new and different needs: and so long as it remains compatible with natural law, it is valid and binding. The modern theory of the state depends upon this development, for it implies that the state is a competent agency to create laws, and it is therefore no longer to be considered an association among others, with rights and functions which are on logical all-fours with others, but is rather above the law, and its responsibility is to create the laws which fix the character of other institutions.

---

[8] Peters and Benn, *op. cit.*, p. 256.

SCOPE OF THE STATE

Questions concerning (1) the relationship of the state to other institutions and associations with the society, (2) the locus of power within the state, (3) the procedures for establishing laws and applying sanctions by the state, (4) the grounds for obligation by those ruled to the state, are the subjects to which we now turn.

It is not particularly useful to begin with to discuss states as actual state of affairs starting with some sort of primitive tribal political organization and working our way through to the modern nation-state. We will rather examine what different people have thought the state to be. In other words, we shall once again try to avoid the pitfall of supposing that some special and essential condition of human association heralds the existence of the state, and that the absence of such a property indicates that the phenomenon in question, whatever else it may be described as being, is not a state. The multiplicity and variety of "sine qua non" which have been thought to be definitely characteristic of the state are well expressed by the following passage from MacIver:

> Some . . . define the state as essentially a class-structure, "an organization of one class dominating over the other class"; others regard it as the one organization that transcends class and stands for the whole community. Some interpret it as a power-system, others as a welfare-system. . . . Some view it entirely as a legal construction. . . . Some identify it with the nation, others regard nationality as incidental or unnecessary. . . . Some regard it as no more than a mutual insurance society, others as the very texture of all our life. To some it is a necessary evil . . . while to others it is the "world the spirit has made for itself." Some class the state as one in the order of "corporation," and others think of it as indistinguishable from society itself.[9]

It is tempting to suppose that the word "state" works in our language to signal the presence of a very special set of political conditions, or to suppose that one of the tasks of a political theorist is to discover that very special set of political circumstances to which the concept "state" may henceforth refer, or, even, to simply stipulate that for purposes of conceptual clarity the concept state shall henceforth refer to this or that

---

[9] Robert M. MacIver, *The Modern State* (London: Oxford University Press, 1926), pp. 3–4.

state of affairs and no other. This latter task, though it may on occasion be a useful one, is, it is easy to see, a purely formal procedure. Anyone is of course free to define any word in whatever fashion he wishes, but to redefine a word which has had broad and established currency in one language will be of no use whatever unless the redefinition takes into account the wide variety of ways in which the concept has been used in the past. A scientist may be prepared to stipulate a new meaning for a word setting a rule for himself and his colleagues to the effect that henceforth the word X will have such and such a *meaning*, that is, that it will, for purposes of ease and clarity, be used in such and such a way, that it will henceforth be appropriate in such and such linguistic contexts and no others, and so forth. But, the language of political theory does not lend itself to formal stipulation in the same fashion. And the reason for this is clear. The language of politics is not a specialized and formalized language; it is the language of the street, the language of our everyday life. The ordinary man in his ordinary everyday conceptual clothes speaks the language of political theory. Our concepts therefore, must be understood to have a linguistic history, so to speak, and our use of such concepts must take into account the fact that if we are to be understood, we must pay our respects to the ways in which people have used the word in the past, and in everyday contexts; for there is no other way of discovering meanings, other than discovering the rules which govern the ways in which a word may be used in our language. We turn now to a brief examination of what people seem to have had in mind when they used the word "state"; we turn initially as usual, to a glimpse of Plato's view of the meaning of the state.[10]

THE STATE AS DEFINED BY PLATO

Ancient Greek has no word which corresponds to the modern term "state." Talk about the "state" then, in Plato or Aristotle is really about the city—the *polis*, the "community"[11] as a unity, rather than the specific part of the community which may be organized for political purposes. The distinction between "society" and "state," a fundamental character-

---

[10] See T. D. Weldon, *States and Morals, A Study in Political Conflicts* (New York: McGraw-Hill Book Co., Inc., 1947), pp. 146 ff.

[11] Cf. *ibid.*, p. 87.

istic of the modern state,[12] has no counterpart in the Greek way of thinking and dealing with social and political life. "The state absorbed and included the entire collective activity of its citizens, a whole outside of which its members could not even be thought of, much less exist. Hence all social life is political life, possibly because in the city-state the political life was in fact so much more 'social' than with us."[13] The absence of a procedure for differentiating between state and society has led to a characteristically modern error regarding what was meant by the word "state" when used by the classical political philosophers. Consider MacIver's observation:

> It is the city-community, not our "state," to which (the . . . Greek political thinker . . . attributed those all-comprehensive functions and powers (of the state). The very word "law" (*nomos*) meant to the Greeks also "custom" or "convention." Nor did Aristotle ever mean what we mean by his famous description of man as a "political animal," he understood by it a being whose life is fulfilled in the city. The Greek tradition, thus misinterpreted, has inspired a modern doctrine of universal partnership within the state which does far less than justice to its original. In respect of social forms, our world has become differentiated far beyond the Greek or even the Roman. The self-government of the city-community was a great achievement, but it could only be a step towards the solution of the great problem of liberty and order, of the union of the individuals within society, until the sphere of political government began to be discovered. The failure to distinguish the state from the community left "Athenian liberty" itself a monument broken and defaced.[14]

For in such a society, one in which the political dimension of life is indistinguishable from the other operations of society, no area of human existence is free from the exercise of domination by the society. As MacIver points out, though Socrates in the *Crito* refuses to evade the death penalty on the grounds that despite unjust character of the law it is better to obey a bad law than to break his covenant to obey the law, he nowhere questions the right of the state to legislate on matters of religious belief or other opinions which, when the modern distinction between state and society is drawn, fall outside of the bounds of legality.

---

[12] Cf. *The Development of the Modern State,* ed. Heinz Lubasz (New York: Macmillan Co., 1964), p. 3.

[13] Charles Howard McIlwain, *The Growth of Political Thought in the West* (New York: Macmillan Co., 1932), p. 5.

[14] MacIver, *op. cit.*, p. 87.

Yet what we must not lose in this discussion is a sympathetic view of the vision of the possibilities of the sort of all-encompassing state which emerges from Plato's *Republic*. In the *Republic,* Plato envisions a state (where state and society are not distinguished one from the other) in which all its constituent parts are natural extensions of expressions, or reflections, of what he takes to be the natural constituents of human character. "States do not come out of an oak or rock, but from the character of the men that dwell in them."[15] Such a state, established in accordance with human nature would consist of social institutions which were no more subject to change than human nature itself, and would be no more arbitrary than the natural fact that men are the sorts of creatures they are. The state is man's character writ large, and thus the predicates which apply to certain attributes of collective mankind apply also to the state. Thus the entire discussion in the first four books of Plato's *Republic* which are given over to a consideration of the question of private and public justice, is an effort to demonstrate that only one sort of state can be *just,* for only one sort of state can approach perfection, for only one sort of state can express the fundamental character of the best in human nature.

Some critics of Plato have argued that the arrangement of social institutions in accordance with different aspects of human nature is a transparent effort on Plato's part to establish philosophical justification for his own elitist prejudices, that only those of upper-class origins and virtues are fit to rule and that they are the only ones capable of deciding what is best for the entire society. Such criticisms, though commonly made of Plato in recent times, only emphasizes the degree to which Plato is committeed to the view that human institutions are just so many expressions of the human mind.

The hierarchy of institutions that Plato justifies in the *Republic* is a further and more difficult issue, and in this context interests us only tangentially. It is true that Plato accepts the view that reason is somehow a higher or morally superior aspect of human character and that the best state ought to be organized such that rational criteria and procedures are used to guide and order the state. But the particular organization of the state and the motives which Plato may have had for organizing the state

---

[15] *Republic,* 544 (p. 297 in Cornford ed.).

in the particular way in which he does are secondary considerations. The central issue here is Plato's insight that "States do not come out of an oak or a rock, but from the characters of the men that dwell in them."[16] What are the consequences for politics of this conception of the state? Consider the story of Socrates' death. In the *Crito* the dialogue which describes the last days of Socrates, the old man has been sentenced to death. The reason which he gives to his friends for refusing the conventional alternative of exile to death, is less revealing in this context than the alternative itself. For this alternative gives us a clear insight into the Greek conception of the state: death and exile. Membership in the political community is a condition of the realization of one's own-self. To live a life worth living requires membership in a political community. Now it may be true that no evidence exists that men have ever lived in conditions of complete anarchy, the Greeks thought of their political community as qualitatively superior to any other. Their language contains words of exclusion such that "varvari" means, synonymously, non-Greek and barbarian. With this way of looking at the world, it is reasonable (though Socrates gave other reasons, and had, no doubt, other motives) to choose death. For only in a political community may one fully realize himself as a human being; to be exiled, is to be deprived of the human conditions of fulfillment as a person.

Such a view of the state suggests that it is far more than a collection of individuals each intent upon pursuing private ends and satisfying private interests. The state, understood in this way, is a moral agent as well, whose functions are not limited to regulating the activity of its citizenry and securing their lives against external forces. For the state is an agency which participates in the moral growth of its individual citizens, whose imperatives have not merely the force of law, but the compelling demand of conscience itself. Just as the destruction between state and society is obscured in Plato's analysis, so is the generally recognized latter-day (18th century) distinction between individual and state. It is meaningless, in Plato's frame of reference to think in terms of the existence of antagonistic relations between state and individual; the individual on the one hand, insisting upon the basicity of his private rights, and the state, on the other, demanding obligations and duties which conflict with the

---

[16] *Ibid.*

rights claimed by individuals. For such an antagonism can exist only under special circumstances: either in cases where an ideology justifies the claim to rights, and political power is limited to exercising restraint against those who threaten the rights of others, or in situations where the traditional bonds of the political community have been loosened or broken, and individuals perceive the social and political world as divided into two parts, one's own interests on the one hand, and the rest of the world, on the other. This last state of affairs might be called "political solipcism."

For Plato, the state is an organism and this implies that no tensions or antagonisms between the parts of the body politic may exist, anymore than they can exist in the bodies of healthy persons. Each part of the organism has a job to do and the health of the entire organism is contingent upon the adequacy of the performance of each constituent element. The state perceived in this way is essentially static—for once the proper set of relations among men is established, the result of change cannot be anything other than decay. The perfect state, i.e. one which cannot become better than it is (since it has arrived at perfection) is a static, unchanging, eternal sort of entity. The essential logic of this proposition is difficult to grasp for those of us who live in times whose predominant ideology is *progress*. Progress after all means that things generally are getting "better and better."[17] However deep such an ideology may have become imbedded in contemporary consciousness (though we are perhaps now becoming increasingly aware of its essential absurdity) it is hardly a view shared by Plato. For Plato, change and instability go hand in hand and his own political experience tended to confirm this view. Coupled with the evidence of political change and decay, is his commitment to the notion that a condition of reality, as opposed to appearance, is changelessness and eternality.

The state according to Plato is (1) indistinguishable from the community as a whole; (2) a reflection of human nature; (3) changeless and perfect in its ideal expression; (4) an organic entity whose parts must function harmoniously; (5) an agency which creates the conditions of

[17] In 1923, Émile Coué made a cult of this sentiment when after arriving in the United States from France established Coué Institutes in which audiences hypnotically recited: "Day by day in every way I am getting better and better." See Frederick Lewis Allen, *Only Yesterday* (New York, 1931), p. 58.

moral and intellectual fulfillment of its citizens' lives; and (6) a moral entity whose imperatives are, ideally, internalized by its citizenry such that (7) no distinction may be reasonably drawn between the self-interest of private individuals and the interests of the state itself.

A popular aphorism, generally attributed to Alfred North Whitehead, alleges that all philosophy is but a footnote to Plato. Certainly, a large part of what passes as political theory owes its earliest formulations to Plato. These pages which we have devoted to a discussion of Plato's theory of the state sets for us the framework of one of the two major analyses of the state which we will consider in this discussion. We shall call Plato's conception of the state, *holistic,* and we shall trace the development of this concept of the state to modern conceptions of that phenomenon. For despite the fact that Plato's *Republic* was never intended to provide an archetype for a political unit larger than the Greek *polis,*[18] or as a model for political phenomena which bear only tangential resemblance to the modern theory of the state, it is nonetheless true that the essential ingredients of the state dreamed of by Plato have their counterparts in modern theories of the state. For an elaboration of the essential attributes of the holistic theory of the state, we shall consider theories of the state offered by Aristotle, Rousseau, Hegel, Marx, and Bradeley. Each will, in his turn, contribute a dimension or aspect which will, we trust, issue in a reasonably clear and adequate model of the holistic theory of the state.

ARISTOTLE'S THEORY OF THE STATE

References to nature, including perhaps those made in our earlier discussions, are systematically ambiguous. Nature teaches nothing in particular and virtually no object or activity, structure or custom or institution cannot be said to be, in some sense or other, natural. Nature

[18] It is important however to distinguish between two different ways in which society and state may be co-mingled. It is possible as Plato seems to have done, to fail completely to distinguish between the political and nonpolitical forms in a society and thus perceive the state as having all those functions which are ordinarily attributed to a variety of social institutions, the social and the political, but making the political institution, the state, all encompassing. The former procedure is not to be confused with latter-day procedures which are characteristic of modern theories of the state.

neither commends nor applauds, neither sanctions nor denies, any atrocity or virtue, for nature is neutral. Attempts, therefore, to justify a political system in terms of its compatibility with nature or, conversely, to denounce the legitimacy of such a system because of its allegedly "unnatural" character, turn chiefly on what is to be meant by nature. Nor is there, as some have supposed, some single conception of nature peculiar or unique to an age. For in each epoch different conceptions of nature have been articulated side by side one with the other. In Greek thought, the concept of nature is, as we have seen, a crucial one, and yet, no consistant theory of nature may be said to emerge unambiguously from that tradition, and a variety of different sorts of political procedures, political systems, and political attitudes have been, among the Greeks alone, tied to theories of nature. The lessons allegedly learned from nature by Thrasymachus and the Sophists are not those of Plato, and those of Plato are not those of Aristotle.

What is not *natural,* is what it is by convention. It is thought that to say that a political system is *conventional* lessens the face of the claim that persons are obliged to obey the commands of the state. Thus, a state that is thought to be the result of human contrivance, rather than an expression of, or outgrowth from, nature, is one which can be altered and where, therefore, the laws and procedures of the state may be judged as being unsatisfactory. What men can create, men can alter. Thus it is important to Aristotle, as it was to Plato, to counter the Sophists' claim that the state is a human creation, for if it were not otherwise, no special claim on the allegiance of its members may be made for a particular set of political institutions. The Sophists examine nature and discover nothing but primary instincts and primitive impulses; Plato finds order and Aristotle discovers a principle of internal development in all natural entities.

With this *caveat* in mind, the statement that Aristotle's theory of state is one in which the state is perceived as a natural entity, is an invitation to consider a problem, rather than the solution of it. "The state (polis)," says Aristotle, "exists by nature and is prior to the individual. (The proof of both propositions is the fact that the polis is a whole, and that individuals are simply its parts.)"[19] By "nature" Aristotle has something in

---

[19] Aristotle's *Politics,* i253a (Barker trans., p. 6–7).

mind quite different from Plato's conception for by describing the state as "natural," by attributing to it a "natural" character, he is saying the following:

(*i*) [The State] is natural because it is the conclusion of a process of human development, in which each step is necessary and natural, the outcome not of human purpose but of instinct struggling toward its goal, while the whole is marked by unbroken continuity, from beginning to end. As the conclusion of such a process, the State is still more natural than any preceding step in the process. The end of a process is more particularly "by nature," as the nearest approach to nature herself: "What anything is, when the process of its development is ended, is called (not only its end, but) its nature"; and the State, as the end of man's process of development and his nearest approximation to Nature herself, is his nature. It is that for which he has been destined by Nature; "the State is natural to him and he is by nature a member of a state." (*ii*) Again, "Nature always works for the best"; and one may convert the proposition, and say, that what is best is the product of Nature. The self-sufficiency which man attains in the State is his *summum bonum* (greatest good); the State is, therefore, the best form of life to which he can aspire; and because it is the best, it is a product of Nature. (*iii*) Finally, "Nature makes nothing in vain." But Nature has endowed men with a faculty of speech which points to social and ultimately to political life. It follows that nature destined man for the state, and that the state is natural. In these different ways, and from these different points of view, the natural character of the State is fully vindicated. It is natural as the result of a process of development, wrought by the agency of Nature . . . : it is natural because it is the best possible: it is natural, because Nature, who works by purpose, and not idly, gave man speech, and thereby destined him for political life.[20]

Nature for Aristotle means the end or soul or purpose of a natural entity. He supposes that every object is subject to four causes, the final cause being the condition or state of full development of a rational object. This teleological conception when applied to associations enables us to perceive the final end or *nature* of all human association and the precise relation which obtains between lesser forms of association and state itself. The condition of ultimate development, of full-realization of associations (as of any entity) is self-sufficiency. Thus, the first form of association, the household or family unit, which satisfies certain natural needs of individual persons, and the second, a collection of households,

[20] Sir Ernest Barker, *The Political Thought of Plato and Aristotle* (New York: Dover Publications Inc, 1959), pp. 269–70.

or a "village" which satisfies other needs, neither form of association arrives at complete self-sufficiency. When, however, we come to the final and perfect association, "formed from a number of villages, we have already reached the *polis,* the state—an association which may be said to have reached the height of full self-sufficiency."[21] Yet, "association" does not properly express the essential unity of the state. Aristotle takes pains to indicate that though the state is the highest form of association, the relations which hold within the state are qualitatively different from those which occur in lower forms of association:

> It is a mistake to believe that the "statesman" (he who handles the affairs of political association) is the same as the monarch of a kingdom, or the manager of a household, or the master of a number of slaves. . . . On this view a man who is concerned with few persons is a master: one who is concerned with more is the manager of a household: one who is concerned with still more is a "statesman," or a monarch. But this is a view which cannot be accepted as correct. (There is an essential difference between these persons and between the associations with which they are concerned.)[22]

His point is that state is not merely a composition of parts which results in a new aggregation, but rather culminates in a new identity.

It is one thing to hold that the state is an organic entity, in the teleological sense which Aristotle proposes, and yet another matter to say what sort of organic entity it may be. Organisms obviously vary one from the other, and though states may be organic, they are not all the same. The kind of organic entity any given state may be depends upon the nature of its internal arrangements. Latter-day conceptions of the organic theory of the state hold, as we shall see, that the individual life of individual persons is utterly submerged in the life of the state. But according to Aristotle, the state supplements man's nature, rather than controls his every faculty.[23] This last point is an important qualification in the articulation of Aristotle's organic theory of the state.

The moral dimension of the state is a further ingredient of its organic character. Indeed, the state's existence is such that it may be said of it that it has moral properties and attributes which we are wont to ascribe only to individuals, viz, that the state may behave courageously, with self-

---

[21] Aristotle's *Politics,* i252b.

[22] Aristotle's *Politics,* i252a.

[23] Aristotle, *Politics,* i252a.

control and justly. But apart from the tendency for Aristotle to predicate moral qualities of states, such that he appears to be suggesting that such properties when so predicated attribute the same sort of moral qualities to states as they do to individuals, he is really arguing for the view that the state is a moral conditioner, part of whose task is to instill certain habits of behavior in individual citizens. As Barker expresses this point:

The true state aims, not at preventing its citizens from doing evil to one another, but at preventing them from being evil or in any way disposed to evil: its law is no guarantor of men's rights as against one another, but a maker of goodness and righteousness among men. Any city which is worth the name has virtue for its object and its care. This is the essential and specific attribute which makes a state: and, without this, habitation in the same territory, relations of intermarriage, and laws regulating the exchange of products, will not make ten thousand men into a State. They are indeed indispensable: a moral purpose is still more indispensable. They are the conditions: it is the essence. Political association . . . is association not in material production, but in moral action; and as, in the sphere of material production, those who have produced, and can offer to the economic association, the maximum of objects, receive in return the maximum of reward, so in this sphere of moral action, those who have done, and can contribute to the spiritual association, the maximum of noble actions, receive the maximum of honors in requital of their work. In this view of the state as a spiritual association, expecting good works and requiting them with honours, we touch the most fundamental part of the *Politics*.[24]

It is a fundamental point not only for the *Politics,* it may be noted, but for the construction of the organic model of the state. The moral dimension of organic conceptions differs drastically from the regulatory and passive function of atomistic or individualistic theories of the state. If the end or purpose of the state is thought to be the good life for its citizens, then it must be assumed either that such a life is possible if individuals are protected from each other and permitted to work toward the satisfaction of their own needs and desires, or on the other hand, that the state must play an active role in creating, establishing, and formulating the conditions and processes necessary to assure a happy life for its citizenry. The key to the difference between the two approaches lies in the fact that the individualistic theories suppose that the individual, rather than the state, supplies the only relevant criterion of what shall

[24] Barker, *op. cit.,* p. 282.

constitute the best kind of life for himself, and what will count as acceptable procedures for acquiring the ends desired (provided that such means are considered legal).

The last point to be made, with respect to Aristotle's conception of the organic theory of the state, concerns the meaning of the word "organic," and its function and justification as a political metaphor. In a general way, it is easy to see that the organic model is metaphorical or analogical. The expression, "organic theory of the state" refers to those theories which suggest that the state is *like* an organic entity. The properties, however, which theorists who subscribe to this view have in mind require precise signification. It is silly to think that *all* the properties which belong to an organic entity belong to the state itself. What then are the characteristics of an organism thought by Aristotle to be applicable to the state?

> The words "organ" and "organic" are fairly frequent in the *Politics,* in the sense of "instrument" and "instrumental." They are words which imply the conception of an end, to which the thing they denote is subservient. Wealth is an "organ" for moral life: slaves, as part of a householder's wealth, are "animate organs." Every organ is limited in size by the end for which it is used: a boat, as an instrument for sailing must be neither too large nor too small to sail. In this respect an organ is like animals and plants, which have equally a certain limited size, suited to the end for which they are designed; and the state is like an organ, as it is also like an animal or plant, in being subject to a necessary limitation of size.[25]

In other respects, however, the state has properties or qualities which are not like those of an organic entity, and vice versa.

> Though like an organ, it is not an organ; it is not an instrument for a purpose beyond itself. But, though it is not organic in the sense of instrumental, may it not be organic in the sense of being a whole composed of a number of organs or instruments? Though not organic in the sense of being part of a system, and instrumental to the realization of a purpose, may it not be organic in the higher sense of being itself a system, composed of parts which are instrumental to the realization of its own purpose? A conception of the State as organic in this latter sense certainly follows upon the teleological view which is everywhere present in the *Politics.* If the State is the end of its citizen's activities . . . it must be a system of which they are the organs or instruments. Its functions are all so many contributions; its life must be the life in

---

[25] *Ibid.,* p. 276.

which they all partake, and by partaking in which they have any life of their own.[26]

The issue facing us here is the *respect* in which we are to suppose the state to be an organism. An "organ" is, in one sense, merely part of a greater whole, yet this is distinctly not the meaning intended by Aristotle. But if the state is perceived as an "organ" in the sense of being a collectivity of subsidiary organs, then perhaps Aristotle's intent becomes clearer. Moreover, if a collectivity of subsidiary organs goes into the making of a larger or greater organic entity, then it is possible to raise the question about the precise relations which hold among these various entities and their relative dependence upon each other. With regard to an organic unity of the sort in question, it must be possible to differentiate organs and their separate function; and yet the relationship of each organ should be one of absolute dependence upon the whole to which it belongs for its life. Putting these two propositions together, we may say that as an association, the state is a system of different organs, which by their membership of the system attain a fullness of life otherwise impossible. So far, the individual is dependent upon the state for his fullness of life; but Aristotle goes further; and lays it down that he is dependent upon the state for his very life. He is able to do this by comparing the state to the human body, and of its citizens to the bodily organs. Because the individual is not full and complete without the state, Aristotle assumes that he stands to it in the relation of an organ to the body, the bodily organ and the citizen being equally and in the same degree insufficient without the body to which they belong. The individual is not only dependent upon the state; he is dependent upon it as absolutely as a hand or foot is dependent upon the body. He exists only in its life and has no meaning or existence except as sharing in its life.

THE STATE AS VIEWED BY ROUSSEAU

In introducing our discussion of Rousseau, we ought to make quite clear the point that no political theorist whom we are attempting to classify as either an organic theorist on the one hand or an individualistic or atomistic theorist on the other hand, falls unambiguously into one of

[26] *Ibid.*, p. 276–77.

these categories without deviation. In Aristotle, we recall that though the bulk of what he had to say indicated that he believed in the organic model of the state, he was nonetheless driven on occasion to make reference to the possibility that there existed transcendental criteria in terms of which states themselves could be judged. We recall, for example, the discussion in which Aristotle makes it clear that it may be possible for a man to be a good citizen, and yet a bad man, if the laws of the state are themselves bad.

If this is so, it would appear that there are criteria over and beyond the state and against which states may be judged, such that the state is not the ultimate arbiter of what is good or what is moral.

By the same token, Rousseau's theory is far more complicated and involved than one might at first expect. And it should be clear that by classifying him as an organic theorist, we are not unaware of the fact that there are those deeply immersed in the literature, who emphasize the social contract aspect of Rousseau's thoughts. To say, as Rousseau does, that man is born free and everywhere he is in chains, and to think of those chains as emanating principally from institutional forms, is to suggest that it is possible for men to exist outside of social and political institutions. And it is clear that if it is indeed possible for men to so exist, then their existence as human beings is not contingent upon their living in a state. Yet, as we shall see, Rousseau is also preoccupied with the problem of the justification of political institutions. And in doing so, Rousseau does no less for himself than to pose the major problem of political theory, namely, how is it possible to establish political institutions whose goals are ultimately the repression of certain natural desires, such that these institutions are compatible with man's ultimate desire to be free. The answer to this question lies in establishing a set of political institutions, which demands of individuals only that which they *ought* to do for themselves. The enterprise, therefore, consists of establishing a state in which antagonisms between different individuals or different interest groups may never arise. Let us consider for a moment what is involved in such an enterprise.

To begin with, we must recognize what is assumed here; namely, that a distinction may be drawn, at least theoretically, between those activities in which I engage, as a private person, that are intended to acquire those ends or goals, which I, as a person, have decided I value, and, the ends, goals, purposes, values, and procedures, which are shared by everyone else in the community in which I live. Atomistic, or individualistic theories of society, interpret this distinction as somehow fundamental. These theories respond to the problem by establishing a set of political institutions, whose goal is the adjudication of disputes which arise between myself and others. In this respect, the state is conceived as a regulatory institution, an artifact, or human contrivance, whose single aim is the preservation of the peace and the establishment of political order. And it is clear that a person living in such a state, must endure the coincident possibility that the free pursuit of his own private interests will stand in need of modification, such that they are made coincident with the desires, needs, and goals of the entire society. According to Rousseau, the limitations of the sort of society described may be overcome if

> . . . each one of us puts his person and all his power in common under the supreme direction of the general will, and we as a body receive each member as an inseparable part of the whole, at that moment, in the place of the particular person of each contracting party, this active association creates a moral and collective body, made up of as many members as there are voters in the assembly, and receiving from this act its unity, its common self, its life, and its will.

It is in this fashion that Rousseau argues that it is possible to establish a form of association where conflicts do not arise, not merely because a private individual has repressed his own personal desires in deference to those of the community, but rather because he recognizes that only when he desires and pursues certain ends and goals which are recognized by the entire community to be desirable does it become possible for him to live a good life. What is the character of the institutions which were supposed to make this good life possible?

Rousseau supposes that there was a time in the past when men lived in a state of nature, that is to say, outside of any sort of social or political organization. The purpose which he has in mind in positing such a state of nature, is to ask whether it is possible to distinguish between what is really natural for human beings and what is artificial in their nature. Life in a state of nature, he concludes, is one which exhibits certain characteristics wholly absent from the existing states and societies which he examines. Thus he writes that political philosophers may know very well what a citizen of London or Paris is, but not what a man is. What then is the truly natural man? Consider Sabine's composite picture of Rousseau's noble savage:

The answer cannot be drawn from history because if natural man ever existed, they certainly do not now. If one tries to make a hypothetical picture, the answer is certain; natural man was an animal whose behavior was purely instinctive. . . . He wholly lacked language, unless in the form of instinctive cries, and without language any general idea is impossible. Consequently, the natural man was neither moral nor vicious. He was not unhappy but neither was he happy. Obviously, he had no property, for property resulted from ideas, forseen wants, knowledge, industry, which were not intrinsically natural but implied language, thought, and society. Selfishness, taste, regard for the opinion of others, the arts, war, slavery, vice, conjugal delict does not endure indefinitely.

For Rousseau asserts in the *Social Contract* that a point is reached in the history of mankind when the: ". . . obstacles to continuing in a state of nature were stronger than the forces which each individual could employ to the end of continuing in it. The original state of nature, therefore, could no longer endure, and the human race would have perished, had it not changed its manner of existence." Moreover, not all forms of political organization are equally satisfactory. The history of mankind is replete, Rousseau thinks, with instances of perverted institutions which ultimately pervert man's natural character. The natural character to which he refers is apparently his instinctive reactions to events rather than the employment of reason in the pursuit of his own self-interest. The cement of society is not reason, but feeling, compassion, and an innate revulsion against suffering in other persons. Given this picture of what men are like by nature, that is to say, prior to their incorporation into civil society, what kind of a state is appropriate to that nature and what kind of a state can emerge from it? The key to the kind of state which Rousseau has in mind must be pursued in an analysis of his conception of the general will. According to Sabine, the general will: ". . . represented a unique fact about a community, namely, that it has a collective good which is not the same thing as a private interest of its members. In some sense it lives its own life, fulfills its own destiny, and suffers its own fate. In accordance with the analogy of an organism . . . [the state] it may be said to have a will of its own, the general will." Rousseau goes so far as to call the state a moral person. He writes: ". . . if the state is a moral person whose life is in the union of its members, and if the most important of its care is the care for its own preservation, it must have a universal and compelling force, in order to move and dispose each part, as may be most advantageous to the whole."

The general will must be understood as a universal and compelling force; as consisting in nothing more but the collective wills of the individual persons who comprise the society. Yet the will of all and the general will are not the same sorts of things, for Rousseau sees the general will as consisting of the collective moral good of the entire society. Thus the general will will always be right. It is never wrong or false, because it is the ultimate criteria of what will be considered right, and against which all of our judgments will be measured. The will of all on the other hand, may well be wrong, for all of us in a given society may collectively will a given policy or purpose or end, and yet, at the same time not realize that we may be mistaken about what is best for us collectively in the same fashion that we may be mistaken about what is best for us privately. Only so was it possible to conceive of a will, which is neither the will of an individual nor majority of individuals nor even of all the individuals in a given society. Indeed, Rousseau considers the possibility that the general will may dictate certain forms of action which none of us are aware of, that is to say, it may well be possible that the general will is unknown. This contingency becomes possible in situations where our calculations about what is best have gone awry.

Let us see if we can make the conception of the general will more clear by comparing it to situations where any one of us as individuals may be mistaken about what is best for ourselves in particular. We may will a certain end or goal mistakenly. That is to say we may have certain expectations from having initiated a given action where those expectations are either not those which we actually desired or where they do not come about. Under such circumstances, it is possible to say that we have erred. We have assumed erroneously that our actual will and our best interests comprised together the real will, that is to say the general will. The general will then, must be perceived as the collectivity of the best part of our individual character. Consider the following passage from Rousseau's *Social Contract.*

Each of us puts his person and all his power in common under the supreme direction of the general will, and, in our corporate capacity, we receive each member as an indivisible part of the whole. At once, in place of the individual personality of each contracting party, this act of association creates a moral and collective body, composed of as many members as the assembly contains votes, and receiving from this act its unity, its common identity, its life and its will. This public person, so formed by the union of all other persons, formerly took the name of city, and now takes that of republic, or body politic; it is called by its members a state when passive, sovereign when active, and power when compared with others like itself.

The text is replete with references suggestive of the organic metaphor. He speaks of the "collective body," "the public person," and "body politic." Such organic metaphors suggest other ingredients of organic theories of the state. Rousseau speaks of the state as a moral and collective body, whose constituent parts when they act in assembly confirms its own unity, common identity, its common life, and its common will. Surely what this expression must mean, when taken together with our earlier discussion, is that the state is formed by the collective unity of moral purpose which comes about when each individual constituent of the community obeys that part of its character which he recognizes as being compatible with that of the general will. Indeed, the general will, as we have seen, is a reflection of the moral consciousness of its individual constituents. The state then must be seen not merely as a collection of those institutions which govern the political life of the people, but as the entire community. And among its functions, in fact its most important function, its *raison d'etre,* is its moral dimension. The state is both a product of the natural, moral sentiment which is exhibited among men in their prepolitical or presocial state. And yet, on the other hand, it is the agency which provides the conditions under which men may lead truly human and moral lives.

Another dimension of Rousseau's reflections concerning the character of the state, ought to be taken into account. It ought to be kept in mind that there is natural tendency to think of the word "state" in Rousseau's usage in ways which are similar to our own contemporaneous use of that concept, yet the concept of state is somewhat more akin to our conception of society or culture than it is to the concept of the state as a political order in Rousseau's sense. This ambiguity concerning the use of the word "state," leads to the conclusion that when Rousseau speaks of the necessity of suppressing dissident political minorities within the society, who, as he says of them, may be forced to be free, he is using the word "freedom" in a perverse way, according to which one is said to be free when one accepts the limitations of one's station and obeys those who are placed in positions of power. However, Rousseau's alleged perversity, with regard to his use of the concept of freedom, rests on a confusion regarding the way in which he uses the word "state." For Rousseau, state does not refer to the political organization of the society, and therefore nothing he says about it can be taken as a rationalization of despotism, as some have charged. He uses the concept rather as a synonym for political community, or for society in general, or even perhaps as a synonym for culture. This is an important point, not merely because it absolves Rousseau of certain charges of totalitarianism, but rather because it emphasizes the extent to which Rousseau is a continuator of the tradition of organic theories of the state. As with Plato, Rousseau does not distinguish carefully between society and state, and where he does so, it is to point out the fundamental basicity of the political community over political institutions.

HEGEL, THE STATE AND HISTORY

In order to discover what Hegel assumes the character of the state to be, we must examine it in the context of the fashion in which it has developed as an institution. For Hegel states are not established, nor do they come about by accident. They come about as the result of a historical development, during which a certain radical alteration of consciousness has taken place among the people who comprise it. It is a simplistic view of history according to Hegel, to assume that it deals with individual human beings. The lowest common denominator of historical discourse is the people or the Volk, or the culture, or the nation, but never an individual as such.

States are not random or accidental phenomena which arise simply because of needs expressed by persons in certain moments in time. They are rather the actors on the stage of history. Prior to the existence of states, if indeed there ever was such a moment in time, history is impossible since the ingredients of history are states themselves. In the earliest moments of existence of the state, in its least mature stage of development, the distinguishing properties of the institution is complete unreflectivity, an utter lack of self-consciousness which characterizes the lives of those who dwell in the state. In such immature and unreflective states, and here Hegel has in mind India and China, the multitude is unaware of itself in the sense that it is not conscious of its potentiality and destiny as a people. It does not recognize its potential vigor or its own unique cultural form. But more importantly, it does not recognize the conditions of its own freedom. Human freedom, according to Hegel, is the result of a long-term process of historical development. It is an ideal which is potentially realizable only when the collectivity has learned to distinguish between itself as a subject of thoughts and desires and the thoughts and desires of which it is a subject.

What all this comes to is that individuals left to pursue their own end and goals, the fulfillment of their private desires, will never be able to do so in a wholly successful fashion because they do not always know what their own best interest is. The very concept of a goal or purpose comes about as a result of membership in a political community. This is not to deny that there are such things as private goals and desires, it is rather to assert that no man can realize all of them since they are neither consistent among themselves nor are they always compatible with the goals and desires of the rest of those who reside in the society. Let us consider an example: at any given moment in time any one of us can provide at a moment's notice a list of those things which we desire. I may desire to escape a Massachusetts winter by vacationing in Florida; at the same time my desire is to keep my job teaching at a university; it is also my desire to complete the writing of this book at a particular date; and, I may desire to spend more time with my family and at the same time to attend a poker party with my academic colleagues. I cannot of course fulfill all of my desires, for some of these are incompatible with each other. I must therefore calculate, think ahead, compare these various desires and estimate the chances of satisfying any one of them as well as the consequences of satisfying them.

Consider another example having to do with perplexities facing the political policy maker: he desires on the one hand to decrease taxes and yet on the other to increase defense spending; he asserts the desirability of decreasing the power of the federal government on the one hand and yet on the other he asserts his intention to work toward the eradication of poverty in rural and urban areas. Clearly, these different desires are altogether incompatible with one another. Neither I nor our mythical policy maker may have our cake and eat it too. Yet, supposing that we could overcome the inconsistency of our desires, suppose for example that we could agree about an order of preference, we would nonetheless have to face the problem that the interests which we express will come into conflict with the desires and aspirations of other persons. And to the extent that the interests of the rest of the community are expressed in the law of the community itself, to that degree will we come into conflict with part of the society. Yet conflict is itself something which we desire to avoid. Indeed, it is thought to be among my basic and fundamental desires. How then is it possible to resolve this paradox? Hegel replies that history is the history of increasing self-consciousness. Self-consciousness of what? Of what does the society or the individuals comprising it become self-conscious? It becomes conscious, says Hegel, of its own potentiality for freedom. What then is freedom? Freedom consists of the awareness that a man's desires are best fulfilled when they are compatible among themselves and where they do not come into conflict with the satisfaction of the desires of others. Such a circumstance can arise only when the very laws of the community, that is to say, the collectivity of those things which those who live in the community desire to become, to use Freud's expression, introjected into the consciousness of each individual citizen.

It is precisely this state of affairs that Hegel is describing when he says that ". . . a state is then well-constituted and internally powerful, when the private interest of its citizens is one with the common interest of the state; when the one finds its gratification and realization in the other—a proposition in itself very important."

The notion of freedom within the confines of the state is a conception which runs counter to our common notion of freedom, of which Hegel writes:

The idea which people most commonly have of freedom is that it is arbitrariness—the mean, chosen by abstract reflection, between the will wholly determined by natural impulses, and the will free absolutely. If we hear it said that the definition of freedom is ability to do what we please, such an idea can only be taken to reveal an utter immaturity of thought, for it contains not even an inkling of the absolutely free will, of right, ethical life, and so forth.

For true freedom, that is to say, freedom in Hegel's sense of that term, can be realized only within a moral order. The moral order which he has in mind is of course his particular conception of the state.

States become, in their progress through history, the embodiment of the rational will. That is to say their laws and customs and institutions become increasingly more internally self-consistent. As the state more adequately reflects and becomes the embodiment of reason, to that degree will the individual who introjects or absorbs the laws and customs of the state, such that they become his own moral code, become himself more rational and therefore free. Rationality is then to be understood when it is considered in the private individual as the perception of the essential moral rightness of the state. The rationality of the state, on the other hand, is to be determined by the consistency of its laws and conventions. And as we have seen, the history of states is the constant progress towards full rationality and towards harmony between the rational will of the individual and the universal will as it is expressed in states. The historical development of states, which most adequately expresses what Hegel seems to have in mind might be well represented if we consider Plato's tripartite division of the state. For Plato, we recall, the state is divided into three parts, each representative of three distinct classes. If we simply historicize Plato's political structure, that is to say, if we place Plato's divisions of the state in a linear progression, we discover that we have, in some major respects, duplicated Hegel's conception. Earlier forms of political organization then will be characterized by those predicates which Plato said applied to the artisan's class. As the state develops then it becomes increasingly more rational until it reaches its fullest development as an agency which provides the conditions of complete human freedom.

BRADLEY'S ORGANIC THEORY OF THE STATE

We have already seen that in organic theories of the state the concept of state and the concept of society and culture are inextricably bound up with each other. The confluence of these two concepts rests upon the attribution of a moral dimension to what we, in our ordinary discourse, consider to be a merely political entity. The organic theorist conceives of the state as a moral as well as a legal agent. We are obliged, therefore, to examine somewhat more closely the relationship which these theorists believe hold between the moral and the legal sector. In turning to an examination of the views expressed by F. H. Bradley, we are in effect turning to a consideration of a holistic theory of state which is not altogether compatible with the earlier organismic theories of the state.

A word of clarification is in order here. We must draw a distinction between what some people have called a "heap" and a "system." A heap is to be understood as a random collectivity of parts which are not related to each other in an internal fashion. That is to say, to remove any member of the heap is to leave both the original material unchanged and to leave the part removed as essentially identical with what it was when it remained a member of the larger whole.

The concept of a system, on the other hand, implies that an organization of entities exists connected one to the other by a set of internal relations. To remove or to alter the position of any one constituent of a system is to change both the system itself as well as the character of the individual in question. A system thought of in this way may be compatible on the one hand with a machine, or on the other hand, with an organism. For in both entities, the criteria of what will count as being a system applies. In other words, a cog removed from a machine leaves the machine altered, and the cog is itself no longer what it was when it played its proper function as a constituent of the machine. Of course the same thing is true of an organism in the sense that an organ removed from a larger organism and deprived of its proper place within that organism is no longer what it was, nor of course, is the larger organic entity, the body, quite the same without its constituent part. Suppose we apply this analysis to the state, as does F. H. Bradley when he writes, "Let us take a man, an Englishman as he is now, and try to point out that, apart from what he has in common with others, apart from his sameness with others, he is not an Englishman—or a man at all; that if you take him as something by himself, he is not what he is."[27]

Bradley continues in this fashion: "What we mean to say is that he is what he is because he is a born and educated social being, and a member

[27] Bradley's *Ethical Studies,* 2d ed., p. 166. Cf. A. J. M. Milne, *The Social Philosophy of English Idealism,* p. 62.

of an individual social organism, that if you make abstractions from all this which is the same in him as in others, what you have left is not an Englishman nor a man, but some, I know not what, residuum which never has existed by itself and does not so exist."[28] The organic theory means that the most distinctively human predicates which may be predicated of any individual, assigns to him properties which are not to be understood as belonging uniquely to him but which are rather properties which he has in common with others. He writes, "In short, man is a social being; he is real only because he is social, and can realize himself only because it is as social that he realizes himself. The mere individual is a delusion of theory; and the attempt to realize it in practice is the starvation and mutilation of human nature, with total sterility or the production of monstrosities."[29]

What does all this teach us with regard to the relationship between morality and legality? He means to say that to live morally is to live socially, and to live socially is to live civically or politically. Thus he says: "Leaving out of sight the question of the society wider than the state we must say that a man's life with its moral duties, is in the main filled up by his station in that system of wholes which the state is, and this, partly by its laws and institutions, and still more by its spirit, gives him the life which he does live, and ought to live."

The meaning of this is clarified by A. J. M. Milne who says:

> When Bradley says that communities must be regarded as the one in the many, his point is that a community is a way of acting achieved by rational agents. They are the many, but they are also one in that they are not a mere aggregate but constitute a systematical unity. Nor is the rational agent in anything apart from his membership of communities. Living and acting socially, however, involves living and acting politically. Social life must be within the framework of an organized political community so that its various forms with their several demands can be harmonized. Thus rational activity, the rational agent's determination of himself, turns out to be the activity of citizenship, an activity which includes all of the forms of social activity. The activity of citizenship, rational activity at its most developed, is then identified with morality.[30]

---

[28] Bradley, *op. cit.*

[29] Bradley, *op. cit.*, 1.1.a., p. 111.

[30] Milne, *op. cit.*, p. 62–63.

Perhaps the best summary of this view is expressed by Bernard Bosanquet in his *The Philosophical Theory of the State:*

The State . . . is not merely the political fabric. The term "state" accents indeed the political aspect of the whole, and is opposed to the notion of an anarchical society. But it includes the entire hierarchy of institutions by which life is determined, from the family to the trade, and from the trade to the church and the university. It includes all of them, not as the mere collection of the growths of the country, but as the structure which gives life and meaning to the political whole, while receiving from it mutual adjustment, and therefore expansion and a more liberal air . . . it follows that the state, in this sense, is, above all things, not a number of persons, but a working conception of life.[31]

Bosanquet continues to complete the picture for us when he writes,

. . . for the force of the state proceeds essentially from its character of being our own mind extended, so to speak, beyond our immediate consciousness. Not only is the conduct of life as a whole beyond the powers of the average individual at its average level, but it is beyond the powers of all the average individuals within a society taken together at their average level. We make a great mistake thinking of the force exercised by the state as limited to the restraint of disorderly persons by the police and the punishment of intentional lawbreakers. The state is the fly wheel of our life. Its system is constantly reminding us of duties, from sanitation to incidents of trusteeship, which we have not the least desire to neglect, but which we are either too ignorant or too indolent to carry out apart from instruction and authoritative suggestion. We profit at every turn by institutions, rules, traditions, researchers, made by minds at their best, which, through state action, are not in a form to operate as extensions of our own minds.[32]

HOLISTIC THEORY

It may be noted that our historical survey of holistic theorists has omitted an analysis of the views of Karl Marx. Marx is after all perceived as one of the intellectual descendents of Hegel and we would have every right to expect that what Marx has to say about the state bears certain affinities to the Hegelian analysis. The fact of the matter is, however, that Marx's analysis of the state is critical rather than didactic. History,

---

[31] Bernard Bosanquet, *The Philosophical Theory of the State,* p. 140–41.

[32] *Ibid.,* p. 141–42.

for Marx, rather than consisting of the unfolding of the idea of freedom is rather a record of the ways in which conflicts among warring classes have occurred and the respects in which these have represented deeper and more fundamental antagonisms which have always existed among men. The holistic character exists not with respect to state, but rather with respect to classes. Thus, Marx is for us, in this connection, a curious figure; for although he is a holist in the sense that he conceives of classes as entities which may have a will and character of their own, quite apart from the will or character of the individuals who constitute the class, he nowhere attributes holistic characteristics to the state itself. For this reason, we have excluded Marx's analysis from this particular discussion.

We have, however, not completed our survey of holistic theorists. Indeed, we have failed to make a number of rather important distinctions within the context of our own classificatory system. We have used the word "organismic" in such a way so as to suggest that the concept of organism and the concept of whole are one and the same. This notion is, of course, entirely misleading. It is misleading because holistic systems are not exhausted by organic metaphors. A theorist who takes the position that the concept of the state may be clarified by drawing an analogy to a machine may well be a holist though he is clearly not an organicist. We must, therefore, be careful to see holism as the name of our type or model, and organicism as one instance, though, as a matter of fact, a rather large class of instances of holistic theories.

In order to clarify this distinction, consider the following passage:

> In the development of political speculation since the year of the French Revolution there may be differentiated a group of theories which undertake to comprehend the State under the general conceptions of organic life. Though these theories differ from one another in their more practical conclusions and in many aspects of their methods, their common object is to show that the juristic and political character of the state can be truly interpreted only by logically associating it with the ideas of animate nature. Their thesis is that the State is essentially like a natural organism in structure and members, in origin and development; or that it is a higher type of the general class of organic existences within which the animal and vegetable kingdom form lower types; or that its genesis, nature, and evolution are determined by the laws of psychic phase, in particular, of the highest type of animal organisms.[33]

---

[33] Coker, *Organismic Theories of the State*, p. 9.

We see immediately then that the concept of holism is the all inclusive one for this particular model, the concept "organic" falls as a subspecies within the larger whole and among the various theories of the state which may be classified as organismic they are so with varying degrees. In fact an examination of organic theories in the 19th century, a period during which such theories flourished, clearly indicates that no general agreement concerning the character of the organismic state may be reached if such agreement is insisted upon on the basis of an analysis of those aspects of the alleged organic state which are emphasized by a particular theorist. We are not surprised consequently to find some theorists speaking of the state as an organic entity in the sense that there exists a harmony of constituent parts. There are others who suppose that the state is a spiritual whole, similar to the spirit of the individual, with spirit meaning mind or psyche. Indeed, there are others who perceive actual states as curious combinations of both contractual, that is to say, atomistic ingredients as well as organismic ingredients.

An excellent example of the latter is Fichte, who, in his *Principles of Natural Right,* says:

> The essential distinction between the citizen and the isolated man is similar to that between the parts of an organic body and the parts of an inorganic body. Every part of the latter has the ground of its destiny in itself; its motive is completely explained through its existence, and its existence through its motive. Every part of a body of the organic world, on the other hand, has the basis of its destiny outside of itself; its motive presupposes its existence, a motive, outside of itself. Similarly with the isolated man who acts simply in order to satisfy his own needs, and these are satisfied only through his own actions; what he is externally he is only through himself. The citizen, on the other hand, has to do and to refrain from doing not merely on his own account, but for the sake of others as well; his highest needs are satisfied through the action of others, without his cooperation. In the organic body each part constantly maintains the whole, and is in maintaining the whole thereby itself maintained; just so stands the citizen in relation to the State.[34]

It is Fichte's point that the criteria of what constitutes an organic entity is that the basis of its destiny lies outside of itself; that is to say, it must be conceived as a suborgan of a larger organism and that is what he understands the relationship between the citizen and the state to be. The

---

[34] See *ibid.*, p. 22; Fichte, *Grundlage Des Naturrechts,* p. 209.

isolated man, on the other hand, is one whose source of determination lies within himself. To the extent that the state contains elements which are themselves determined, which are understood by Fichte, to constitute unassimilable elements, to that degree does the state contain a mechanical dimension in contradistinction to an organic one. The point here is that any given state may contain elements which are internally related to each other and insofar as they do, to that degree are they organic entities. Yet on the other hand, any state may contain elements which are externally related to the other constituents of the State and which therefore constitute a mechanical or mechanistic dimension of the state.

The possibility of a heterogenous state which contains both organic and mechanical elements is pointed out here to indicate once again that our models of respective states must be taken as idealized abstractions of the actual theories put forth by individual thinkers. This *caveat* is intended to enable the student to avoid the temptation of describing any given political theorist as an organic theorist or an atomistic theorist without considerable qualification. It would be a serious error if any such description were intended to be anything more than an introduction to an analysis of what that particular theorist means by the expression organic or atomistic.

Another example of the way in which the different conceptions of organicism may be confused under the same heading is to consider the fact that a leading concept which has appeared as an ingredient of virtually every conception of the organic theory of the state, namely the concept of reason, is, despite its ubiquitous character not an essential property of organismic theories. Indeed, though we have encountered the concept of reason as a necessary condition for the very possibility of a state with such thinkers as Aristotle and Hegel, there appears an apparent incongruity between appeals to the organic metaphor on the one hand to establish the legitimacy of the state, and to appeals to reason on the other. Consider for example the observation made by Milne: "The members of a society are selfconscious; they know themselves to be members and fulfill their functions in the light of this knowledge. The organs in an organism are not selfconscious and do not know that they are organs. They fulfill their functions blindly and automatically. A society lives in the thought and volition of its members; the life of an organism is a complex process of natural events."[35] The observation that there is an inconsistency between the operation of will and reason on the one hand, and the automatic functionalism of an organ on the other, is compatible with another notion of the organic theory of the state which emphasizes the instinctive and automatic, rather than rational and functional aspects of organic entities. We have seen for example in Rousseau where moral sentiment and compassion, rather than reason, comprised the cement of social and political organization. And we shall see when we turn to an examination of holistic theories, and those political ideologies which have been based upon such theories, that reason is not a necessary condition of, and indeed may be an unassimilable ingredient of, organic concepts.

Holism, groups, and classes

If it is both reasonable and convenient to describe states as organic, or to use organic entities or other holistic devices as metaphorical explanations of how states work, then it is natural that some will suppose that other forms of association may be clarified with similar metaphors. We have mentioned in an earlier passage that according to Marx a class is a holistic entity. It is commonplace in any analysis of the philosophy of Karl Marx to observe that the state in all presocialist societies is an instrument for the repression of the exploited classes. The state, according to Marxists, is nothing more than a police agency which functions in such a way so as to maintain and extend the power of the economically enfranchised classes, that is to say, of those who own the means of production and distribution. There is nothing in this notion which would suggest a holistic or organic theory of state. States are merely instruments of repression, and in all presocialist societies, that is, all societies arranged along class lines, states are nothing more than agencies of police power. Frederick Engels expresses the Marxist notion of the state as follows:

As the State arose from the need to hold class antagonisms in check, but as it arose, at the same time, in the midst of the conflict of these classes, it is,

[35] Milne, *op. cit.*, p. 63.

as a rule, the state of the most powerful, economically dominant class, which, through the medium of the state, becomes also the politically dominant class, and thus requires new means of holding down and exploiting the oppressed class. Thus the state of antiquity was above all the state of the slave owners for the purpose of holding down the slaves, as the feudal state was the organ of the nobility for holding down the peasant serfs and bondsmen, and the modern representative state is an instrument of exploitation of wage labor by capital.[36]

Whatever may be the character of this nonholistic theory of the state, a subject to which we will return at a later discussion, we must nonetheless inquire about the character of Marxist notion of the *class*.

A class is defined or understood in terms of the relations which that particular group of people bear to the way in which objects are produced and to the ownership of those objects. The criteria of membership in the capitalist class is the ownership of the means of production and distribution, though at times Marx speaks of others who do not own a direct interest in the means of production and distribution though they may be broadly classified as professionals or managerial persons whose interests lie with those of the capitalist class.

Class, it would appear then, is a matter of interest, and interest is a function of the relations which obtain between persons and the right they may have to control both their own labor and the labor of others. Thus, in capitalist societies, it is to the interest of the capitalist class to create and maintain certain political forms to preserve its own particular relationship to production and the means of distribution. In the same sort of society, it is to the interest of the proletarian class to alter those existing forms so as to eliminate both the condition and the possibility of their servitude.

Now the important point in this discussion is that it is possible for classes to have interests which no individual can recognize or acknowledge as his own personal interest. Thus, it may be that I am a member of the proletarian class, though I neither own property, nor do I have control over the disposition of the goods which I produce, nor, indeed, do I have any alternatives with regard to the way in which I will dispose of

---

[36] Excerpt from the *Origin of the Family, Private Property and the State*. Cf. L. Feuer, p. 392.

my own labor and skill. For these reasons, it may be said that I am a member of the proletariat. It is Marx's position that the class of which I am a member has certain interests and that among these is the elimination of the capitalist class. Such a state of affairs will come about once the proletarian class becomes self-conscious, that is to say, once the class becomes aware of its own vigor, its own potentialities, its historic destiny. Yet, I personally may be unreflective in this regard and indeed, I personally may adhere to a moral system or system of belief in which I suppose my own interests to be best served if I am given an opportunity to become a member of the capitalist class. Under such not very absurd circumstances, it would appear that I am a member of a class defined in accordance with the interests of the class where I may be neither aware of what those interests are or, indeed, if I were aware of them, where I would deny that they are my own interests. Thus, it is possible, and this is Marx's meaning, for a class to have interests quite apart from, and possibly even different from, the interests of its constituent members, or at any rate, what its constituent members claim its interests to be. This conception of class is altogether compatible with the holistic concept.

Similarly, it is possible to attribute other psychic properties to groups and other social collectivities, other than classes. Consider for example the following passage from the French sociologist Emile Durkheim:

> Our individual reason is, and has the same value as, that collective and impersonal reason called science which is, both in its constitution and in its processes, pre-eminently a social thing. Our aesthetic faculties, the fineness of our tastes, derive from art, which is again a social thing. It is to society that we owe the power over matter which is our glory. It is society that has freed us from nature. It is not then to be expected that we think of it as a mental being higher than ourselves from which our mental powers emanate. This explains why it is that when it demands of us those sacrifices, great or small, that make up our moral life, we bow before its demands with deference.
>
> The believer bows before his God, because it is from God that he believes that he holds his being, particularly his mental being, his soul. We have the same reasons for experiencing this feeling before the collective.[37]

Here again, we encounter the propensity of social theorists to ascribe to social entities, groups, classes, associations, and states, properties

[37] Emile Durkheim, *Sociology and Philosophy*, p. 73.

which in our ordinary discourse we are generally inclined to ascribe only to individuals.

Holism, metaphysical and methodological

To this point in our discussion we have been concerned with what might be classed metaphysical holism, that is to say, with theories which suppose or allege, that among the various objects which we encounter in the universe are collectivities which would not be what they are were they reducible to their various constituent parts. This way of perceiving the world leads us to deny that it is constituted to a variety of individual and particular entities which are themselves ultimately reducible, at least in imagination, to simpler and less complex properties and qualities. The theory of holism alleges that states or groups or associations like classes, possess a reality as great or greater than the reality of particular things. Holism construed in this way is a metaphysical theory because it makes a commitment about the sorts of things which actually exist in the world. Yet it is important to distinguish between holism as a metaphysical theory and holism as a methodological theory. For it becomes immediately apparent to us that if we reject the metaphysical assumptions upon which holism is based, we are faced with the problem of justifying any talk about collectivities. We should then be in an exceedingly difficult situation for we would be reduced to accepting a theory of language in which only those terms which denote concrete objects would have any sense for us. But there is a way out of our difficulty. If we think of collectivities like states or classes or the forms of association, as having properties which may be correctly ascribed to them provided only that those properties may be ascribed to the individual members which comprise that collectivity, we would nonetheless be justified in speaking of such collectivities without having made an untenable metaphysical commitment concerning their reality. Suffice it to say that metaphysical holism provides us with a way of looking at the world which assumes or asserts something about the sorts of objects which are to be found there. Methodological holism, on the other hand, provides us with a way of thinking about the world without commitments as to its ultimate constituents, that is to say, wihout requiring that we commit ourselves as to whether there are such entities.

The ingredients of holism

Proposition 1. The state has an existential status independent of that of the individuals who compose it.

Proposition 2. The state has interests, goals, and purposes which may be different from those of the individuals who compose it.

Proposition 3. The state is a moral entity, and consequently functions as a moral, as well as a legal arbiter.

Proposition 4. The state is instructive in the sense that it exists for the moral improvement (perhaps intellectual improvement as well) of its citizenry.

Proposition 5. Being truly human is possible only within, and under the influence of, the state.

Proposition 6. State and society are inextricably linked, and in the best of such states no conflict is expected to arise between the constituent members and the requirements of the state itself.

Proposition 7. To obey the law of the state is to do not merely what is legal, but what is right.

Proposition 8. The rightness of such obedience is perceived by the citizen if only he examines the dictates of reason or the dictates of conscience.

Holism and ideology

It is only natural to suppose that there exists a relationship between the various dimensions of the concept of holism and some particular ideology or other. Indeed, an examination of the preceding list of the state leads us to believe that the ideology most compatible with these concepts is some variant of totalitarianism. In fact there is a long and important tradition of critical interpretation which alleges that totalitarian ideology stemmed from, or are outgrowths of, ways of looking at the state which are compatible with the theories of Plato and Hegel. A poignant and perhaps moving example of this interconnection between theory and ideology, and between ideology and concrete historical events concerns a passage from the dedication of L. P. Hobhouse in his *The Metaphysical Theory of the State* where, in a note to his son, then a pilot for the R.A.F., Hobhouse writes the following soon after a raid by the German Air Force on London:

As I went back to my Hegel, my first mood was one of self satire. Was this a time for theorizing or destroying theories, when the world was tumbling about our ears? My second thoughts ran otherwise. To each man the tools and weapons that he can best use. In the bombing of London I had just witnessed the visible and tangible outcome of a false and wicked doctrine, the foundations of which lay, as I believe, in the book before me. To combat this doctrine effectively is to take such part in the fight as the physical disabilities of middle age allow. Hegel, himself, carried the proofsheets of his first work to the printer through the streets crowded with fugitives from the fields of Jena. With that work began the most penetrating and subtle of all the intellectual influences which have sapped the rational humanitarianism of the 18th and 19th century, and in the Hegelian theory of the God state all that I had witnessed lay implicit.[38]

Hobhouse continues in a somewhat less melodramatic fashion. To characterize the holistic state or as he calls it the metaphysical view of the state and to indicate the respects in which it differs from nontotalitarian conceptions, he writes:

Here precisely lies the issue between two views of the state. In the democratic or humanitarian view it is a means. In the metaphysical view, it is an end. In the democratic view, it is the servant of humanity in the double sense that it is to be judged by what it does with the lives of its members and by the part that it plays in the society of human kind. In the metaphysical view, it is itself the soul guardian of moral worth. In the democratic view the sovereign state is already doomed, destined to subordination in a community of the world. In the metaphysical view, it is the supreme achievement of human organization. For the truth let the present condition of Europe be witnessed.[39]

Though we will consider at some length fascist notion of the state, it is of interest to see that Hobhouse's allegation is not without some foundation. Consider for example, Benito Mussolini's characterization of the fascist state:

Fascism desires the state to be strong and organic. . . . The fascist state . . . anticipates the solution of certain universal problems . . . in the ethical field by the need felt for order, discipline, obedience to the moral principles of

---

[38] L. P. Hobhouse, *The Metaphysical Theory of the State,* p. 6.
[39] *Ibid.,* p. 137.

patriotism. . . . Far from crushing the individual, the fascist state multiplies its energies, just as in a regiment a soldier is not diminished but multiplied by the number of his fellow soldiers. . . . The state possesses a moral code rather than a theology. . . . The fascist state expresses the will to exercise power and to command. . . . Fascism . . . in short, is not only a law giver and a founder of institutions, but an educatory and a promoter of spiritual life. It aims at refashioning not only the forms of life but their content—man, his character, and his state. To achieve this purpose it enforces discipline and uses authority, entering into the soul and ruling with undisputed sway.[40]

Now these passages appear on the face of it to confirm Hobhouse's inference that fascism or totalitarianism has its roots in a holistic or organic theory of the state. Unfortunately, this inference will not do. For although it may be true that fascism has its roots in a given theory of the state, it cannot reasonably be argued that holism implies, in a logical sense of "imply," a given ideology to the exclusion of all others.

The possibilities of such an interpretation became apparent to us in our discussion of Rousseau. A continuation of that segment of Rousseau's thought which may be characterized as democratic may be found in the work of T. H. Green. According to Green:

Society begins in the consciousness of a common good, of common interests. These interests necessitate definite interrelations. It is recognized that order and organization are part of the actual life of the community. Individuals become no longer atomic units, but integral parts of (more or less dimly) recognized whole, clothed with various but appropriate rights and duties. Force, sovereign power, is in no sense the originator of these rights, though it cooperates in sustaining the regular performance. Every society is constituted and held together by a conscious, intelligent, recognition of a common good.[41]

Another expression of the way in which democratic theory may be justified with reference to a holistic theory, which rests upon a conception of the general will similar in many ways to Rousseau's concept of the general will, stems from analysis like the following:

The notion that the man who values, guards, cultivates his own individuality is setting himself in opposition to the interest of society is a profound misunderstanding. It is the essence of democracy that the public interest cannot flourish without the cultivation of the individual's interest in himself. The

---

[40] Benito Mussolini, *The Doctrine of Fascism,* p. 42, 43 and 17.

[41] William Henry Fairbrother, *The Philosophy of Thomas Hill Green,* p. 128–29.

Together-Will will be the aggregation of real and vigorous individual wills; otherwise it becomes that devouring monster, mass emotion, goaded by unconscienable and overweaning individual will.[42]

A similar view is expressed by Chapman who notes an intimate connection between Rousseau's conception of the state and the theory of state most compatible with modern liberalism:

Both Lindsay (the modern liberal) and Rousseau think of the state as essentially the institutional expression of man's moral purpose, which purpose includes recognition of an obligation to neutralize his selfish tendencies and their effects. For them, the state is the means by which man releases his moral potential and seeks to realize goodness and justice; it is not merely a device by which men are enabled to control one another. Neither pictures man as the egoistic yet plastic creature of the utilitarians. Both see man's need for liberty in his capacity for moral growth, in his perfectibility as Rousseau would say.[43]

All these passages indicate that in the minds of some theorists it is at least possible to justify democratic political institutions with reference to holistic theories of the state.

Holism and communism

In discussing the communist theory of the state it is important to distinguish between the way in which communist theorists perceived the state as it functions in presocialist, precommunist society and its mode of operation in postsocialist society. In prerevolutionary society, we have seen that the state is conceived of as an instrument of repression. And, if we are to take Marx and Engels literally, the condition of society in postsocialist era is one in which the state had withered away entirely, that is to say, communist society requires no repression since it is classless and thus force and coercion have no function. But the curious thing is that what little Marx and Engels have to say about the conditions of life which obtain in this communist society, it bears a distinct resemblance to the idealized community of saints described by Rousseau. The idyllic state of affairs generated by this classless society is brought about because men no longer compete among themselves for the objects which they

[42] Carleton Kemp Alan, *Democracy and the Individual,* p. 105.

[43] John W. Chapman, *Rousseau—Totalitarian or Liberal?* p. 143.

produce once they have gained complete control over nature. The concept of interest is herein interpreted as meaning almost invariably economic interest and therefore, if the basis of competing economic interests is removed, that is to say, if there is no longer a scarcity of goods, then competition is also removed. Under such circumstances, there is no longer any point in talking about individuals pursuing their own private interests, for those interests are satisfied. The transition to this communist state is understood by Engels in the following way: "All socialists are agreed that the political state, and with it political authority, will disappear as a result of the coming social revolution, that is, that public function will lose their political character and be transformed into the simple administrative functions of watching over the true interests of society."[44]

This postcommunist state is therefore not a political entity but truly an administrative body which is geared to protect society's interests. The community is depoliticized and conflicts do not arise because men have satisfied their needs. Now all this is, of course, absurdly utopian. The theory of the communist state or nonstate and the reality are two quite different matters. If we examine briefly the reality, we notice that in socialist societies, at any rate, individual expressions of the will of individual persons are subordinate to those of the state, and, indeed, that the state is itself an agency which cannot be justified in terms of reference to the ideology of communism alone. Obviously, no efforts are made in the Soviet Union today to proceed with what is allegedly the next step of historical development, namely, the establishment of communism and the sort of community we have described. There are good reasons offered by Soviet theoreticians which account for this practical deviation from theoretical intentions. Nonetheless, the reality provides us with a picture of an ideology which has its roots in holistic thinking.

---

[44] L. S. Feuer in *On Authority*, p. 481.

4

The concept of the state, II

IN THIS CHAPTER we will discuss atomistic theories of the state. Our purpose will be to construct a model of atomistic theories drawing historical ingredients from a variety of diverse political thinkers—from the Sophists to the Utilitarians.

THE SOPHISTS

Ernest Barker once observed that early Greek thought had a natural tendency to accept the order of the state, its laws, and its agencies of enforcement without question.

> Men were born, and lived, and died, under old customary laws, whose origin no man knew. It was dimly felt that they were divine; it was certainly recognized that they were rigid and fundamental. Custom was Lord of all things . . . the sense of an inevitable order of all human life was so powerful, that by comparison the life of the earth, with all its flux and change, with its lightening and tempest, well might seem incalculable and indeterminate. In human life all was appointed. You did *this* and *that* followed. It was not so in nature.[1]

But human affairs do not follow a pattern uninterrupted by the vicissitudes of history. And as the traditional stability of what might be described as a tribal community began for a variety of reasons to erode, men began to recognize the variations from one society to another in

[1] Ernest Barker, *Political Thought of Plato and Aristotle,* p. 28.

customs, values, and standards of conduct. Thus, as Barker writes: "While the study of physics had worked towards the conception of a single underlying substratum of all matter, the anthropological study of the human world worked towards the conception of an infinite diversity of institutions. The old relation was inverted: nature abode by one law, and men hovered between many."[2]

The relativism engendered by the recognition that no one single standard of conduct or one single way of perceiving the world was the correct or valid one, found its way into the fabric of the way in which men thought about political institutions. The sentiment which emerges from this condition is best expressed in the aphorism attributed to the Sophist Protagoras who wrote: "Man is a measure of all things."

The world is the way in which all men perceive it, which is to say, that objects of knowledge are based ultimately upon man's experience. And since men then felt free to raise questions about all aspects of their lives, it is only natural that they raise questions about the character of human institutions and the laws of states.

Such were the questions raised by the Sophists and the very asking of them in the first place constitutes a revolution in the way in which men have learned to approach political matters. The morphology of this development is fairly clear: so long as men perceived human institutions as the sorts of things which could be taken for granted, based upon habit and custom, and beyond the capacity of human reason, it was the natural world that appeared to be chaotic and unpredictable. When, however, the natural world became a proper object of human inquiry and men came to recognize that it was possible to subjugate nature, to understand that nature is subject to understanding through the apprehension of laws of conformity, the power of human reason, which could be efficacious with regard to natural phenomena, was turned upon the analysis of human institutions themselves.

The distinctive characteristic of early Greek metaphysics is the search for a single underlying theory of explanation in terms of which all natural phenomena could be understood. The search for such an underlying substance appears to us today as absurd or perhaps amusing. Thales thought that the substance of which all things were constituted was

---

[2] *Ibid.*, p. 29–30.

water. Heraclitus argued that the substance in question was fire, and so for Empedocles, and Anaxagoras. And thus, the natural transition which has taken place in every era in which men have learned to have confidence in the method with which they pursue empirical issues concerning the natural world, those methods are then turned to the analysis of moral and social and political matters. Thus, when men's historical experience enable them to apprehend the diversity of customs, habits, and constitutions from one culture to another, the world of human institutions took on the aura which the physical world was once thought to possess, namely, as chaotic, disorganized, and without foundation. The task then is to try to discover the fundamental rules of political and social life in a manner which is similar to the way in which men began to uncover the fundamental characteristics of objects in the natural world. Thus, men began to perceive formalized human relationships in institutions as reducible to purely hedonistic impulses, as an elaborate ideology which obscures the fact that basic human drives consist of pleasure and the satisfaction of individual needs. Just as the multiplicity of natural objects in the world are themselves reducible to one basic underlying substance, so is the diversity of human institutions, customs, habits, rules, constitutions, etc., reducible to the pursuit of pleasure and the avoidance of pain. This conception of human motivation is at the foundation of a theory of individualism. We find the political theory produced by this individualism put into the mouth of Glaucon, Plato's protagonist, in the second book of the *Republic*. Here, Glaucon states what might be taken to be the first suggestion of a theory of the social contract:

What people say is that to do wrong is, in itself, a desirable thing; on the other hand, it is not all desirable to suffer wrong, and the harm to the sufferer outweighs the advantage to the doer. Consequently, when men have had a taste of both, those who have not the power to seize the advantage and escape the harm decide that they would be better off if they made a compact neither to do wrong nor to suffer it. Hence, they begin to make laws and covenants with one another; and whatever the law prescribed they called lawful and right. That is what right or justice is and how it came into existence; and stands halfway between the best thing of all—to do wrong with impunity—and the worst, . . . which is to suffer wrong without the power to retaliate. So justice is accepted as a compromise, and valued, not as good in itself, but for lack of power to do wrong; no man worthy of the name, who has that power, would ever enter into such a compact with anyone; he would be mad if he did. That, Socrates, is the nature of justice according to this account, and such circumstances in which it arose.[3]

Glaucon offers a view of the state as the product of the interested action of ordinary men without reference to a natural order or without referring to the state as a divine institution. It is brought about through the direct action by men who, in a previous condition of nature, were preyed upon by the beasts. This conception of the social contract is one which works toward the justification of the existence of a state, though the justification is grounded neither in nature nor in history, but rather in utility. The pragmatic character of this conception of the way in which the state comes about lies in the fact that men created it in order to bring about a certain purpose, namely the equalization of their powers which does not exist in a state of nature. Perceived from this point of view, the contract is a bargain entered into by those who would in a state of nature be considered the weaker and who create the state as an agency which enables them to subdue the stronger. Looked at in this way, we detect the flaw in justifications of political institutions with reference to utility. For the benefit in such a state accrues not to all but to the weaker. The other side of this coin is expressed by Thrasymachus who, in the *Republic,* argues essentially that the state is indeed a convention but one which works against the laws of nature and is therefore an unwarranted and unjustifiable perversion of the relations which would exist among men in a state of nature. And what are those relations? Thrasymachus says that "if each has thus the right to satisfy himself according to his powers . . . , it follows that the strongest have the greatest right, because they have the greatest power."[4] Following this reasoning, it is easy to see that a theory of individualism coupled with a theory of the social contract may on the one hand imply an egalitarian society whose institutions insure equal treatment to all those who are parties to the contract, yet looked at from another perspective may imply a critical ideology which rejects the state because it is a perversion of nature, a nature which dictates that might makes right.

[3] Cornford's ed., p. 43–44.

[4] *Ibid.*, p. 37.

Aristotle

Aristotle, as we have seen earlier, draws a distinction between a good man and a good citizen. The suggestion that it is possible to be a good man on the grounds that one adheres to certain universal principles of conduct, and to be a good citizen on the grounds that one obeys the law of the land implies that circumstances may arise where an individual may be considered to be a good citizen and yet a bad man. This peculiar circumstance comes about when the law of the land is incompatible with universal rules of conduct. Although there is no suggestion in Aristotle of the social contract, one of the ingredients of a moderate individualism lies in the distinction between a man and a citizen itself. For to draw the distinction is to suggest that it is conceptually possible to abstract and judge a man according to criteria which are different from those employed in judging a citizen.

Cicero

We turn now to a very brief examination of Cicero's analysis of the state—the way in which the state has come about, and the relationship which obtains between the various individuals who compose the state and that entity itself. The following passage is quoted from Cicero's, *On the Commonwealth:*

The Commonwealth, then, is the people's affair; and the people is not every group of men, associated in any manner, but is the coming together of a considerable number of men who are united in a common agreement about law and right and by the desire to participate in mutual advantages. The original cause of this coming together is not so much weakness as a kind of social instinct natural to man. For the human kind is not solitary, nor do its members live lives of isolated roving; but it is so constituted that, even if it possessed the greatest plenty of material comforts [it would nevertheless be impelled by its nature to live in social groups]. . . . [These gregarious impulses] are, so to speak, the seeds [of social virtue]; nor can any other source be found for the remaining virtues or, indeed, for the Commonwealth itself. Such groups, therefore, brought into being for the reason I have mentioned, first settle themselves in a fixed abode that they might have dwellings. And when they have fortified this abode, either by taking advantage of the natural features of the land or by building artificial works, they call such a group of buildings, with the places set aside for shrines and for common use, either a town or city. Consequently, every people which is a number of men united in the way I have explained, every state, which is an organization of the people, every commonwealth, which, as I have said is the people's affair, needs to be ruled by some sort of deliberating authority in order that it may endure. This authority, in the first place, must always be relative to the peculiar grounds which have brought the particular state into being. It must, in the second place, be delegated either to a single man, or to certain selected persons, or it must be retained by all members of the group.[5]

Consider the first sentence of the passage quoted above. First, a condition for the establishment of a commonwealth requires the unity of a considerable number of people; secondly, of people who are organized in a special sort of way which involves a common agreement about law and rights. Thirdly, the impulse to organize into a political unity lies in the mutual advantages which such a unity promises. The state is not the product of individual or collective weakness and fear in a state of nature, but rather the product of man's fundamental social nature. What is of interest to us here is the fact that Cicero is referring to a kind of a state of nature superseded by a social contract which, if not explicitly entered into, is nonetheless implied by the observation that unity is the result of a common agreement about law and rights and by the desire to participate in mutual advantages.

It has been said that the existence of a universal law, eternal in duration and divine in character, is a presupposition of Cicero's theory of the state. If we combine Cicero's commitment to the theory of natural law on one hand with his conception of man as an individual who possesses a social nature, we discover the key to his theory of the state. Individual persons have in fact a dual citizenship; their social nature requires that they recognize certain obligations and duties to the state in which they live and their conditions as human beings requires that they observe demands placed upon them by the natural law. This condition is an extention of Aristotle's distinction between man and citizen discussed in the preceding paragraphs. Indeed, Cicero confirms this interpretation in his discussion of the sort of structure an individual state ought to have. Thus he writes:

---

[5] *On the Commonwealth,* Book I, proposition XXV and XXVI.

When . . . the supreme power is in the hands of one man, we call that man a king, and that form of government a monarchy. When it is in the hands of certain selected persons, the state is said to be ruled by the will of an aristocracy. And a state is democratic—for that is the term used—when all authority is in the hands of the people themselves. Any one of these three forms of government, while not, of course, perfect nor in my judgment the best, is nevertheless a passable form of government, if the bond holds which originally united its members in the social order of the commonwealth; and one may be better than the other.[6]

The important thing is that men belong to states, no matter what the character of a particular state may be, and yet at the same time as individuals they belong to universal mankind. Moreover, whatever the character of the particular state in which they are citizens, there are certain attributes or properties which may be predicated of them by virtue of their status as individual men. All men are, for example, equally endowed with reason and are therefore, equal by nature. All men, whatever their citizenship, exhibit a belief in goodness, they applaud virtue and detest barbarity. In these respects, they possess human qualities independent of any particular form of political organization.

Machiavelli

General statements about political theory and about political theorists have a tendency to suffer from two rather severe limitations. If on the one hand, they are too general, they tend to be useless and uninformative and yet, if on the other, they are narrow and informative, they are apt to be false. There is a strong temptation to argue that every political theorist normally treated in a study of the Western political tradition says what he says against a background of commitments and presuppositions concerning the world at large. In other words, it is said that the way in which men have looked at political institutions is very often, perhaps even almost always, a function of how they look at the world generally. Put bluntly, metaphysics implies in a nontechnical sense of that concept, politics. The generalization appears least tenuous in the light of classical political theory where the connection between inquiries into the nature

---

[6] *Ibid.*, para. XXVI.

of ultimate reality and analysis of human institutions was close and obvious. Indeed, in Plato we found it difficult to draw the distinction.

Nicolo Machiavelli appears on the face of it to present us with an exception to our general rule. Machiavelli raises no questions about the nature of ultimate reality or about the character of the natural world. His book, *The Prince,* may be, and has been, read as a manual concerning the arts of ruling. Yet an analysis of how to rule properly and successfully must take into account the nature and character of the individuals ruled. And in this connection, Machiavelli makes a variety of important assumptions about what he takes to be human nature. Thus he writes in the *Discourses:*

> . . . all those who have written upon civil institutions demonstrate . . . that whoever desires to found a state and give it laws, must start with assuming that all men are bad and ever ready to display their vicious nature, whenever they may find occasion for it. If their evil disposition remains concealed for a time, it must be attributed to some unknown reason; and we must assume that it lacked occasion to show itself; but time, which has been said to be the father of all truth, does not fail to bring it to light.[7]

In *The Prince,* a similar sentiment is expressed in advising the ruler as to whether it is better to be loved more than feared or feared more than loved.

> The reply is, that one ought to be both feared and loved, but as it is difficult for the two to go together, it is much safer to be feared than loved, if one of the two has to be wanting. For it may be said of men in general that they are ungrateful, voluble, dissemblers, anxious to avoid danger, and covetous of gain; as long as you benefit them, they are entirely yours; they offer you their blood, their goods, their life, their children . . . when the necessity is remote; but when it approaches, they revolt.[8]

The picture of human nature offered by Machiavelli is that of human beings who live static lives, who are selfish, acquisitive, restless, and perpetually discontented. They are creatures with no motives and no interests except those supplied by their own egoism. Though Machiavelli does not describe this condition of mankind as that of the state of nature, it is nonetheless a picture of what he thinks men are by nature. Men are

---

[7] *Discourses,* p. 117.

[8] *The Prince,* p. 61.

isolated egos each striving to satisfy their own private ends, living a life closely analogous to that of beasts in a jungle. The creation of political institutions is simply a device to insure a degree of security which cannot exist without a community with a political structure. The state has no justification other than the maintenance of peace where peace is construed as security and stability. Yet it is important to see that the state does not alter the basic constituents of human nature. Men are no less selfish or egoistic or treacherous within the confines of political organization than they are without such institutions. The political community does not alter human nature, it merely takes human nature as a basic fact of life. The purpose of a political organization therefore, is to organize power, covertly rather than overtly, such that the *anomic* condition of the prepolitical community is overcome and security and stability is achieved.

The Prince may be interpreted as a textbook in the arts appropriate to the administration of power in a society constituted of men of the sort which Machiavelli describes. The prerequisite for political community and therefore a condition for the successful administration of a prince lies in the perception of the true character of man, and particularly in the fact that though human nature is essentially static, it is also pliable. The ruler does not make an effort to change men's basic character but merely to channel and manipulate his self-serving propensities in such a way that the society is preserved and its interests advanced.

A further fact is man's natural tendency to be led astray by self-produced illusions. Men cling to certain habits of mind and character no longer appropriate to present and future events, habits based on fantasy insuring a sense of security unwarranted and unsupported by the world of everyday affairs. This vital fact about human nature must be carefully exploited by the ruler. For it provides him with the opportunity to manipulate social institutions while preserving their outward form, in such a way that they enable him to solidify, secure, and extend his power.

What is crucial to our consideration of Machiavelli in this respect is the simple fact that the Prince must understand what men are and to exploit this understanding so as to preserve the society despite the essentially nonsocial properties of those who are ruled. The Prince has as his task the manipulation of the natural aggressiveness of human nature which makes struggle and competition a normal feature of every society. The Prince must accept the fact of natural competition and struggle which exists among those whom he rules and establish an equilibrium or balance between opposing interests. Yet it is important to see that the natural competition which Machiavelli accepts as a condition for a healthy society is competition based not upon political, but rather upon social or economic matters. Men, according to Machiavelli, compete for the goods of life, and for political power only indirectly so far as these enable them to acquire the goods of life. Political power on the other hand remains ultimately in the hands of the ruler.

In this discussion we have encountered an analysis of human nature based upon an individualistic theory which makes no commitment with respect to the theory of natural law and natural rights. Indeed, for Machiavelli, there are no such rights or laws other than those which the ruler finds convenient to bestow upon those ruled. What is critical to our discussion is that individuals are perceived as consisting of atomic units each pursuing their own interests and their own ultimate ends. The political community does not change this basic fact about human beings, but rather the organization of power and the centralization of authority, takes this basic datum into account and structures itself accordingly.

Thomas Hobbes

The 17th and 18th century are times of revolution, both institutional and intellectual. The issue of individualism was debated as an aspect of a greater and more encompassing intellectual revolution whose beginning point is the analysis of what things simply are. No area of inquiry was completely free from the analytic onslaught; analysis meant reducing physical objects into atoms; thinking into impressions and images; ethics into primary instincts and utility; society into individuals who compose it; religion into ignorance and fear. The method of reductive analysis, that is to say, the reduction of complexities into the constituent simples which compose them has its roots in two, quite different historical and institutional forms. On the one hand, the method has its roots in the scientific revolution of the 17th century. On the other hand, it is an expression of a general way of looking at the world which derives from the ideology of the Protestant Reformation.

The method of reductive analysis is the method of classical mechanics. Just as the pre-Socratic Greek philosophers sought to reduce the varied phenomena of nature to a single underlying principle, in a similar fashion the classical physicists of the 17th century attempted to reduce all phenomena to mechanics. Christian Huygens, the 17th century physicist, declared: "In true philosophy one conceives the cause of all natural effects in terms of mechanical motions. This . . . we must necessarily do, or else renounce all hopes of comprehending anything in physics."[9]

A similar view directed towards the procedures which must be employed in the comprehension of the structure of the physical world is expressed by the following: "Mechanics is the beginning and foundation for all planetary natural science. It is the most general natural science, insofar as one attempts to reduce, on the strength of the postulate of the permanence of material substance, all natural phenomena given to external sense to the phenomena which mechanics study, that is, to motions of bodies and of their parts."[10] And again: "The highest object at which the natural scientists are constrained to aim, but which they will never reach, is . . . in one word, the reduction of all the phenomena of nature to mechanics."[11] The same view is expressed by Helmholtz who writes: "The object of the natural sciences is to find the motions upon which all of the changes are based, and their corresponding motive forces—to resolve themselves, therefore, into mechanics."[12]

If we raise a question concerning the character of classical mechanics, we discover that the heart of the enterprise lies with the fundamental axioms or laws of bodies in motion. Once again, the parallel with the early Greek physicists becomes apparent. Just as their reductive analysis in the explanation of natural events was taken by the Sophist to provide a methodology and a set of presumptions about human society, in the same way the methods and assumptions of classical mechanics were applied to the historical world of social phenomena. Thus, if the physical world consists of bodies in motion and if there are laws which can be

---

[9] *Treatise on Light,* n.d. p. 3.

[10] Wilhelm Wundt, *Logik,* Vol. 2, 3d ed., p. 274.

[11] G. Kirzhoff, *Concepts of Modern Physics* (New York, 1884), p. 18, quoted by J. B. Stallo.

[12] *Ibid.;* see also E. Nagel, *The Structure of Science,* p. 154–55.

discovered in terms of which explanations and predictions concerning natural events are possible, then is it not also possible to conceive of the social world as comprised of individual human atoms in motion? And is it not reasonable to suppose that here too there are universal rules or general laws in terms of which explanations and predictions are possible? In other words, there are certain things about the behavior of natural bodies which allow for the formulation of general laws. Consider for example, Newton's third law of motion: "To every action there is always opposed an equal reaction: or the mutual actions of two bodies upon each other are always equal, and directed to contrary parts." Is it possible for us to discover a comparable law which explains the behavior of human beings? The search for such laws lies in the very foundation of a good deal for what passes for political inquiry in the 17th and part of the 18th century. (Consider for example the full title of David Hume's most important work: *A Treatise of Human Nature: Being an attempt to introduce the experimental method of reasoning into moral subjects.*)

The other expression of reductive analysis is ideological or philosophical rather than scientific. In our discussion of Machiavelli we noted that he had succeeded in uncovering a new dimension of political life in the sense that his theory revolved around an emphasis upon the concept of interest. The older concept of community, of a political society which rested upon common interests, common purposes, and common goals was replaced by a theory which reflected the disintegration of community itself. This crisis in community was not a local phenomenon limited to the Italian city-states with which Machiavelli was preoccupied. Institutional decay is closely tied to the decay of the one single monolithic institution which endured during the first thousand years of the modern era, namely, the church. The problem for the theorists of the Protestant Reformation was to put together again a world which their own theological revolution had undone. The new conception of the church was that of a voluntary association in which each individual member faced the prospect of coming to terms with his own soul and his own salvation by himself. Individualism in this theological sense was a response to and a reaction against the monolithic community established by Christianity. Thus, the reformation theorists in encouraging the sense of individuality necessary to alter the structure of the traditional community created at the same time the conditions for society without community. The proliferation of the reformation church into a variety of segmented groups, each consisting of individuals tenuously related to each other, and members of the group by virtue not of having subscribed to canon or dogma of the church, but rather by the possession of an inner experience to which the individual alone could testify, made the possibility of unity and cohesion, if not impossible then at least improbable. To each individual person was left the task of deciding which path he will pursue in achieving salvation. It is manifestly clear that the problem which confronts the Protestant theologians concerning the incongruities between the church as an institution, traditionally a tightly knit unity, and the new individualism of the Protestant man is precisely the problem which confronts political theorists who must establish a foundation for the practice of government and the conduct of political life despite the fact that the society was no longer a community.

The concept of individualism provides us with a foundation for two distinctly different, although perhaps related, foundations for looking at the world. On the one hand, individualism is the ideology of liberalism, promising freedom and egalitarianism. On the other hand, it is the foundation and the expression of the breakdown of community, of disorder, doubt, uncertainty, and fear. In the succeeding discussion we shall see how each of these conditions stemming from a theory of individualism is developed. On the one hand, we shall consider Hobbes for whom the fact of individualism, that is to say, the anomic condition of man implies the necessity of the strongest possible sort of political organization. The same fact of individualism, though conceived of in a somewhat different fashion by John Locke is thought to imply a considerably more modest form of political organization.

As every student of political theory knows, Hobbes is the first major social contract theorist in Western political thought. Yet a theory of contract rests upon certain assumptions, the most obvious of which is that it is possible to describe a condition of man which precedes the contractual act itself. Just as this assumption enables the theorist himself to hypothesize about the natural character of man prior to his incorporation into civil society, so does it allow the student of political thought to comprehend a political thinker's conception of what human nature is.

Hobbes thus stands at an intellectual and historical intersection. He is a scientist who inherits the reductive analysis of classical mechanics and he is a philosopher who lives at a time of institutional disintegration and a renaissance of individualism. Science gives him the method, reductionism and history provide him with a new vital fact, individualism. The mechanism which reveals the character of these individuals is the concept of the state of nature. Since it is in the state of nature itself which makes it possible to witness the operation of the fundamental laws of human nature, what, we may ask, is life like there?

According to Hobbes man is by nature self-regarding. He is concerned principally with the satisfaction of his own natural appetites as well as the satisfaction of those appetites which he acquires for power, riches, honor, and command. Such appetites are insatiable and thus no man can ever have too much power. Men are, therefore, natural competitors, predatory animals, competing with each other for riches, honor, and command. Even the language of morality must be understood in terms of this psychological egoism. Good is merely whatever a man desires and evil is that which he is averse to. Imagination serves only to intensify his desire and give it a greater horizon. It enables him to become interested in another person's goods, for even when he does not have the power to acquire those goods, he feels pleasure or pain at the thought of himself situated as that other person is. Pity, taken together with imagination, enables man in his natural state to experience grief. For grief is nothing more than the sensation one feels when he supposes that the pain suffered by another is the pain to which he himself might be subjected.

In the state of nature, there are neither legal nor moral prohibitions. The desire to establish rules and laws is a function of the desire to impose a degree of unity upon this chaos which insures a degree of peace and security required for the satisfaction of private interests. Thus, the terrible experiences of man in the state of nature teach him in the only way in which such creatures can learn that peace is preferable and desirable and that a continual state of war is so terrible that any form of political organization is preferable to life in a state of nature.

The alternative to a "short, nasty, solitary, and brutish" existence was the establishment of a convenant whose principle condition was the acceptance of a sovereign. The covenant is a promise then, which reads something as follows: "I authorize and give up my right of government myself, to this man, or this assembly of men, on this condition: that thou give us thy right to him, and authorize all his actions in a like manner." This agreement is the beginning of civil society and social institutions.

Hobbes may be the first contract theorist in the age of the enlightenment, though he is by no means the last. We shall delay our discussion of the validity and the utility of social contract theory until later. Suffice it to indicate, that the kind of political organization which comes about as a result of the covenant discussed is closely tied to the concept of human nature revealed in an examination of the conditions of life in the state of nature. Hobbes' state of nature is a condition of economic scarcity, in which men vie like beasts for the limited quantity of goods available to them. They are frightened, fearful, insecure, and wretched creatures whose principle concern is the satisfaction of the basic necessities of life and the satisfaction of appetites. They are bodies in motion and despite their conscious character act in ways which are as predictable as the paths traced by inanimate bodies. The sort of political organization they are prepared to settle for may be, as indeed it turns out to be in Hobbes, repressive and tyrannical. Men, being what they are, require harsh masters; and the state of nature being what it is, is infinitely less desirable than a state which promises peace and security.

The logic of the social contract argument implies that the force of authority established and codified by the contract more closely approximates the exercise of sheer power in proportion to the rigidness of life in a state of nature. The authority of the sovereign, however, is indeed authority rather than power merely, because the contract authorizes the creation of a sovereign.

The significant difference between the state of nature and a commonwealth is that in the latter, the sovereign acts to guarantee that which could not be guaranteed in a state of nature, namely, peace and security. Therefore, the sovereign must be perceived as one who acts, not as a member or a party to the contract, but rather as the people's representative in the sense that the people authorize the sovereign to secure these benefits. Peace and security are the benefits of life in a political community because it is peace and security which men cannot have in a state of nature. The political commonwealth, then, is expected to provide those conditions of life which men desire, but which they cannot acquire for themselves in a state of nature. The legitimacy of the sovereign depends upon successful creation of those conditions. If life in a state of nature is exceedingly difficult, then the expectations which men have of commonwealth are proportionately modest. The result is that men are prepared to endure a great deal at the hands of a sovereign, so long and so far as the sovereign guarantees peace and security. As we shall see, if we conceive of life in a state of nature and of human nature in general as being of a gentler and more humane sort, the expectations which men have of social and political organization are increased and their tolerance to endure the arbitrary and capricious exercise of political power is decreased.

For Hobbes, the authority of the sovereign must be unlimited, shared with no other agency of government and perpetual. The sovereign, therefore, is the creator of the law, the soul agency for determining where and how the law will apply, and, moreover, he functions as the judge and jury determining what constitutes a delict of law and punishes those who have behaved in ways which are perceived to be undesirable. Under such circumstances the concept of civil liberty makes no sense whatever. Civil liberty lay, according to Hobbes, only with those actions which the sovereign has decided to allow. Nor does it make any sense to speak of the sovereign doing an *injury* to a subject since such a possibility is rendered logically impossible by virtue of the fact that the sovereign is authorized by the consent of those governed to do whatever may be necessary to secure peace and security. Anything at all might turn out to be prejudicial to security and thus no limitation on sovereignty could be imagined. Thus, with Hobbes we see delineated a vast area of political space, so to speak. Both Machiavelli and Hobbes perceive the exercise of political power as legitimately extending to every area of social life and all this comes about as a result of the identification of political power with sovereign power and because of the rampant social atomism of life in a state of nature.

Locke

With Locke the principle of individualism is further articulated and refined; a way of looking not merely at the political world, but at the world generally. For Locke's intellectual accomplishments revolve around his formalization of the principles of the philosophical movement known generally as British Empiricism. It was this school of thought which set itself the problem of providing an analysis of some fundamental philosophical questions, particularly issues which might be characterized as epistemological in nature. Locke's principle concern as a philosopher must be understood in terms of his effort to construct a theory of knowledge in which any statement that can be properly characterized as an object of knowledge is grounded in human experience.

Locke's epistemological commitments converge in one important respect with those of Hobbes. For both Locke and Hobbes conceptual knowledge is interpreted as a construction derived from a variety of individual perceptions which taken together, according to rules, form the content of the concept itself. Consider an example: The concept which I possess of the complex object, "dog," is the product of a variety of instances of individual dogs which I have perceived during the course of my perceptual life. My concept, then, could not contain ingredients with which I had not been previously familiar. It is easy to see then that though both you and I may use the word "dog" in most contexts without encountering disagreement or ambiguity, it is nonetheless possible that we might encounter a situation where, because your individual experiences and mine may have been different, we would not agree about whether the given entity is a dog or not. Though such instances would perhaps be rare with regard to the concept "dog," they may well become more common when we consider concepts of a more abstract character. What is important here is that our individual concepts are outgrowths of different patterns of experience and although there may be objective criteria for determining the truth of propositions based upon our individual experiences, the fact of the matter seems to be that each one of us perceives the world in a way which is peculiar and unique to our own position in it. The particular image which I may have in mind when I use the general term "dog" may well be, and most often times will be, different from another's. It is in this fashion that we understand how individualism may function as the foundation of a theory of knowledge on the one hand, and as the presumption of a political theory on the other.

Moreover, the mechanics of Locke's empiricism involves once again the principle of reductionism. The world may appear as a series of complex objects which stand in certain definable relations to each other, but the meaning of the concepts which we hold of such objects is determined by our ability to reduce in thought that object to its constituent simples. Just as the concept "apple" is reducible to its constituent simples, namely, sphericity, redness, and sweetness, so must more elaborate and complicated concepts like "state" be reducible to its constituent simples, namely, individual persons, relations, and domain.

It is in this fashion that Locke's principles of empiricism support the individualism of his political theory. The second manifestation of this individualism is a function of his theory of natural rights, a conception which has been discussed at considerable length in our analysis of the theory of natural law. It is often said that this segment of his theory, namely, the notion that there are individual rights which are thought to be natural parts of a man's essential being is incompatible with the principles of empiricism which are articulated in his *Essay Concerning Human Understanding*. However, it may be more fruitful to suppose that Locke's reference to rights may simply be a way of saying that there are certain moral values which are simple and irreducible constituents of human character, and which are not the production of men as members of a political community. In other words, natural rights may be construed as moral sentiments which may not be subject to being reduced to simpler qualities. The alternative to this interpretation of natural rights is to believe that Locke violated his own principles of empiricism in asserting the existence of rights which could not be confirmed on truly empirical grounds, that is to say, on the basis of experience alone. Whatever the virtues of this argument it is important to see once again that the concept of the state of nature enables us to determine those properties and characteristics which are essentially predictable of human beings quite apart from their institutional affiliations. We turn then to an examination of Locke's conception of the state of nature.

In his major work entitled, *An Essay Concerning the Truist Original, Extent and End of Civil Government*, Locke says of the state of nature: "To understand political power aright, and derive it from its original, we must consider what state all men are naturally in, and that is a state of perfect freedom to order their actions and dispose of their possessions and persons as they think fit, within the bounds of the law of nature, without asking leave, or depending upon the will of any other man."[13] To this extent, Locke is saying little more than Hobbes has with respect to the utility of positing the notion of the state of nature. The difference between them, however, is a function of how we are to understand the expression "law of nature." For Hobbes the law of nature or the expression natural law meant simply the force or power which could be exercised by one atomistic entity over another. For Locke, however, the state of nature is not a condition of pure anarchy:

> But though this be a state of nature, yet it is not a state of license; though man and that state have an uncontrollable liberty to dispose of his person or possessions, yet he has not liberty to destroy himself, or so much any creature in his possession, but where some nobler use than its bare preservation calls for it. The state of nature has a law of nature to govern it, which obliges everyone; and reason, which is that law, teaches all mankind who will but consult it, that, being all equal and independent, no one ought to harm another in his life, health, liberty, or possessions.[14]

Though men are in a state of nature, an examination of the dictates of their own reason teaches a moral lesson, namely, that no man ought to harm another with respect to another's life, health, liberty, or property. Such moral lessons or moral sentiments did not exist in Hobbes' state of nature. Nor do they exist in Locke's state of nature as a function merely of the recognition that others have certain rights which ought to be respected and who will in turn recognize one's own rights. For this arrangement would already suggest that the mutual recognition of rights is the product of a *quid pro quo,* and that one's rights have no other foundation but mutual recognition. On the contrary, Locke wishes to say that a person's right to his own body, to the health thereof, to be free, and to his own property are substantially self-evident rights. There is no further explanation required to justify the attribution of such rights to individuals apart from the assertion that anyone who examines the dictates of reason will recognize the self-evident and the irreducible character of these moral maxims.

---

[13] Locke, Second Treatise, section 4.

[14] *Ibid.,* section 6.

The difficulty with the state of nature is not what we would at first imagine it to be, namely, that there will invariably be those who in the pursuit of their own private interests will abrogate those of another. Locke does not propose to argue that political organization is a utilitarian device to which men are prepared to accede simply because situations will arise in a state of nature where individual rights will be violated by the few whose bad will leads them to engage in nonrational conduct. The fundamental defect of life in a state of nature is that each individual person must function as a judge in meting out the punishments appropriate to those who have engaged in such conduct. Thus he writes that it is unreasonable for men to be judges in their own cases and that self-love will naturally make men partial to themselves and their friends. Only confusion and disorder will follow when each man takes upon himself the responsibility of judging and punishing those who have in one way or another abrogated his natural rights.

This is so because: ". . . in the state of nature there wants a known and indifferent judge, with authority to determine all differences according to the established law. For everyone in that state, being both judge and executioner of the law of nature, men being partial to themselves, passion and revenge is very apt to carry them too far, and with too much heat in their own cases, as well as negligent and unconcernedness, to make them too remiss in other men's."[15]

And finally, in the state of nature men lack the power to support and execute a sentence or punishment levied against those who have transgressed upon other person's rights. It is for these reasons that mankind:

> . . . notwithstanding all the privileges of the state of nature, being but in an ill condition, while they remain in it, are quickly driven into society. Hence it comes to pass that we seldom find any number of men live any time together in this state. The inconvenience is that they are therein exposed to by the irregular and uncertain exercise of the power every man has of punishing the transgressions of others, make them take sanctuary under the established laws of government, and therein seek the preservation of their property. It is this that makes them so willingly give up every one his single power of punishing, to be exercised by such alone as shall be appointed to it amongst them; and by such rules as the community, were those authorized by them to that purpose,

---

[15] *Ibid.,* section 125.

shall agree on. And in this we have the original right and rise of both the legislative and executive power as well as of the governments and societies themselves.[16]

It is easy to see that the major expectations which men have of political organization, of executives and legislators, is one which requires that these agencies create and maintain the conditions of life superior to those which could be legitimately anticipated by the individuals who organized institutions from the starting point provided for them by Hobbes. When men enter or become parties to social and political institutions, it is with the reasonable expectation that the area of authority permitted such institutions will be articulated within the framework of those rights which they have by nature. And, since it is clear that men come to social and political institutions with moral convictions discovered through a capacity with which all men are equally endowed, namely, their reason, it is only natural that they will insist that no human agency can legitimately exercise power or restraint on those areas of life which fall outside the terms of the agreement which establishes those institutions themselves.

Though Locke is not clear about the distinction between social institutions on the one hand and political institutions on the other, it is manifestly clear that he means to say that there are at least two distinct contracts involved here. For unlike Hobbes, Locke's concern is with the constriction of legitimate political power and consequently with the diminution of political space, so to speak, rather than as with Hobbes, the contraction or expansion of what may be legitimately seen as subject to political control.

Indeed, in many respects, Locke's picture of the state of nature suggests that that condition is itself a kind of society. There are many relations which obtain among the individuals who compose the state of nature, the most obvious of which has to do with commercial activity. And despite the fact that no formal agency exists which regulates the economic activities among individuals within a state of nature, such mutually recognized regulations did in fact exist. It may be true that men are moral quite apart from whether there exists social institutions or not, but what is certain is that their morality dictates that here are certain

---

[16] *Ibid.*, section 127.

limitations to what may be considered to be acceptable in social intercourse. The basis of the contract then, is that of an agreement in which men voluntarily and consciously enter, and appears to be essentially one which establishes political institutions and perhaps legal procedures for the adjudication of disputes which arise in the conduct of every day affairs.

What Locke may be credited with in this regard is an awareness that power has many manifestations and that political power is but one instance of the way in which men control other men's lives. This is what we mean when we speak of Locke's constriction of political space. In turning to an analysis of what is involved in Locke's conception of consent, it will be important for us to recognize that though consent may be a vital ingredient when it comes to establishing political institutions, the establishment of social institutions is to a considerably lesser degree a conscious and voluntary act.

Let us consider now for a moment how Locke has provided us with the foundation for a theory of the state. First, Locke's notion of human nature echoes the traditional Christian conception of man as being a curious and perhaps incompatible mixture of appetitive self-interest and reason. This curious mixture of properties attributed to man in a state of nature enables Locke to make his case against Hobbes. He is able to say men are sufficiently rational as not to require a Hobbesian sovereign, and yet contentious enough to require that they surrender their natural rights and powers to a civil society. Those men in a state of nature whose conduct is governed by self-interest, unmodified by reason, sometimes thought by Locke to be a group small in number, and other times thought to be a larger part of the whole, makes the necessity of restraint apparent to those whose conduct remains compatible with reason and therefore consistent with the requirements of natural law. In this way, the state is thought to be an agency which comes into existence for the sole purpose of creating the conditions under which one may secure rights which are properly his by nature.

It is in this context that the concept of consent plays a large role in understanding the character and limits of political power and of the justification of the agencies which exercise that power.

In an earlier discussion concerning Hobbes, we mentioned, but did not comment extensively, on the role played by consent in the establishment of political institutions. The history of the use of the theory of consent is a precarious one at best. For it is a consent arrived at by the submission of those who are subject to power, instead of being the foundation or the justification for the exercise of power by those who have authority bestowed upon them. Hobbes appears to be saying that where there is a relationship which consists of the exercise of power by one person or group over others, then the group over whom the power is exercised must have given its consent, though no other evidence other than the fact that some men stand in a subservient relationship to others may exist. This is no doubt a curious and perhaps mistaken way to use the concept of consent. The extent and degree to which this may be mistaken is best indicated by the way in which Locke himself uses this concept. For Locke it is not a question of defining consent as an act in which a man consents whenever he encounters a situation where he has more to lose than to gain by not consenting. Indeed, Locke's purpose in applying the concept of consent is to determine the limits of legitimate exercise of political power, whereas Hobbes' intent was to establish the unlimited character of the authority of rulers. Moreover, for Locke true consent is personal, deliberate, and "express," and the act of consent does not rest upon need as it does in Hobbes. For if it did, it might make sense to say, which it does not, that the authority exercised by a father over a child is based upon the child's consent. But a child has no choice, and therefore in Locke's sense of consent could not be said to be giving his consent to the authority which is exercised over him by his father.

The temptation however, to read Locke as intending to attribute to the concept of consent a meaning comparable to that in Hobbes' use is partly justified by an observation which Locke makes with regard to the relationship between political and paternal power. Thus he writes, ". . . it was easy and almost natural for children by a tacit and almost natural consent, to make way for the father's authority and government. They had been accustomed in their childhood to follow his direction . . . and when they were men, who was fitter to rule them?"[17] But this confusion rests upon a more subtle distinction in a theory of consent, according to Locke.

The theory of consent is an answer to the question about what makes

---

[17] *Ibid.*, section 75.

government legitimate. The legitimacy of political power he thinks, rests exclusively upon the consent of the governed. He writes that men make themselves by their own consent members of some politic society. Consent, therefore, must be personal, deliberate, and free, and every man must consent for himself alone, because only his own act can bind him. This sense of consent has sometimes been called the "explicit sense," sometimes the "stronger sense," both descriptions referring to the act of consent as something free, deliberate, and personal. It is in this sense that Locke says "whatever engagements or promises anyone made for himself, he is under the obligation of them, but cannot by any compact whatsoever bind his children or posterity."[18] The consequences of such a theory of consent become immediately apparent to us when we consider that if political obligation to a centralized power is to be based upon a private and personal act which binds the actor alone and not his descendants, then each generation, and indeed each member of a new generation, must reaffirm the terms of the contract and personally consent to political society if that institution is to have a sustained existence and an orderly life.

It is apparently clear to Locke that this arrangement would not do. The continued, independent, and orderly existence of a political community cannot depend upon a theory of contractual renewal similar in character to a fraternity initiation ceremony, or an aboriginal circumcision ceremony, or a Bar Mitzvah. Locke meets the problem of continued consent of the original contracting parties from one moment in time to another and of succeeding generations who are not directly parties to the contract in a fashion which he supposes would make it possible for the civil society to outlast the first and subsequent political disagreements among its citizens. He does so by introducing the concept of tacit or indirect consent.

Tacit consent was introduced by Locke to overcome the objection that the original or express compact could not explain why later members, who might not have been parties to the original agreement, were nevertheless obliged to accept the commands of political authority. The notion of tacit consent is the effort to meet this problem and Locke intends to meet it by suggesting that when an individual, despite the absence of

---

[18] *Ibid.*, section 116.

any explicit act of consent on his part, has enjoyed the benefits of membership in the political community, he has *ipso facto* given his consent to the political organization of the community which makes the enjoyment of those benefits possible.

In interpreting the significance of this argument and showing how the concept of consent as the foundation for political obligation works, we shall follow an interpretation of Locke which derives from some observations by Sheldon Wolin. Wolin challenges the conventional interpretation of Locke's theory of consent which alleges that the consensual basis of Locke's political society rests upon each member's voluntary and express promise to keep the terms of the contract. According to Wolin, the express contract must play a subordinate role in maintaining the continued loyalty of the members of the community over a long period of time.[19] Locke's solution to this problem lies in the introduction of the notion of tacit consent. Yet, tacit consent is a precarious foundation upon which to rest political obligation, for though it may imply that one benefits from living in a society which is well ordered and whose rules and laws governing conduct and the institutions which assure that the application of these laws and rules will be justly accomplished, it is by no means clear that anyone gives his tacit consent simply by profiting from the order established by any given government to that particular government itself.

It may be true as Locke suggests that people may consider themselves obliged to obey the rules and regulations which govern such disparate activities as inheriting property, using the highways, or sending one's children to school, simply on the basis of the fact that they actually engage in such conduct. Yet, these examples of tacit consent are not sufficient to support the loyalty to a political institution which would not be necessary for the continued and ordered existence of a state. In fact, it would appear that tacit consent as a foundation for obligation would work in a state of nature as well. This is partly because a state of nature very closely resembles a society like any other except for the fact that it possesses no independent agency, namely, a political agency which functions as a disinterested body whose purposes the adjudication of disputes in an equitable fashion.

---

[19] Wolin, *Politics and Vision,* p. 311.

Consider how Locke expresses the distinction between express and tacit consent:

Nobody doubts that an express consent of any man entering into any society makes him a perfect member of that society, a subject of that government. The difficulty is, what ought to be looked upon as a tacit consent, and how far it binds, i.e., how far shall anyone be looked on to have consented, and thereby submitted to any government, where he has made no expressions of it at all. And to this I say that every man that hath any possession or enjoyment of any part of the dominions of any government doth thereby give his tacit consent, and is as far forth obliged to obedience to the laws of that government during such enjoyment as anyone under it; whether this his possession be of land to him and his heirs forever, or a lodging only for a week; or whether it be barely traveling freely on the highway; and in effect it reaches as far as the very being of anyone within the territory of that government.[20]

This argument does not close the issue for Locke, for it becomes immediately apparent that the concept of tacit consent expressed in this way is altogether incompatible with the facts. Certainly, the conditions of tacit consent would hardly apply to a stranger passing through a given territory, or to a foreigner who lives a large part of his life under an alien government where despite the fact he may gain from the privileges and protection of that government, cannot be said to become a subject of that commonwealth.

It soon becomes apparent that the foundation of political obligation which involves the concept of tacit consent depends not on any of the privileges and enjoyments which come about from residing in a civil society, but from one such privilege, in particular, namely, property. By this act of consent then,

. . . whereby anyone unites his person, which was before free, to any commonwealth, by the same he unites his possessions, which was before free, to it also; and they become, both of them, person and possession, subject to the government and dominion of that commonwealth, as long as it hath a being. Whoever therefore from henceforth by inheritance, purchases, permission, or otherwise, enjoys any part of the land so annexed to, and under the government of that commonwealth, must take it with the condition it is under, that is, of submitting to the government of the commonwealth under whose jurisdiction it is as far forth as any subject of it.[21]

---

[20] Locke, *op. cit.,* section 119.

[21] *Ibid.,* section 120.

In other words, tacit consent must be understood in an even narrower sense than we have suggested. As Locke says, ". . . submitting to the laws of any country, living quietly and enjoying privileges and protection under them makes not a man a member of that society."[22] It is specifically the enjoyment of property rights which puts a person who though not among the original convenantors, that is, not himself having expressed explicitly his consent, is nonetheless as much obliged as those who have given their express consent.

There is however in this connection one important qualification, namely, that the obligation anyone is under by virtue of his tacit consent "begins and ends with that enjoyment"[23]:

> . . . so that whenever the owner, who has given nothing but such a tacit consent to the government, will be donation, sale, or otherwise, quit the said possession, he is at liberty to go and incorporate himself into any other commonwealth, or to agree with others to begin a new one . . . in any part of the world they can find free and unpossessed. Whereas he that has once by actual agreement in any expressed declaration given his consent to be of any commonweal is perpetually and indispensably obliged to be and remain unalterably a subject to it, and can never be again in the liberty of the state of nature; unless, by any calamity, the government he was under comes to be dissolved, or else by some public act cuts him off from being any longer a member of it.[24]

Here Locke says that anyone who becomes a member of a commonwealth by virtue of tacit consent in the sense that he has enjoyed the protection of property is obliged to submit to the government unless he is prepared to give up his rights to that property and to return it to the commonweal. Those, however, who are members of the commonwealth by virtue of a declaration of express consent, may as he says never be again in the liberty in the state of nature and are forever obliged to be subject to the commonwealth. Thus, when he comes to the end of this discussion he writes that nothing can make any man a member of the commonwealth "but his actually entering into it by positive engagement, and express promise and compact."[25]

---

[22] *Ibid.,* section 122.
[23] *Ibid.,* section 121.
[24] *Ibid.,* section 122.
[25] *Ibid.,* section 122.

It seems apparent that Locke rested his theory of the state and of civil society on a concept of consent which in one sense is hopelessly narrow and which in another is uselessly broad. For if consent must be deliberate and voluntary and if a man's duty to obey a government rests upon such a notion of consent, then most people at most times and in most places have no duty of obedience. If on the other hand it is construed in the tacit sense then whatever creates the duty of obedience must be consent. The doctrine of tacit consent in this case is then no different than that encountered in Hobbes with all that theory's attendant difficulties.

There are two more major points in Locke's analysis of the concept of civil society to be considered. Firstly, Locke writes that the act of the whole must be considered to rest upon the consent of the majority. The practical considerations which lead to this conclusion are obvious for if the act of the whole society meant the consent of every individual in it, the state would become an impossibly unwieldy instrument in which no actions at all would take place. In Locke's demonstration that civil society requires majority rule, he draws the distinction between individual consent and majority consent only to show that individual consent is an impossible requirement. If one's goal is the preservation of his property, whatever means the majority accepts to accomplish that end, the individual must give his assent. The existence of this civil society then rests upon express consent at least so far as the original convenant is concerned. However, when the matter is any given issue which confronts the state the simple majority is sufficient to determine and justify the actions of the state.

The second remaining point is a continuation of the first and has to do with the distinction between civil society itself and the political institution which is part of that civil society. There is no question but that part of Locke's task in this respect is to show that the legitimacy of government rests upon consent and that the boundaries of legitimate exercise of political power are circumscribed by the rights which men claim for themselves and those which they are prepared to surrender to this greater agency. In this respect, it must be remembered that the state is established to perform a certain set of tasks and that any state which transcends the purposes for which it was devised is one which may no longer claim the obligation of its members to obey. It is under these circumstances that the state or its character may be changed and in fact dissolved, for the consent on which it is established is qualified by the successful performance by the state of certain tasks.

The point here is that whatever consent may be involved in establishing a civil society, it is not a contract which may be abrogated and from which individual members may be released from obligation in the same way in which the contract establishing the state may be abrogated, leaving the state subject to alteration and dissolution. Consent may be at the foundation of the exercise of political power in general, but not of any particular government and certainly not of a government which does not function responsibly. In fact, Locke is unimpressed with the specific claims which any particular form of political organization might make with regard to its greater efficiency or greater legitimacy. Though he thinks that it is best that legislative authority should be bested in collective bodies of men and though he thinks that the executive and the legislative powers ought to be separated, he does not suppose that any particular form, even monarchy, is preferable to any other provided only that they are established by common agreement either tacitly or explicitly.

THE UTILITARIANS

Bentham and Mill

In turning to Mill, we come to a consideration of a theory of human nature formulated without the conveniences of a theory of a state of nature. And yet, it is a theory of human nature which evolved from the powerful philosophical speculations of the 18th century English enlightenment. David Hume had successfully demolished the prospect that a theory of social contract or of state of nature could be used as a device for discovering the natural and undistorted properties of human nature. Part of what Mill contributes to the discussion concerning individualism lies with the assumptions with which he begins.

It is possible to discuss and to analyze the concepts of individualism as the foundation for political organization without further committing oneself to the highly artificial and perhaps questionable assumptions involved in a state of nature or a social contract theory. For although Mill has certain prejudices based on his imagery of what men are essentially, these rarely become elevated to the level of principle. Among these prejudices is the notion that: ". . . civilization in every one of its aspects is a struggle against the animal instincts. . . . It has artificialized large portions of mankind to such an extent that of many of their most natural inclinations they have scarcely a vestige or a remembrance left."[26] The animal instincts to which Mill refers must be understood as the foundation for the ethical theory articulated by the founders of Utilitarianism, Jeremy Bentham, and James Mill. We turn first to an examination of Utilitarian ethical theory, a theory which is necessary if we are to understand, or perhaps reconstruct, the theory of the state implied by Utilitarianism and refined explicitly by Mill, himself.

What may sound more like a call to arms rather than a sober introduction to a philosophical theory, Bentham writes that:

> . . . nature has placed mankind under the governance of two sovereign masters, pain and pleasure. It is for them alone to point out what we ought to do, as well as to determine what we shall do. . . . They govern us in all we do. . . . In words a man may pretend to abjure their empire: but in reality he will remain subject to it all the while. The principle of utility recognizes this subjugation. . . . It is that principle which states the greatest happiness of all those whose interest is in question, as being the right and proper, and only right and proper, and only universally desirable end of human action.[27]

Leaving alone the issue as to whether or not this is a descriptive statement which asserts that men do in fact act in this fashion or whether it is an ethical assertion to the effect that they ought to do so, the principle in question runs clearly contrary to the notion that any conduct or object has an intrinsic value independent of those who may or may not desire it or value it. Indeed, as Mill put the point: "The creed which accepts as the foundation of morals, Utility or the Greatest Happiness Principle, holds that actions are right in proportion as they tend to promote happiness, wrong as they tend to produce the reverse of happiness. By happiness is intended pleasure, and the absence of pain; by unhappiness, pain, and the privation of pleasure."[28] The theory of life on which this theory of morality is grounded is: ". . . that pleasure, and freedom from pain, are the only things desirable as ends; and that all

---

[26] *Principles of Political Economy*, II, pp. 373–74.

[27] Bentham, *Principles of Morals and Legislation.*

[28] Mill, *Utilitarianism,* chap. 2.

desirable things are . . . desirable either for the pleasure inherent in themselves, or as means to the promotion of pleasure and prevention of pain."[29]

At first glance, the principles of utilitarianism then, as a moral theory seems to be reducible to the following formula: "This is good" = "I desire this" = "This gives me pleasure." On the face of it, this principle appears to be indistinguishable from a theory of thoroughgoing hedonism. How can such an equation ever give rise to the necessary ingredients of a theory of morality, namely, as explicit notion of right and wrong conduct? As the formula appears, it may provide an individual person with a notion of what is right for him or wrong for him but there does not seem to be any place in it to provide for the general happiness. Mill is here relying on a kind of natural empathy, not altogether unlike that of Hobbes where the idea of the pleasure of another is naturally pleasurable itself.[30] That such a person would engage in conduct which would lead to the general happiness is an assumption which rests upon whether or not such a person wants the pleasure of another and in fact seeks his pleasures in that fashion.

But this analysis is certainly at variance with the facts. All sorts of occasions can and do arise when one seeking his pleasure does so and perhaps must do so at the expense of others and therefore at the expense of the general happiness. Mill replies that although a relationship exists between an individual seeking his pleasure and doing so in accordance with his own animal instincts, it is nonetheless true that the instincts appropriate to the human animal are not those appropriate to lesser animals and indeed, the kinds of pleasures that will be appropriate to human beings are different in quality than those which are appropriate to swine: "The comparison of the Epicurean life to that of beasts is left as degrading, precisely because a beast's pleasures do not satisfy a human being's conceptions of happiness. Human beings have faculties more elevated than the animal appetites, and when once made conscious of them, do not regard anything as happiness which does not include their gratification."[31]

Part of what is involved in being a human being and of having instincts appropriate to human beings is the appreciation and the desires

---

[29] *Ibid.*

[30] Cf. Karl Britton, *John Stuart Mill* (London, 1953), p. 48.

[31] Mill, *op. cit.,* chap. 2.

for pleasures of the intellect, of the feelings and imagination, and of the moral sentiments—pleasures, in short, qualitatively higher than those appropriate to lower animals, that is to say, mere sensation. The most reasonable question we can ask in this connection concerns the criteria which allow us to distinguish between those pleasures which are qualitatively appropriate to human beings and those which are appropriate to lesser animals. Moreover, which of those pleasures appropriate to human beings are higher than others? The answer which Mill gives to this question is a vital one because it will provide us with criteria for deciding which actions fall within the realm of political adjudication and those which do not. That is to say, the famous criterion of self-regarding and other-regarding actions which Mill puts forward in his essay *On Liberty* must be understood as a criterion which is built upon his answer to the question concerning the way in which we must decide between higher and more valuable pleasures on the one hand, between the pleasures of Socrates, and lower pleasures on the other, the pleasures of piggery.

The problem is: If pleasure is the criterion of value and if what is pleasurable is also valuable, does it follow that if most of us prefer reading the novels of Mickey Spillane and Ian Fleming to the pleasures of reading Shakespearean sonnets and listening to Bach, then the literary productions of the former, since they are on the face of it more pleasurable, are also the more valuable aesthetically. Here is Mill's reply:

If I am asked what I mean by difference of quality in pleasures, or what makes one pleasure more valuable than another, merely as a pleasure, except its being greater in amount, there is but one possible answer. Of two pleasures, if there be one to which all or almost all who have experience of both give a decided preference, irrespective of any feeling of moral obligation to prefer it, that is the most desirable pleasure. If one of the two is, by those who are competently acquainted with both, placed so far above the other that they prefer it, even though knowing it to be attended with a greater amount of discontent, and would not resign it for any quantity for the other pleasure which their nature is capable of, we are justified in ascribing to the preferred enjoyment a superiority in quality, so far outweighing quantity as to render it, in comparison, of small amount.[32]

The key words in this passage are "competently acquainted with both." If one, therefore, is competently acquainted with both Shakespeare and Spillane, he will recognize the former to be "placed so far

[32] *Ibid.*

above the other" that he will prefer it despite the fact that reading Shakespeare may be "attended with a greater amount of discontent" than reading the latter. Is there then some rule for understanding which of various pleasures those who are "competently acquainted with both" will choose? Mill thinks there is such a rule and that it has to do with the faculties employed in the experiencing of various pleasures. Thus he writes:

> Now it is an unquestionable fact that those who are equally acquainted with, and equally capable of appreciating and enjoying, both do give a most marked preference to the manner of existence which employs their higher faculties . . . a being of higher faculties requires more to make him happy, is capable probably of more acute suffering, and certainly accessible to it at more points, than one of an inferior type; but in spite of these liabilities, he can never really wish to sink into what he feels to be a lower grade of existence.[33]

The reason for this refusal, Mill thinks, rests upon a natural human sentiment, namely, the love of liberty and personal independence, but most especially upon a sense of dignity "which all human beings possess in one form or another, and in some, though by no means in exact, proportion to their higher faculties, and which is so essential a part of the happiness of those in whom it is strong, that nothing which conflicts with it could be, otherwise then momentarily, an object of desire to them." All of which is not to say that all human beings will agree equally about what is most pleasurable and therefore most valuable. For as Mill writes, "It is indisputable that the being whose capacities of enjoyment are low, has the greatest chance of having them fully satisfied; and a highly endowed being will always feel that any happiness which he can look for, as the world is constituted, is imperfect."[34]

In summarizing this argument, Mill writes: "It is better to be a human being dissatisfied than a pig satisfied; better to be Socrates dissatisfied than a fool satisfied. And if the fool, or the pig, are of a different opinion, it is because they only know their own side of the question. The other party to the comparison knows both sides."[35]

Thus, the political question for us becomes, what sorts of institutions in general, and what kind of state in particular can make it possible for

[33] *Ibid.*
[34] *Ibid.*
[35] *Ibid.*

men, not merely, as with Locke, to live lives in accordance with moral principles discoverable through analysis of what men are by nature, but rather to create the conditions under which men may work toward the creation of an epoch which will consist ultimately of conclusions reached on the basis of an experiencing of life in accordance with certain fundamental sentiments which are natural to them.

Moral principles are created when two distinctly different conditions obtain. Where, firstly, human beings have the intuitive capabilities or potentialities of moral sentiment, and secondly, where the social and political conditions are such that a variety of experiences are available to them such that they are able to choose judiciously among them and thereby create a moral system based upon the informed choice of the higher pleasure.

The key to understanding Mill's theory of the state is to become aware of his concern for the value and development of individual character. And both of these aspects of character require that the individual be permitted an experimental way of living partly because variety is itself pleasurable and partly because variety allows for the development of a more noble character by enabling men to test the possibilities which life, experience, and nature permit. What are the barriers which thwart the realization of the kind of life Mill thinks human beings ought to lead?

Historically, Mill thought the most powerful threat to individual and collective liberty lay in the tyranny of political rulers. Thus he writes in the *Introductory* of his essay *On Liberty* that: "The struggle between Liberty and Authority is the most conspicuous feature in the portions of history with which we are earliest familiar, particularly with that of Greece, Rome and England. But in old times, this contest was between subjects, or some classes of subjects, and the government. By liberty, was meant protection against tyranny of the political rulers."[36] The earliest effort of men was to set limits to the "power which the ruler could be suffered to exercise over the community; and this limitation was what they meant by liberty." The development of political liberty then became a function of the gradual distribution of power, such that an increasing number of persons within a given society could collectively exercise power over the various magistrates of the state and create political insti-

[36] *Ibid.*, chap. 1.

tutions in which the ruling power emanated from the people themselves. Thus, ". . . in time . . . a democratic republic came to occupy a large portion of the earth's surface, and made itself felt as one of the most powerful members of the communities of nations; and elective and responsible government became subject to the observations and criticisms which weighed upon a great existing fact."[37] Yet, a new and greater danger arose, where the people themselves collectively exercised oppressive power over a part of their number. The result is the creation of a tyranny of the majority and its limitations as a tyranny are not limited merely to political considerations. Indeed, political tyranny, even a tyranny by those who constitute a majority over a minority may be neither as repressive nor as reprehensible as the tyrannical repression exercised over matters which are not political in nature.

> Society can and does exercise its own mandates: and if it issues wrong mandates instead of right, or any mandates at all in things with which it ought not to meddle, it practices a social tyranny more formidable than many kinds of political oppression, since, not usually upheld by such extreme penalties, it leaves fewer means of escapes, penetrating much more deeply into the details of life, and enslaving the soul itself. Protection, therefore, against the tyranny of the magistrate is not enough: there needs protection also against the tyranny of the prevailing opinion and feeling; against the tendency of society to impose, by other means than civil penalties, its own ideas and practices as rules of conduct on those who dissent from them; to fetter the development, and, if possible, prevent the formation, of any individuality not in harmony with its ways, and compels all characters to fashion themselves upon the model of its own. There is a limit to the legitimate interference of collective opinion with individual independence: and to find that limit, and maintain it against encroachment, is as indispensable to a good condition of human affairs, as protection against political despotism.[38]

The syndrome which Mill has in mind has been often expressed by critics of democratic societies, even sympathetic critics like deTocqueville who writes that: ". . . the public, therefore, among a democratic people, has a singular power, which aristocratic nations cannot concede; for it does not persuade others to its beliefs, but it imposes them and makes them permeate the thinking of everyone by a sort of enormous pressure of the mind of all upon the individual intelligence."[39]

---

[37] *Ibid.*

[38] *Ibid.*

[39] deTocqueville, *Democratic America,* Vol. 2, p. 11.

The heterogeneity of values imposed upon all of culture in this subtle and tacit fashion, this insidious destruction of individuality and uniqueness, are the most evil kinds of repression to which men are susceptible, according to Mill.

> It is not by wearing down into uniformity all that is individual in themselves, but by cultivating it, and calling it forth, within the limits imposed by the rights and interests of others, that human beings become a noble and beautiful object of contemplation; and as the works partake the character of those who do them, by the same process human life also becomes rich, diversified, and animating, furnishing more abundant aliment to high thoughts and elevated feelings, and strengthening the tie which binds every individual to the race, by making the race infinitely better worth belonging to. In proportion to the development of this individuality, each person becomes more valuable to themself, and is therefore capable of being more valuable to others.[40]

What does Mill mean when he speaks of "the rights and interests of others"? We have been analyzing the concept of individualism as it occurs in the political writings of those who justify and establish the legitimacy of political power and of government in general by reference to the individual rights and individual moral commitments which human beings have *qua* human beings. Yet here we encounter a concept of individualism which goes further and perhaps deeper than the concepts of individualism hitherto considered. For in these earlier theories, individualism and individuality were as much metaphysical theories or epistemological theories as they were moral theories.

Indeed, one could hardly say that any values could be attached to the fact of being an individual person, except perhaps as an explanation, as in Locke, of the origin of moral sentiment. But for Mill, the issue of the value of individual expression and the cultivation of individual uniqueness is a positive one, which allows for the improvement not merely of the individual himself, but of the society and of the species.

Now to draw a limit requires that we know both sides of the limit. Hence, in asking the question, "What are the limits of permissible interference by the state and by the society in individual human lives?" we are at the same time asking, "What are the limitations to be imposed upon individual expression and individual action?"

The preceding analysis suggests at least one of the tasks that a

---

[40] Mill, *op. cit.,* chap. 3.

properly constituted government must perform. For one thing, because it is an easier matter to locate the source and initiate remedies for inequities perpetrated by the state than those perpetrated by society, it is the task of such a government to determine what the rights and interests of its citizens may be in order to protect them against the excesses of society. For another, it is the task of government to directly promote the happiness and virtue of its individual citizens, not by performing as a moral teacher, but by creating the circumstances which allow individual citizens the opportunity to discover and to implement the area of interest common to them all and in terms of which the kind of life appropriate to the species could be realized. In this respect, Mill is clearly at variance with his predecessors, Bentham and the elder Mill.

According to Bentham, the state must take people as they find them and its object is to create the conditions under which individual persons may secure their own best interest assuming also that an area of common interest may be found such that the area of private interest and of public interest could be made to coincide. All, however, were agreed that the proper sort of government to accomplish these ends was democratic and representative. (J. S. Mill was, in this regard, clearly committed to the notion that not all peoples everywhere at every given time are capable of establishing such institutions.) Representative government, moreover, while it promotes the happiness and virtue of its individual citizens is itself improved by virtue of the increment of merit among its own constituency.

Now we are obliged to return to a consideration of the criterion which determines the extent and limitation which must guide representative government in the proper performance of those responsibilities which belong to it. In other words, what are the legitimate areas of governmental action and what precisely is the province of private conduct which falls outside of the possibility of formal political restraint?

The answer to this question is the occasion for a vast and complex series of arguments by those who have set themselves the task of interpreting Mill. Mill's own words are clearly ambiguous on this issue, but not so ambiguous as to remove the possibility of stating the criterion in question with a reasonable degree of clarity. In different places throughout his writings he states the criterion more or less as: "The government may rightfully intervene in all actions on the part of individual citizens which *affect* others; it may rightfully intervene in all actions which *affect the interest* of others; it may rightfully intervene in all actions which *harm* others." All conduct may therefore be divided into two kinds: self-regarding actions, and other-regarding actions. Which of the three interpretations concerning what will be taken as an instance of self-regarding of other-regarding actions Mill actually has in mind is not always clear. The most likely interpretation, however, is that the power which can be legitimately exercised by society over the given individual is limited to those occasions when the individual is engaged in conduct where he affects or may affect the *legitimate interest* of others. (The expression, *legitimate interest,* must be clearly distinguished from actions which affect others, since it is possible to affect others and yet leave their interests untouched. How one is affected by a theatrical performance depends partly on one's tastes, but the interests of the business man would be affected by a tax on business property no matter what his tastes or susceptibilities. A legitimate interest then is something which depends upon social recognition and refers to the sort of behavior a man can legitimately expect from others.

Unfortunately, it is not an easy matter to decide, once a theory of natural rights has been abandoned, what a legitimate interest would be. Or, what sort of agency would be appropriate to determining whether a legitimate interest had been infringed upon. Though a clear criteria for determining such legitimate interests and rights is not forthcoming in Mill's writings, he does, nonetheless attempt to provide us with what might be called loosely, a rule, for making decisions about those occasions which are not. He writes in this respect: "With regard to the merely contingent injury which a person causes to society, by conduct which neither violates any specific duty to the public, nor occasions perceptible hurt to any assignable individual except himself, the inconveniences are ones which society can afford to bear, for the sake of the greater good of human freedom."[41] It would be a mistake to suppose that this is an adequate procedure in terms of which it would be possible with a minimum degree of ambiguity to decide what constitutes a proper occasion for societal intervention and what does not. The difficulty with this and similar criteria calls for a separate discussion elsewhere.

---

[41] *Ibid.*

Among the various issues discussed regarding the role and function of state and society in Mill's works, we have emphasized to the degree thought appropriate the concept of individualism. Yet, it is clear that the individualism of Locke and that of Mill differ in some important respects. The role of the state is no longer analogous to a policeman who regulates heterogenous activities and conduct in which individual persons strive to satisfy private interests in accordance with privately held rights defined by nature and protected by law. The state has neither a moral obligation nor the moral competence to meddle or in any way alter what nature has prescribed, according to Locke. The moral neutrality and disinterested role of the state is a theme which has run thus far uninterruptedly through those theories which we have characterized as individualistic. Mill, however, is the first whose sentiments on this issue are at least ambiguous. Though men may create value systems by virtue of the lessons learned through the rational and sensitive analysis of their experiences with life, they have obligations to, and are subject to, sanctions from society itself. They are inextricably bound up with the rest of society in a variety of ways and with respect to a wide variety of relations which fall well outside the immediate considerations of formal political and legal institutions. Conduct is at least in part a matter of habit as well as of reasoning which serves to promote individual happiness. And it is in the light of these assumptions that Mill must come to terms with the tradition of Utilitarian individualism on the one hand, and on the other, with the fact that the collective experience of the species provides the environment which sets the conditions for the development of habitual responses and reasoned conclusions about moral conduct. Furthermore, Mill is, unlike the earlier Utilitarians, fully conscious of the evolutionary dimension in both human experience and human institutions. In *Representative Government*, he writes "It is, then, impossible to understand the question of the adaption of forms of government to states of society without taking into account not only the next step, but all the steps which society has yet to make."[42] It is in this connection that Mill emphasizes the importance of the political education which a government may provide and the importance of inculcating,

---

[42] J. S. Mill, *Representative Government*, Everyman ed., p. 201.

by the state, a set of political values which will benefit the people at large and thereby improve the character of government itself.

Mill's attitude in this regard may be expressed in the words of Charles Horton Cooley, who in his *Human Nature and the Social Order,* implies that those who accept an evolutionary point of view are led to the conclusion that: ". . . we see that the individual is not separable from the human whole, but a living member of it, deriving his life from the whole through social and hereditary transmission. . . . He cannot cut himself off; the strands of heredity and education are woven into all his being. And, on the other hand, the social whole is in some degree dependent upon each individual, because each contributes something to the common life that no one else can contribute."[43] This, of course, sounds suspiciously as though a major concession is being made to organic theorists and indeed, this is in part so. For Mill came to realize, an observation which is at the heart of the distinction between classical and modern liberalism, that the state, considered merely as impartial and disinterested arbiter which operates only on occasions where conflicts of rights have arisen, constitutes an interpretation wholly inadequate to the demands of advanced industrial society.

The state cannot function as a passive arbiter and at the same time allow for a new flowering of individual life and inner character on behalf of its citizenry. The paradox is, of course, not Mill's alone. It has, in effect, become our own problem, that is to say, a problem in modern America. It is most clearly manifested in the disputes which take place in the political marketplace which revolve around the issue of the welfare state. The question is one of maximizing political liberty on the one hand, that is to say, drawing rigorous limits to the way in which the state may act with regard to private domain of individual persons and yet at the same time play an active and moral role in the education and improvement of its peoples.

For us in the United States, it is a very recent phenomenon that the government explicitly recognizes that it has a positive role to play in the elimination of social ills and of social injustice. It is generally agreed that it is only since the days of the New Deal and explicitly perhaps only in

---

[43] C. H. Cooley, *Human Nature and the Social Order* (New York, 1902), p. 35.

the past few years that an agency of government would be established with the primary responsibility of eliminating pockets of poverty among our population. The United States is perhaps among the last of the major Western countries to recognize its moral obligations to actively provide minimum standards of life to its citizenry.

5

The concept of freedom, I

A BOOK WHICH is about some chief problems in political thought must at the very outset of a discussion of the concept of freedom distinguish between a variety of different ways in which this concept has been used such that "freedom" in a political sense is understood in ways quite different from the myriad context in which the word may appear in a multiplicity of disciplines. There are, obviously, many different ways and a variety of different criteria which might be used in clarifying how one is to go about a discussion of the concept of freedom.

VARYING INTERPRETATIONS OF FREEDOM

The schema which we impose on our analysis of the concepts of state consisted in distinguishing in a general way between two quite different assumptions about the character of state. These new ways in fact provide us with criteria for distinguishing between two different ways of talking about the concept of freedom. Indeed the meaning of the word "freedom" as it is used in the context of holistic theories is quite a different one from that expressed by the same word when it is used in connection with atomistic or individualistic theories. The distinction to which we refer here has been called "the distinction between negative and positive freedom." Consider Professor Isaiah Berlin's statement of the distinction.

The first of these political sense of freedom or liberty . . . which I shall call the "negative" sense, is involved in the answer to the question "what is the area within which the subject—a person or group of persons—is or should be left to do or be what he wants to do or be, without interference by other persons?" The second, which I shall call the positive sense, is involved in the answer to the question "What or who is the source of control or interference, that can determine someone to do, or be, one thing rather than another?" The two questions are clearly different, even though the answers to them may overlap.[1]

Let us put the same point another way. The central question confronting those whom we have characterized in an earlier discussion as individualistic or atomistic theorists concerned the issue of drawing proper and legitimate limits to the kind, extent, and quality of authority which can be used to limit the area of conduct of individual persons. Implicit in perceiving the problem of the range and extent of authority in this fashion, is the notion that within a given class of conduct no restraint or coercion is seen as legitimate and that this class of conduct is one with regard to which the individual is free. Freedom, therefore, in this connection refers to conduct with which no human being or human agency interferes. Once again quoting Berlin:

If I am prevented by others from doing what I want I am to that degree unfree; and if the area within which I can do what I want is contracted by other men beyond a certain minimum, I can be described as being coerced, or, it may be, enslaved. Coercion as it is understood here implies the "deliberate interference of other human beings within the area in which I wish to act. You lack political liberty or freedom only if you are prevented from attaining your goal by human beings.[2]

It is clear then that negative freedom is a theory of freedom which is implied by a theory of individual liberty and of individual rights. So far as this is so, Locke and Mill (and to a certain degree Hobbes as well) are the representatives of this conception of freedom. For the assumption is that such conditions of freedom are both necessary and desirable if the kind of classical liberalism articulated by Mill and Locke is to be established. Indeed, negative freedom is perceived by Mill and others as a prerequisite for the advancement of civilization. The utilitarian justi-

---

[1] Isaiah Berlin, *Two Concepts of Liberty* (Oxford University Press, 1958), p. 7.
[2] *Ibid.*

fication for defining and protecting an area of personal, individual freedom where coercion may never be justified establishes the conditions under which men may exhibit the spontaneity, originality, genius, and courage which marks the character of life in advanced civilizations.

Although historically this conception of liberty appears to go hand in hand with democratic political thought, logically freedom is in a sense not necessarily connected with democracy or self-government. For democracy is a response to the question "Who governs me?" and not necessarily an answer to the question "How far does government interfere with me?" Berlin, for example, writes as follows:

> Liberty in this sense is principally concerned with the area of control, not with its source. Just as a democracy may, in fact, deprive an individual citizen of a great many liberties which he might have in some other form of society, so it is perfectly conceivable that a liberal-minded despot would allow his subjects a large measure of personal freedom. The despot who leaves his subjects a wide area of liberty may be unjust, or encourage the wildest inequalities, care little for order, or virtue, or knowledge; but provided he does not curb their liberty, or at least curbs it less than many other regimes, he meets with Mill's specifications.[3]

It ought to be fairly clear that the concept of negative freedom rests upon a variety of assumptions not the least of which is that each individual person is free when he performs two tasks, to wit: he knows what his best interest is or at any rate he rejects whatever distinctions may be drawn between what he knows his best interest to be and what his best interest might be apart from what he supposes it to be. Secondly, given the assumption that he knows what his best interest is and that what he takes his best interest to be is in fact his best interest he is permitted to pursue his best interest free from human or institutional restriction. The notion of positive freedom, however, depends upon making the very distinction which is denied in the analysis of negative freedom.

The notion of positive freedom depends upon the postulation of the existence of two selves. Consider the following passage quoted from Berlin which helps make this concept plain:

> One way of making this clear is in terms of the independent momentum which the metaphor of self-mastery acquired. "I am my own master": "I am

---

[3] *Ibid.*, p. 14.

slave to no man": But may I not be a slave to nature? or to my own "unbridled" passions? Are these not so many species of the identical genius "slave" —some political or legal, others moral or spiritual? Have not men had the experience of liberating themselves from spiritual slavery, or slavery to nature, and do they not in the course of it become aware, on the one hand, of a self which dominates, and, on the other, of something in them which is brought to heel? This dominant self is then variously identified with reason, with my "higher nature," with the self which calculates and aims at what will satisfy it in the long run, with my "real" or "ideal" or autonomous self, or with myself "at its best"; which is then contrasted with irrational impulse, uncontrolled desires, my "lower" nature, the pursuit of immediate pleasures, my "empirical" or "heteronymous" self, swept by every gust of desire and passion, needing to be rigidly disciplined if it is ever to rise to the full height of its "real" nature. Personally the two selves may be represented as divided by an even larger gap: the real self may be conceived of something wider than the individual (as the term is normally understood), as a social "whole" of which the individual is an element or aspect: a tribe, a race, a church, a state, the great society of the living and the dead and the yet unborn. This entity is then identified as being the "true" self which, by imposing its collective or "organic" single will upon its recalcitrant "members," achieves its own, and, therefore, their "higher" freedom. The perils of using organic metaphors to justify the coercion of some men by others in order to raise them to a "higher" level of freedom have often been pointed out. But what gives such plausibility as it has to this kind of language is that we recognize that it is possible, and at times justified, to coerce men in the name of some goal (let us say, justice or public health) which they would, if they were more enlightened, themselves pursue, but do not, because they are blind or ignorant or corrupt. This renders it easy for me to conceive of myself as coercing others for their own sake, in their, not mine, interest. I am then claiming that I know what they truly need better than they know it themselves. What, at most, this entails, is that they would not resist me if they were rational, and as wise as I, and understood their interests as I do. But I may go on to claim a good deal more than this. I may declare that they are actually aiming at what in their benighted state they consciously resist, because there exists within them an occult entity—their latent rational will, or their "true" purposes—and that this entity, although it is belied by all that they overtly feel and do and say, is their "real" self of which the poor empirical self in space and time may know nothing or little; and that this spirit is the only self that deserves to have its wishes taken into account. Once I take this view, I am in a position to ignore the actual wishes of men or societies, to bully, oppress, torture them in the name, and on behalf, of their "real" selves, in the secure knowledge that whatever is the true goal of man (happiness, fulfillment of duty, wisdom, a just society, self-fulfillment) must be indentical with this freedom—the free choice of his "true" albeit submerged in an articulate, self.

This paradox has been often exposed. It is one thing to say that I know what is good for X while he himself does not; and even to ignore his wishes for its—and his—sake; and a very different one to say that he has *eo-ipso* chosen it, not indeed consciously, nor as he seems in every day life, but in his role as a rational self which his empirical self may not know—the "real" self which discerns the good, and cannot help choosing it once it is revealed. This monstrous impersonation, which consists in equating what X would choose if he were something he is not, or at least not yet, with what X actually seeks and chooses, is at the heart of all political theories of self-realization. It is one thing to say that I may be coerced for my own good which I am too blind to see: and another that if it is my good, I am not being coerced, for I have willed it, whether I know this or not, and am free even while my poor earthly body and foolish mind bitterly reject it, and struggle against those who seek to impose it, with the greatest desperation.

This magical transformation, or sleight of hand can no doubt be perpetuated just as easily with the "negative" concept of freedom, where the self that should not be interfered with is no longer the individual with his actual wishes and needs as they are normally conceived, but the "real" man within, identified with the pursuit of some ideal purpose not dreamed of by his empirical self. And, as in the case of the "positively" free self, this entity may be inflated into some super-personal entity—a state, a class, a nation, or the march of history itself, regarded as a more "real" subject of attributes than the empirical self. But the "positive" conception of freedom as self-mastery, with its suggestion of a man divided against himself, lends itself more easily to his splitting of personality into two: the transcendent dominant controller, and the empirical bundle of desires and passions to be disciplined and brought to heel. This demonstrates (if demonstration of so obvious a truth is needed) that the conception of freedom directly derives from the view that is taken of what constitutes a self, a person, a man. Enough manipulation with the definitions of man, and freedom can be made to mean whatever the manipulator wishes. Recent history has made it only too clear that the issue is not merely academic.

The consequences of distinguishing between two selves will become even clearer if one considers the two major forms which the desire to be self-directed—directed by one's "true" self—has historically taken: the first, that of self-abnegation in order to attain independence; the second, that of self-realization, or total self-identification with a specific principle or ideal in order to attain self-same end.[4]

---

[4] *Ibid.*, pp. 16–19.

The conception to which Berlin refers is clearly compatible and indeed a continuation of what we have hitherto called "organic theories." But it ought also to be clear that Berlin's condemnation of positive conceptions of freedom on the grounds that they suppose individuals to be unaware of what may be best for themselves may be expressed as well in terms that are clearly not totalitarian. A reading of this passage, quoted above, brings to mind the real will theory of a Hegel or Rousseau or perhaps even a Spinoza. Taking the latter as an example, however, it may be demonstrated that a positive conception of liberty can be stated in terms which makes it sound attractive indeed. Consider the following passage from Spinoza's *Tractatus Politicus:*

> The last end of the state is not to dominate men, nor to restrain them by fear; rather it is so to free each man from fear that he may live and act with full security and without injury to himself or his neighbor. The end of the state, I repeat, is not to make rational beings into brute beasts and machines. It is to enable their bodies and their minds to function safely. It is to lead men to live by, and to exercise, a free reason; that they may not waste their strength in hatred, anger and guile, nor act unfairly towards one another. Thus the end of the state is really liberty.[5]

Of course, the attractiveness of this passage disappears when we analyze it more closely. If it is true that the end of the state it to free each man from fear so that he may act without injury to himself then it follows that the state is the agency which decides what sort of conduct would indeed be injurious to oneself. If the state is the agency which enables men's minds and bodies to function safely, then it is presumably the state that must decide what constitutes which is safe conduct and which is not. Again, if the end of the state is to prevent men from wasting their strength, then the state becomes the agency which must decide what is useful and desirable conduct and what is not.

The point here, seen in juxtaposition to Mill's position on this matter, is that the state has a moral obligation and indeed, has as its end, its *raison d'etre,* the protection of persons not merely from the rapacious conduct of others, but from the individual's own weaknesses of will, spirit, and character. It is clear as Berlin asserts that this theory rests upon a presumption about human character, to wit, that there exists a

---

[5] Spinoza, *Tractatus Politicus,* chap. 20.

real, final, ultimate purpose or end in human affairs which may be apprehended through the exercise of reason by a rational, real self but which indeed may be obscurely perceived or perceived not at all by the empirical self. Those who subscribe to a negative notion of liberty may not be prepared to deny any more than they are prepared to assert the truth of this metaphysical allegation.

From the point of view of the notion of negative freedom, the existence of a rational will on the one hand, and an empirical will on the other hand, or a real self on the one hand and an empirical self on the other, is fundamentally irrelevant. What is relevant is that each particular individual is considered to have a legitimate opportunity to judge what is best for himself by himself. On this theory, the chief or principal assumption is that no agency of government may legitimately dictate to any of its citizens the terms of his own best interest. That is not to say of course that the state may not legitimately rule certain forms of conduct as contrary to the best interests of the society as a whole. It is to say, however, that agencies of the state are barred from coercive and oppressive measures on the grounds that such coercion is for the ultimate benefit of the individual and that such coercion has as its goal rendering private conduct of individuals compatible with the best interests of the individuals in question.

Thus the distinction between negative and positive conceptions of freedom provides us with another framework in terms of which the concept of freedom may be analyzed. There are, of course, other such frameworks and we are obliged to consider what some of these may be.

Determinism

The problem of freedom may be conceived in a nonpolitical or, as it were philosophical, fashion. In some ways, an analysis of the concept of freedom whose complimentary concept is determinism rather than coercion or control is both the logically and historically prior theory. That is to say, discussions of the concept of freedom in the political context presuppose that an adequate answer may be given to a logically prior question concerning the very possibility of human freedom. Let us proceed to an examination of how this problem might be posed.

Disputes which arise with regard to the question about men's freedom in the conduct of their affairs and the extent to which their conduct may be determined by autonomous forces generally conceal an ambiguity. The ambiguity concerns the meaning of the concept "determine." The concept "determine" may mean on the one hand that an action is subject to causal explanation, and on the other hand, it may mean that the action in question could not be avoided. Those who have addressed themselves to this problem have not always been careful to distinguish between which sense of determinism they have in mind. It is one thing to say that behavior is determined in the sense that there are causes and that the conduct in question may be explained in terms of those causes and quite another question to say that behavior is unavoidable.

Causal explanations are the very heart of scientific explanations. The scientist almost invariably assumes the truth of the principle of the uniformity of nature. He assumes, that is, that events have causes and when certain initial conditions obtain, certain other events will follow. It is an easy matter to see how this assumption operates in the physical sciences. The physicist, for example, argues that given a universal law or theory, together with a set of statements about the initial conditions which obtain at a given moment, it is possible to predict some future event. This is the sense in which we mean to say that an action is determined when the event in question actually takes place. To whatever degree the social scientist operates in the same fashion that the physical scientist does, he makes similar assumptions. He assumes, for example, that given certain data about social or political or individual behavior and given certain general behavioral maxims which function in ways comparable to the way in which universal laws or theories in physics function, it ought to be possible to predict how groups and individuals will behave at some future moment in time. The assumption, when it is made, is a plausible one when the conduct in question does indeed occur. In this way, it is sometimes alleged that the conduct of groups and individuals are determined in a way similar to the conduct of particles in motion. Although no one would want to dispute the fact that the degree of confidence one may have in the predictions offered by the social scientist may not approach the degree of confidence that the physical scientist may have concerning the conduct of particles in motion, the limitation is less dependent upon qualitative distinctions than upon quantitative ones. The social scientist merely assumes that the character of his data is such that he cannot know enough, or cannot state as many initial conditions, as the physical scientist may. For the social scientist this is a practical rather than a theoretical limitation. For he continues to assume and so far as he functions as a scientist, must assume, that it is, at least in theory, possible to know enough about groups or given individuals to make more secure predictions about how the group or the individual will behave at some future moment.

Assumptions about the uniformity of nature may be justified particularly when the assumption is made in the social sciences or in psychology with reference to those relevant factors which determine future behavior. It is a commonplace argument, for example, to say that my current behavior is determined by causes over which I have no control. My personal habits, my profession and the competence with which I conduct it, my relationship toward my children, toward my wife, friends, colleagues, the way in which I spend my leisure time, the sorts of political attitudes I have, the moral system to which I subscribe, the kind of house I buy, all of these, and of course many other things, are all determined in the sense that they may be understood and explained in terms of traits genetically inherited, the moral imperatives articulated and introjected in the immediate social environment, historical and cultural facts which determine the kind of environment in which I live, and so forth.

Similarly, certain interpretations of history, constitute elaborations of this theme. The most obvious example which comes readily to mind is the interpretation of history and culture offered by Hegel and Marx. According to this theory, the principles which operate in culture and in history do not merely determine the collective behavior and conduct of societies but may even, as in the case of Hegel, lie beyond human comprehension. The laws which govern historical development are deterministic in the sense that the art, philosophy, science, and political institutions which may exist in a given moment in time are products of historical developments and in turn determine the very conditions of individual lives. Accordingly, men are not free either with regard to the institutional arrangements which predominate in a given society nor with regard to the social conditions which determine the content of their lives.

Another example of determinism at work lies in the area of human consciousness. All of us are familiar with Freud's claim that all actions previously thought to be merely accidents or peculiarly inexplicable phenomena are in reality the symptoms or effects of causes which may be discovered through an analysis of the unconscious and of the unresolved conflicts which may be discovered there. Consequently, phenomena like dreams, or slips of the tongue, or slips of the pen are causally determined as indeed are the more sophisticated and more complex actions of men.

An objection has been raised concerning the inclusion of Freud among those who have offered deterministic arguments for human conduct. Consider for example the following passage quoted from *Social Principles in the Democratic State:*

> If . . . we look more closely at these so-called laws in psychology we find, in the main, that they do not give sufficient explanations of *human action,* of what human beings do deliberately, knowing what they are doing and for which they can give reasons. Freud's brilliant discoveries, for instance, were not of the causes of *actions* like signing contracts or shooting pheasants; rather they were of things that *happen* to man. . . . These might be called "passion" more appropriately than "action," and in this respect they are similar to what we call "fits of passion" or "gusts of emotion." Men do not dream or forget a name "on purpose" any more than they are deliberately subject to impulses or gusts of emotion. One class of laws in psychology, then, gives causal explanations which seem sufficient to account for what *happens* to a man, but not for what he does.[6]

The objection seems plausible on the face of it, but a closer examination indicates that it may be an example of question-begging. For if we distinguish between what happens to a man and what he does on purpose, we may merely be restating the very distinction between being free and being determined. The whole deterministic argument seems to be not that he does nothing on purpose, though of course he may have reason for what he does but rather that everything which he does is a consequence of what has happened to him. Therefore, it does not appear that the distinction helps to clarify since it appears to be merely a restatement of what is precisely at issue, namely, the degree to which men are in fact determined by those things which happen to them.

Moreover, the extent to which a causal explanation is a genuine explanation depends upon whether the laws or theories in question state sufficient rather than merely the necessary conditions for the occurrence

---

[6] S. I. Benn and R. S. Peters, *Social Principles in the Democratic State* (London: George Allen & Unwin Ltd.), pp. 199–200.

of the event. The distinction between necessary and sufficient conditions is an important one. A team of carpenters may be a necessary condition to the construction of a building, but they are clearly not sufficient. In this connection, Peters and Benn are correct in pointing out that some sorts of psychological explanations, particularly those which claim that intellectual performances depend upon the antecedent physiological conditions or mental processes, are offering very much more than a statement of the necessary conditions for such activities. Consider for example the following passage:

> We have in mind here the contributions made by physiological psychologists and those who have studied cognitive skills like learning, remembering, and perceiving. Part of what we mean by such terms is that human beings obtain a norm or standard. Remembering is not just a psychological process; for to remember is to be *correct* about what happened in the past. Knowing is not just a mental state; it is to be sure that we are *correct,* to have good *grounds* for our conviction. To perceive something is to be *right* in our claims about what is before our eyes; to learn something is to *improve* at something or to get something right. All such concepts have norms written into them. In a similar way, . . . a human action is typically something done in order to bring about a result or in accordance with a standard. Such actions can be said to be done more or less intelligently and more or less correctly only because of the norms defining what are ends and what are sufficient and correct means to them.[7]

The physiological psychologist is concerned principally with the processes involved, rather than with the norms involved such that it would be possible to judge the actions and questions correct or incorrect, intelligent or stupid. If this is so, that is if norms must indeed be taken into account if sufficient conditions are to be stated for the occurrence of various kinds of human behavior, then a strictly naturalistic explanation for the occurrence will not be enough.

There is, moreover, another peculiar characteristic of causal explanations when they occur in the social sciences which are somehow disanalogous to comparable explanations in the physical sciences. Consider for example the following passage again from Peters and Benn:

> . . . the problem of the freedom of the will arose mainly in connection with the type of action that is palpably different from a mere movement or process—an action that is preceded by deliberation and choice. For, roughly

[7] *Ibid.*

speaking, a "willed action" was usually taken to mean one in which we think before we act, when we make up our minds in terms of considerations which are relevant to the matter at hand before we act. [These difficulties are] connected with the fact that into the human beings' deliberations about what he is going to do will be introduced considerations about what he is likely to do, which the social scientist may have published. A scientist may discover a causal law connecting the properties of clover with a certain effect upon the digestive organs of sheep. But, when he publishes his findings, the sheep cannot take account of them and modify their behavior accordingly. But with men it is different. Many causal connections discovered by psychologists may only hold good provided that the people whose actions are predicted in accordance with the law remain ignorant of what it asserts. And it is practically impossible to ensure that this is the case. So, if people know the causes on which a prediction of a certain type of behavior is based, and if they deliberate before acting, they may do something different from what is predicted, just because they recognize these causes. A prediction may thus be valid only on the assumption that the people concerned remain unconscious of the causes on which it is based. Otherwise, it may be no more than a warning.[8]

This argument, which is quite often used by those who wish to show that there is an important disanalogy between the methods employed by the natural scientists and the methods employed by the social scientists is not altogether convincing. For one thing, it would be possible to treat the additional piece of information about the prediction concerning the piece of behavior that is to take place as another variable which could be taken into account. No doubt it is possible to predict that on a certain day and on a certain time there will be a traffic jam on a given highway. Supposing that this prediction is well publicized, motorists may avoid the place at the time indicated. And consequently, the prediction is disconfirmed by virtue of the fact that it functioned not as a prediction but as a warning and that the warning was generally heeded. It is not at all clear why the explanatory model cannot take this phenomenon into account simply by treating the prediction as another piece of information which, if programmed into the data on which the prediction was originally based would act as a self corrective.

What all this comes to is that determinism may be construed in different ways and that these ways are not carefully distinguished. To this point we have been discussing causal determinism, though we have

[8] *Ibid.*, p. 200–201.

not clearly resolved the question as to whether or not such deterministic principles exclude the possibility for making a case for human freedom. It may well be that the kind of freedom we have in mind when we use the concept to stand as an antithesis to determinism requires that determinism be interpreted not as causal explanation, but rather as *unavoidability*.

One more example may help to clarify part of what is involved here. Suppose a patient undergoing psychoanalysis announced to his analyst one day that he intends to be married. The analyst may very well understand the patient's intent as determined, in the sense that it is the sort of desire which is a natural outgrowth of the patient's working through his unresolved conflicts. He may suppose for example that the patient is excessively anxiety ridden and suffers from an unresolved oedipal complex and that his desire to seek a solution in matrimony is caused by these conflicts. The desire or intent to be married then, is perceived by the analyst as causally determined by certain unconscious factors. One might say that the patient in this regard is not making a free choice but that rather his choice is determined by the psychological factors in question. But suppose the analyst asks the patient for his *reasons* for wanting to be married. The patient might reply by saying that he is lonely and this is a solution to his loneliness, or that his prospective bride is wealthy and will enable him to continue with his analysis, or that he would like to have children, or perhaps that he no longer wishes to cook for himself. Now, it is clear that the patient is offering reasons for a prospective action, and that these are the result of reflection and deliberation. Yet, the kind of explanation which each offers for the prospective conduct is quite different. The analyst will not deny that there may in fact be good reasons for the patient's decision to be married, although it is clear that this is not the sort of explanation which the analyst himself is offering for the same phenomenon. It would seem then that any explanation which purports to be an adequate one must take into account not merely what the analyst perceives as the causes for the action, but the reasons which the patient has offered on behalf of that action. On a strictly causal analysis, in psychological terms, only the analyst's explanation would count. And it is perfectly clear that a good deal of what is involved in this exercise of will would be omitted.

The problem of unavoidability is a different matter. Someone may be perfectly prepared to admit that his actions have causes and yet at the same time deny that this admission implies that the actions in question are unavoidable. Consider the explanation offered by Benn and Peters for the unwarranted assumption that causal explanations imply unavoidability.

This assumption that any action for which causes can be produced is therefore unavoidable is surely a mistake occasioned by the peculiar circumstances of the rise of science. It so happened that scientific advance, which consisted in the discovery of far reaching causal laws, coincided with the wide spread theological doctrine of predestination and with the metaphysical picture of the universe as a vast piece of clockwork in which human beings, like cog wheels, were pushed on a set pattern of movement. God, as it were, constructed the clock and set it going. If the clock could be seen as a whole, men could see what the future had in store for them and what movements determined that their fate should be this and no other. Causal discoveries reveal the springs and levers which pushed men toward their appointed destiny. The tacit assumption is therefore developed that wherever causes could be found for actions, they were also unavoidable. Causes, being pictured always as internal pushes and pulls, were thought somehow to compel a man. And this picture suggests compulsion whether such causes are properly to be regarded as necessary or as sufficient conditions for human action. Men were therefore regarded as being not free because they were the victims of peculiar internal sort of compulsion exercised by the causes of their behavior. They were thus not able to avoid doing what they did.[9]

Now it is clear from this that a stimulus-response psychology, crudely interpreted, in the light, say, of a Hobbesian theory, is compatible with the cog-wheel metaphor and lends itself easily and plausibly to the assumption that if actions may be understood in terms of the stimulus-response then they are indeed unavoidable.

The logic which governs the use of the word "avoidable" in our ordinary discourse is similar in certain important respects to the way in which we use the word "selfish." It makes no sense for example to say that all human beings under all circumstances are selfish. And it makes no sense because a word which has a contrasting job to do in our language would now be presumably appropriate in all contexts. If this were so, there would continue to exist a dimension of conduct which had hitherto been called selfish and marked off from other sorts of conduct

[9] *Ibid.*, p. 205.

which could not now be described as it was in the past. We would in effect be doing away with whatever utility the concept has in our ordinary discourse. A similar result takes place in dormitory bull-sessions concerning altruism and egoism. It is a relatively easy matter though perhaps not a very profitable one to demonstrate how all behavior may be understood as being egoistic. The incorrigible protagonist can reasonably though perhaps not correctly insist that martyrdom itself is to be understood in terms of the masochistic pleasure afforded a person who permits himself to be martyred. Yet it is clear that from such disputes, few discoveries about human behavior are to be made. We succeed only in impoverishing our language and in blunting the conceptual tools which might ordinarily be used to understand and explain human conduct.

If we examine the meaning of the word "avoidable," the same sort of analysis provided in the preceding discussion seems to apply.

To argue that all human conduct, because it is causally determined is also unavoidable is obviously to say that all human conduct is unavoidable. Yet an examination of our ordinary language indicates that we do indeed recognize some forms of conduct to be the result of a kind of compulsion. Our intention when action is characterized as compulsive is to distinguish it from forms of conduct which are not.

The foregoing considerations lead us to involvement in a further problem, namely, the issue of assigning responsibility. Moral language to whatever extent it is a language of praising and blaming rests on the general assumption that there exists a moral agent of whose conduct it may be said that the agent in question may have done other than what he in fact did. To blame or praise someone for his conduct in what might be generally regarded as a moral context assumes that the agent did what he did freely. "Freely" is to be understood in this context as a piece of conduct which takes place without coercion or compulsion. We do not ordinarily assign praise or blame if the agent could not have done otherwise, if, that is, he was compelled or required by outside agencies to perform the action in question.

Perhaps the issue becomes somewhat more clear to us if we consider the following passage:

Determinism erases none of the ordinary distinctions between free and coercive action. It may be thought to do so, since the thesis that all behavior is "determined" by character and circumstances sounds rather like saying that character and circumstances "make" us do whatever we do; and this again sounds as if we are not "free" to do anything else, and are coerced. Again, when determinists say . . . that natural laws determine our behavior, they may seem to be saying something very similar to what we are saying if we assert that civil laws "require" us to behave in certain ways; and this again suggests that all our actions are coerced or compelled.

It may not strike the reader as a natural mistake to pass from the thesis that behavior is determined to the thesis that it is compelled, or coerced. Very likely he is not tempted to draw such inferences. It has been supposed, however, that the thinking of some philosophers has moved precisely in this way; in fact it has been asserted that the whole controversy about determinism has its source in the confusion of "determine" with "coerce" or "compel."

However this may be, it is clear that to say that all behavior is determined is not at all to say that it is unfree in the sense of coerced. To see that this is so, we need only examine what we mean when we say someone did something freely, without coercion. If, for instance, a man's wife reminds him that he married her "of his own free will," what is she saying? She is denying that he was hypnotized, that anyone guided his hand when he signed the marriage document, that anyone held a shotgun at his back or held dire threats of any kind over him when he said "Yes." He was not physically forced, nor was he coerced by threats. On the contrary, she is saying that, after full consideration of the alternatives, he did what he thought he wanted most to do.

Determinism does not deny that people often make "free" choices in this sense. What determinism asserts is that free choices are determined—that they could have been predicted.[10]

Precisely the same point is made in a somewhat more elaborate fashion by Peters and Benn who write as follows:

As a matter of fact men *sometimes* do seem to be acting under this sort of compulsion. This is what makes the prisoner of the past picture of determinism so plausible. For example, a man under post-hypnotic suggestion will do, when he wakes, what the hypnotist told him to do in his trance. He cannot be dissuaded nor sidetracked by rational arguments. He will act as if there were something in him which *compells* him to act in this way. And it was because the language which Freud and Marx used to record their causal speculations—their talk of forces, drives, impulses, etc.—creaked with compulsion, that an indefinite extention of the concept of acting under compulsion was intimated. But we are inclined to say that a man is not responsible for his actions, and for being hypnotized, not because we know their causes,

[10] Richard B. Brandt, *Ethical Theory, The Problems of Normative and Critical Ethics* (Englewood Cliffs, N.J.: Prentice-Hall, Inc., 1959), p. 514.

but because he behaves so oddly when we try to get him to do something else. It is this which suggests compulsion or subjection to some irrational irresistible force. For irresistible impulses are those which, on the whole, people seem unable to resist. Very often, too, we speak of compulsives when we know nothing of the causes of their obsessive preoccupation. We describe their actions as compulsive because we apply a crude battery of tests to them, not because we have done a piece of detective work on their causes. For instance, if a man is really a kleptomaniac, we have classified him as such because we have found that reward and punishment, praise and blame, rational argument, etc. make no difference to his stealing. The causes in general must be distinguished from the special type of causes that have unavoidable affects. For there are *some* causes that do conform to this pattern. For instance, it is claimed by Bowley of the Travisdock Clinic that certain kinds of deprivation of maternal care in early childhood, not only cause traits like unfriendliness, distractibility, etc., but also constitute causes leading to unavoidable effects. Deliberation and resolution, praise and blame, reward and punishment, change of environment—all these devices are of no use. . . . His reasoning is irrelevant to what he does. In such cases there is some point in saying that a man cannot help doing what he does, that his behavior is unavoidable. The causes, too, seem sufficient to explain his behavior; for it falls into the category of something happening to him rather than of his doing something deliberately. But many have mistakenly generalized such sensational examples and have thought that whenever causes can be found for a person's behavior, he cannot help doing what he does. But this does not follow at all. The facts even of this sort of case are highly disputable and psychologists have produced few other such examples of causes with unavoidable effects. The mere production of causes is of itself irrelevant to the question whether a man could reasonably be said to have been able to avoid doing what he did. It is only if we know in *general* that a certain type of cause tends to lead to unavoidable effects that the production of a cause is relevant to the question of responsibility. And then, of course, this type of *cause* must be produced; not just *any* cause. For most causes do not in fact compel. Perhaps the notion of compelling or impelling is itself only appropriate in cases where things *happen* to a man, where causal explanations are also sufficient.[11]

The philosophical discussion of the problem of freedom is not exhausted by an analysis of the problem of determinism. There are other, perhaps less traditional or formal ways, in which the problem of freedom has been approached by political philosophers. Among the most important of these stems from an analysis of political concepts offered by

[11] Peters and Benn, *op. cit.*, p. 208.

T. D. Weldon. We have examined Weldon's position with regard to the analysis of other sorts of political concepts, and it may be of some utility to examine his analysis of the concept of freedom.

Freedom as value

One of the inescapable facts about freedom is that hardly anyone is opposed to it. And having said so it is easy to see that the word "free" does less of a job in our language of *describing* a particular state of affairs than it does to *commend* to us a particular state of affairs. No analysis of the concept which restricts itself to the kinds of descriptive jobs it may do in our language can be considered as complete. The question which is proper to ask in connection with these concepts is to ask how is it possible to contradict the allegation that someone is free? Suppose we are faced with the allegation that X is free. The natural challenge to that question seems to be "No, he is a slave" or "No, he is still married" or "He is in prison" or something of that sort. "He is free" is an incomplete sentence. The natural challenge to it is "free from what?"[12]

It is Weldon's point that in any discussion of the concept of freedom it is necessary to distinguish between various uses of the concept of freedom which are not rigidly separated in ordinary speech. Consider for example the way in which Weldon distinguishes between "free from" and the expression "free of":

> At first sight it looks as if "free from" was just an idiomatic way of stating a negative. "He is free from want" is equivalent to "He is not in want," "He is free from infection" to "He is not infected." But this is not the whole story. "Free from" is normally used only when an affirmative was or might reasonably be expected. We do not say that notoriously wealthy people are free from poverty or that notoriously healthy ones are free from disease. "He is free from anxiety" usually means the same as "He is not anxious now" (but he was 'till he heard from his wife or until the doctor told him it wasn't cancer). "Freedom from fear" is like "Out of danger." Both imply that something would or might have happened although it in fact did not.
>
> We also talk commonly about "free to. . . ." "Smith is free to go abroad if he wants to" (there is no law to prevent him and he can pay for his ticket); "he is free to leave the house" (he is not ill or paralyzed and the door is not locked). It looks as if these can be translated into "free from" statements

[12] Weldon, *Vocabulary of Politics,* p. 70.

without any change of meaning, but this is not the case. They are more hypothetical (if he wants to) and more positive. "Free from" merely implies that something is not there (though it might be). "Free to" suggests that conditions for doing something not favorable (though the agent might not want to do it).[13]

This distinction may on the face of it appear to be highly academic. Yet a moment's reflection will demonstrate its applicability to making certain kinds of somewhat more concrete distinctions in viewing the way in which political institutions operate. Indeed, it is Weldon's view that the distinction between "freedom to" and "freedom from" plays an important role in distinguishing between the political and economic organization characteristic of the capitalist idea on the one hand the communist view on the other:

To put it shortly the capitalist idea was that freedom from . . . was very important and freedom to . . . rather a luxury except insofar it was a kind of freedom from. . . . The Communist view now reverses this valuation, and capitalism insofar as it has come to accept New Deals and welfare states has considerably changed its position "You are free to go to the doctor if you want to" does not in this country [England] mean simply "You may do so if you have enough money to pay his fee. The police will not stop you." There is less talk of freedom from want and fear and more of freedom to work and receive a living wage. Freedom to . . . is what really matters and freedom from is much less in evidence. The difference is sometimes marked by talking about the positive as distinguished from the negative State.[14]

The chief point which Weldon makes or thinks he makes is that in view of the distinction, does it in fact make sense to ask which of these two uses of the concept of freedom is really Freedom? Thus he writes: "When 'freedom' is thus clarified it becomes clear that most of the traditional questions about it involve a hopeless muddle.[15]

Indeed, polemics which come about as a result of raising the problem of freedom in the traditional context are not real problems at all. The allegation that there is less freedom in the United States now than there was a hundred or fifty years ago because there are more laws and regulations and there are therefore more restrictions on freedom is not incom-

---

[13] *Ibid.*, pp. 70–71.
[14] *Ibid.*, p. 71.
[15] *Ibid.*, p. 72.

patible with the observation that there is more freedom today than ever before because there is less unrestricted arbitrary behavior and therefore more protection of freedom. These are not incompatible or contradictory statements because they play on the ambiguity of the word "freedom," confusing on the one hand "freedom to" with the meaning of the expression "freedom for." A question like "How can freedom and authority be reconciled with one another?" or, a statement like, "Will, not force, is the basis of the State," and similar sorts of questions seem to call for general answers, and attempts at offering such answers invariably lead to vacuous, banal, and generally unhelpful kinds of propositions.

The upshot of this entire discussion is that there is nothing to be gained by raising such questions or by making efforts at answering them. The difficulty involved is clarified only when we come to consider talk about freedom to be talk which involves making appraisals or formulating value judgments. The term cannot be used, it is argued, descriptively. Peters and Benn, as well as Weldon conclude that the word "free" denotes, not as we might expect, a particular state of affairs or quality of action, but rather the state of mind, the preference, bias or prejudice of the person or persons who use the word. The argument appears to be that the word "free" if it denotes anything at all refers to the feeling of the speaker, and the attitudes which he has about particular political arrangement. How then do we extricate ourselves from a situation in which a key political concept appears to have no descriptive or analytic utility but which functions apparently only as a sign to denote a subjective state?

We have learned in our consideration of other political concepts that when we encounter an ambiguity, the solution lies not in the arbitrary legislation about the contexts in which the use of the word will be appropriate and those in which its use would not be appropriate but rather through an examination of the ways in which the concept in question has been used in the systematic articulation of political systems by political philosophers. We must turn therefore, once again, to the data available to us which, in this case, means an analysis of the way in which the word "free" has been used by selected historical figures and, the construction of several models which represent characteristic analysis of the concept "freedom."

IDEALISTIC CONCEPTS OF FREEDOM

For both Plato and Aristotle the ultimate end or goal or good of human life is self-realization. Whatever properties which the classical Greeks would recognize as constituting virtues must be seen as contributing in some fashion or other to this ultimate end. Consider the following passage from Book IX of the *Republic:*

> Bearing in mind, then, the analogy between state and individual, you should tell me what you think of the condition of each in turn. To begin with the state: it is free under a despot, or enslaved?
>
> Utterly enslaved.
>
> And yet you see it contains some who are masters and free men.
>
> Yes, a few; but almost the whole of it including the most respectable part is degraded to a miserable slavery.
>
> If the individual, then, is analogous to the state, we shall find the same order of things in him: a soul laboring under the meanest servitude, the best elements in it being enslaved, while a small part, which is also the most frenzied and corrupt, plays the master. Would you call such a condition of the soul freedom or slavery?
>
> Slavery, of course.
>
> And just as a state enslaved to a tyrant cannot do what it really wishes, so neither can a soul under a similar tyranny do what it wishes as a whole. Goaded on against its will by the sting of desire, it will be filled with confusion and remorse. Like the corresponding state, it must always be poverty stricken, unsatisfied, and haunted by fear. Nowhere else will there be so much lamentation, groaning, and anguish as in a country under a despotism, and in a soul maddened by the tyranny of passion and lust.[16]

Plato is here directing his attention to the argument that the tyrant is among the freest of men because he does precisely what he wishes to do independent of both external constraint and internal restraint. Plato's point is that such a man is not merely unfree but is rather an absolute slave because a more profound examination of his character will reveal that he, least of all men, does what he wishes. Now this is a curious assertion. And Plato's justification for his assertion enables us to examine the principle ingredient of the *idealistic conception of freedom.*

---

[16] *Republic,* Book IX, para. 577b.

According to Plato, freedom means doing what one wills, and thus the most free among us is he who does what he wills. But isn't this exactly what we mean when we talk of a tyrant? Is not a tyrant one whose actions are altogether free of restraint? Indeed, Plato's replies, a tyrant is precisely such a man but a man whose whole self is in abeyance for his character is enslaved to one shred or fragment of human nature. The tyrant can do nothing that he really desires (desire here means desirable as well). The really desirable is that which is desirable to the real or true self, and the real self means the whole self.

Throughout the moral philosophy of Plato and Aristotle there runs the conception from an order not only of the physical but of the moral world to which we must conform if we would be at our best, or, in other words, if we would satisfy our nature: and along with this goes the kindred idea that the higher nature is, so to speak, the truth of the lower, that is that the lower nature finds what it aims at in the satisfaction of the higher. Freedom, accordingly, or doing what one wills, is not the power to satisfy any and every desire, but the power to satisfy those desires in which the whole self finds satisfaction.[17]

Freedom then must be seen as a phenomenon internal to the individual and not merely as a special sort of relationship which obtains among individuals. A man who is master of himself is free as opposed to a man who is a slave of self, who is unfree. One who is master of himself conducts his life in accordance with those principles which are compatible with what is highest in the human soul, as opposed to the tyrant who is the most unfree of men because he operates in accordance with what is worst in his soul. This conception of internal freedom as a property or characteristic of self-realization is the central core of idealistic analysis of the concept of freedom. We continue now to an elaboration of what will constitute our first model of the concept of freedom.

In the ordinary acceptation of the word "freedom," the meaning most of us attribute to that term, is simply that to be free is to be able to act and conduct our lives independent of institutional coercion exercised by agencies of the state. This formula is so much a part of our rhetoric that it is exceedingly difficult for us to imagine an analysis of the concept of

---

[17] R. L. Nettleship, *Lectures on the Republic of Plato* (London, 1906), p. 317.

freedom such that social and political coercion may be required to promote freedom as an end or goal. Rousseau's expression "forced to be free" strikes us on the face of it to constitute a blatant contradiction. Let us consider for a moment the context in the *Social Contract* in which Rousseau uses this peculiar locution: "In order then that the social compact may not be an empty formula, it tacitly includes the undertaking, which alone can give forth to the rest, that whoever refuses to obey the general will shall be compelled to do so by the whole body. This means nothing less than that he will be forced to be free; for this is the condition which, by giving each citizen to his country, secures him against all personal dependence."[18] In a previous discussion we have tried to understand the meaning of this expression in terms of Rousseau's conception of the state which, as he perceives it, is essentially a moral entity, which must by its very nature assume as part of its responsibility the well being of its citizenry. This is far from an absurd notion and we find it stated in terms far more compelling in the writings of T. H. Green and Thomas Carlyle.

True freedom it is thought does not consist merely in the freedom to do what one wishes to do, but rather in doing the thing which is considered worth doing. Carlyle put the point as follows:

> Surely of all the rights of man this right of the ignorant man to be guarded by the wiser, to be, gently or forceably, held in the true course by him, is the indisputablest.[19]
>
> Liberty? The true liberty of a man . . . consisted in his finding out, or being forced to find out, the right path, and to walk thereon. To learn, or to be taught, what work he actually was able for; and then by permission, persuasion, and even compulsion, to set about doing the same. . . . You do not allow a palpable mad man to leap over precipices; you violate his liberty, you are wise; and keep him were it in straight waist coats away from the precipices! Every stupid, every cowardly and foolish man is but a less palpable mad man: his true liberty were that a wiser man, that any and every wiser man, could, by brass collars, or in whatever milder or sharper way, lay hold of him when he was doing wrong, and order and compel him to go a little righter.[20]

---

[18] Rousseau, *The Social Contract,* Everyman ed., p. 18.

[19] Carlyle, *Chartism,* p. 157.

[20] Carlyle, *Past and Present,* p. 212.

Put in these terms, it is neither surprising nor absurd to suggest that if the ultimate intent and purpose of life consists in the development of inborn potentialities of goodness and beauty and reason[21] then it is not difficult to make a case that society and the state have a responsibility for compelling such persons who by virtue of ignorance or indolence do not conduct themselves in such ways as to develop these potentialities.

If the real development of individual life requires that persons work, then efforts made by the state or society to compel persons to work are perfectly legitimate.

A man who will not work according to what abilities the gods have given him for working has the smallest right to eat pumpkin, or any fraction of land that will grow pumpkin, however plentiful such land may be; but has . . . a *right* to be compelled . . . to do competent work for his living. . . . If it be his own indolence that prohibits him (from working), then his own indolence is the enemy and he must be delivered from it: [that is] the first "right" he has.[22]

Carlyle himself sees education as a vehicle of redemption, though the system which he has in mind is, as Carlyle himself recognizes, close to the moral code of a drill sergeant. He writes:

Beyond all other schooling one often wishes the entire population could be thoroughly drilled; into cooperative movement; into individual behavior, correct, precise, and at once habitual and orderly. . . . The One Official Person royal, sacerdotal, scholastic, governmental of our times, who is still thoroughly a truth and a reality, and *not* in great part a hypothesis and worn out humbug . . . is the Drill Sergeant who is master of his work, and who will perform it.[23]

The same sentiment concerning the problem of freedom, is expressed by Fichte, who, as well as Kant, distinguished clearly between freedom of the will, that is to say, internal freedom, and freedom from the arbitrary interference of others, that is to say, external freedom. According to this articulation of the concept of freedom, understanding the problem only in terms of the absence of external restraint by governmental control is to offer a severely adumbrated and myopic theory. It

---

[21] M. Storrs, *The Relation of Carlyle to Kant and Fichte,* p. 91.

[22] Carlyle, *The Nigger Question,* p. 355.

[23] Carlyle, *Shooting Niagara,* p. 41.

implies only the right to do as one pleases, which is interpreted according to this theory as nothing more than being permitted to be a slave to one's passions and senses. According to Fichte, true freedom is internal freedom and its possibility is contingent upon the recognition that the state must set forth the outward conditions under which moral freedom, i.e., internal freedom, is to be achieved.[24] The role then which the state must play in its efforts to create the conditions under which men may realize what Fichte calls "internal freedom" is to increase external coercion by repressing and removing those external objects and institutions which allow men to "do what they wish," which is nothing more than being allowed to be a slave to one's passions or sense. The curious circumstance which comes about, therefore, is that internal freedom can increase only as external freedom decreases. Consider for example the following passage:

> . . . if you wish to influence him (the people) at all you must do more than merely talk to him, you must fashion him and fashion him in such a way that he simply cannot will otherwise than you wish him to will. . . . The recognition of and the reliance upon "free" will in the pupil is the first mistake of the old system, and the clear concession of its impotence and futility. By confession that . . . the will still remains "free"; i.e., hesitating, undecided between good and evil, it confesses that it neither is able nor wishes to . . . fashion the will. . . . On the other hand, the new system or education must consist essentially in this that essentially destroys the freedom of the will . . . and produces on the contrary strict necessity in the decisions of the will. . . . Such a will can henceforth be relied upon with confidence and certainty.[25]

Here again we encounter Plato's conception of freedom in which it is alleged that freedom, true freedom, is the internal exercise of control over those parts of one's character which may be considered base, and the establishment of an internal unity of character and personality which enables the complete fulfillment of that which is essentially human.

Underlying the speculation of Plato, Carlyle, Fichte, and others whose conceptions of freedom will receive our attention directly, is one basic fundamental assumption. Almost without exception, it is assumed, that there is one single end or goal or purpose or meaning in human life and

---

[24] Fichte, *Die Staatslehre,* p. 390.

[25] Fichte, *A Justice to the German Nation,* pp. 20–21.

therefore in human institutions. The realization of that end or goal, is thought to depend upon the circumstances established at least in part by political institutions. It is the task of the state, therefore, to create the conditions under which the human spirit may blossom and fulfill itself in accordance with a set of moral principles which are held to be irrevocably binding and unquestioned. It is natural then to conclude, when such an assumption is made, that it is the task of the state to make men good, to enable them, indeed, to assist them, to overcome those forces which thwart and pervert the personal moral progress of each individual. The concept of internal freedom, then, offers a complete justification for external repression in the sense indicated. That is to say, the struggle or conflict which must be resolved for the good life and fully realized self to be possible is a struggle which takes place not between individuals and institutions, but rather a conflict which takes place within the individual himself.

Political freedom then is understood in the way in which one might understand the resolution of moral conflicts as they occur within the internal life of individual persons. One supposes that this is the context in which one is to understand Rousseau's famous expression that it may be necessary to force persons to be free. For the ambiguity of the expression "forced to be free," makes the issue in question clear to us. Force and freedom may be incompatible only on the condition that we misunderstand the ambiguity involved in the use of the concept "freedom." By "force" Rousseau and others have meant only the introduction or removal of obstacles which encourage or prohibit the development of internal freedom.

This view may be elaborated in a consideration of the arguments of T. H. Green. Though Green does not press the view that the state is obliged to enforce morality directly or even that the state under any circumstances ought to do so, his reasons are not themselves based on arguments of morality, but rather on a point of logic. He writes,

> The question sometimes put, whether moral duties should be enforced by law, is really an unmeaning one, for they simply cannot be enforced. They are duties to act, it is true, and an act can be enforced, but they are duties to act from certain dispositions and with certain motives, and these cannot be enforced. The enforcement of an outward act, the moral character of which

depends on a certain motive and disposition, may often contribute to render the motive and disposition impossible.[26]

Green's point is one we've encountered earlier. What sense does it make to say that someone acts morally if the act in question is one which is the result of the exercise of coercion or threat of coercion from sources external to himself? Clearly, we would want to distinguish carefully between those situations where we know that we ought to do something and where we do in fact do it because we choose to, and those situations where we do what we do (whether we think that we ought to do it or not) because we are fearful of punishment. It is Green's point that the state cannot function as a moral enforcer because the very conception of a moral enforcer is a contradictory one. The will, the impetus, to perform an act which may be characterized as moral must come from within ourselves and not be the result of external force, threat, or intimidation.

However convenient the conclusion might be that Green's admission concerning the degree to which the state may legislate or enforce conduct in the realm of morality, is justified the fact of the matter is that Green subscribes to an interpretation of the state in which the state is obliged to interfere with the actions of its citizens in the cause of morality.[27] According to Green, freedom consists in acting in accordance with the dictates of a free moral will. Whenever certain conditions arise which make it impossible for the free moral will to function, it is the duty of the state to frame laws which remove these hindrances or obstacles to freedom. Among the obstacles which may arise are, for example, drunkenness or ignorance. Under such circumstances, the state has an obligation to regulate, for example, the sale of liquor or to make education compulsory. Indeed, any obstacle which interferes or may interfere with the free development of any individual's faculties is subject to being removed, modified, or regulated by the state. As Ernest Barker in his *Political Thought in England,* puts the point: ". . . [a boy] has a capacity for doing things worth doing, worth doing for him, and worth doing for the community, which the community for his sake

---

[26] T. H. Green, *Lectures on the Principles of Political Obligation* (Ann Arbor, Michigan: University of Michigan, 1967), section 134.

[27] See William McGovern, *From Luther to Hitler* (Cambridge: Houghton Mifflin Co., 1941), p. 175.

and for its sake has the right to liberate by removing the ignorance which hinders the action of his capacity."[28]

Just as a law requiring education in order to enable persons to "freely" develop their faculties is justifiable and indeed required, by the same token, any law which makes it difficult or impossible for individuals to debase or dehumanize themselves is equally legitimate. Thus, according to Green, persons are in no sense free to allow themselves to be put under the influence of their animal passions or free to be slaves to the baser parts of their character; and since domination by a passion for drink is a form of slavery, the state has an obligation to remove this obstacle to freedom by limiting, or curbing, or even eliminating the use of liquor. Green says: ". . . to argue that an effectual law in restraint of the liquor traffic would be a wrongful interference with individual liberties to ignore the essential condition under which alone every particular liberty can rightly be allowed the individual, the condition may mean that the allowance of that liberty is not . . . an impediment to social good."[29]

Moreover, just as the state is obliged to remove moral obstacles to freedom; so it is obliged to remove material or economic obstacles. True freedom in the economic sphere requires that the state regulate and control the economic behavior and activities of individual persons. Thus he is able to say:

> . . . we do not mean merely freedom to do as we like irrespective of what it is that we like. . . . We mean a positive power or capacity of doing or enjoying something worth doing or enjoying, and that something which we do or enjoy with others. . . . When we measure the progress of society by its growth in freedom, we measure it by the increasing development and exercise of the whole of these powers of contributing to social good with which we believe the members of the society to be in doubt. . . . The mere removal of compulsion, the mere enabling of a man to do as he likes, is in itself no contribution to true freedom."[30]

It is apparent that there is no area in life which may be considered in the conventional or negative sense of freedom to be in fact free. For

---

[28] Ernest Barker, *Political Thought in England: 1848–1914*, rev. ed. (Oxford: Oxford University Press, 1947), p. 52.

[29] T. H. Green, *Works*, 2d ed. (New York: Kraus Reprint Corp., 1889–90), section III, p. 384.

[30] *Ibid.*, p. 371.

whatever activity, conduct, or behavior which may be judged to be incompatible with the social good and therefore incompatible with the "fullest development of one's capacities" may be altered in a coercive fashion by the power of the state.

Few political theorists have attributed to the concept and idea of freedom the centrality which it possesses in Hegel's political system and in his theory of history. Indeed, according to Hegel, the history of the world must be understood in terms of its progress toward freedom. Although Hegel sometimes uses the concept in a way which commends it to the liberal tradition, the real meaning of the concept is precisely antithetical to the liberal's use. Freedom, according to Hegel, does not consist merely in the absence of external restraints and coercion. It does not mean merely the freedom that an individual may have to do what he wills with his own faculties and his own possessions; it means rather that the individual is obliged by virtue of the fundamental laws of his own nature and existence to develop those moral and intellectual and spiritual powers which are his by nature. How are we then to construe the expression "the fundamental laws of man's own nature"? Do we mean that a man develops his own capacities in accordance with his rational dispositions which are private to himself, or do we mean reason in the sense that it is the expression of the rational institutions of which he is a part as, for example, the state? Hegel clearly has the latter in mind, and it is therefore possible for him to conclude that to act in accordance with abstract reason is to act in accordance with the laws of the state, and to act in accordance with the laws of the state means to act in accordance with the inner rational essence of each individual person. Thus freedom means no more than submission, for it is only by submitting to the laws of the land that men become free.

The justification for this curious argument lies in the simple fact that isolated individuals apart from social and political organizations cannot, under any circumstances be said to be free. And this is so because freedom requires the development of one's faculties and such faculties cannot be developed in isolation from a social and political context: "It is impossible for the soul, as a principle of action, to unfold its powers to any degree without the submission of the individual to certain specific duties which he himself had no share in imposing, in which he only comes gradually to recognize as the adequate and necessary expression of his own freedom and personality."[31] The process of what is involved in "gradually to recognize" the moral necessity of submission and the perception of such submission as a condition for freedom is well expressed by one of Hegel's commentators who writes as follows:

> The State has [a] . . . double relation to the individual. On the one hand, the individual must be aware that the State is something external to him, determining him, and even constraining him. The State must stand above every private interest within it and must have power to mold any of its factors, however powerful that factor may be. To it, any member may appeal for protection and defense against any other; it is the supreme judge and has supreme right. On the other hand, the individual must know that the State is not an alien power, but the expression and the realization of his own rational principle. It is only his caprice which is constrained; his genuine will is emancipated and maintained. . . . His purposes obtain their content and significance from the social world; and the ends which he seeks are social. Consequently, he can achieve these ends in their fullness, that is to say, realize himself only if he takes account . . . of the principle by which it is constituted. *An antisocial act attacks its own substance and is opposed to itself."*[32]

This last sentence, "an antisocial act attacks its own substance and is opposed to itself" depends upon the notion that any individual is composed of two different and unique selves: a private self and a social self. The social self transcends immediate and parochial interests. Life is perceived as a striving to become something which, at a given moment, we are not. Life is a process of becoming. Liberty, or freedom refers to a condition to be sought not to something we possess. Freedom requires the constant effort, an unending struggle to assert that part of our character which represents the social self—a voice which we obey, at any given time, to an imperfect degree.

It is in this sense that we are said to submit to a law which inhibits a private particular wish, but which makes it possible to assert our true self. To the degree that all of us in such a system of government are subject to the will of the rational self which is represented by that government to that degree have we established self-government.

It is an easy matter to see the ambiguity which works on the word

---

[31] C. E. Vaughan, in his *Studies in the History of Political Philosophy,* Vol. 2, p. 147.

[32] Reyburn, *Hegel's Ethical Theory,* pp. 233–34. Italics mine.

"self." When we speak of self-government, we may on the one hand mean that the people collectively govern themselves, and on the other, that each individual person exercises self-control in the governing of those impulses which may be incompatible with the requirements of the social whole. (There is a third sense of self-government which is compatible with a theory of anarchy. We may for example speak of self-government as though it implied that any given individual would determine the criteria in terms of which his own conduct and behavior would be determined, without reference to external or institutional welfare or requirements.)

There is, moreover, a peculiarity concerning the logic which governs the use of the word "freedom": "As to the sense given to freedom, it must of course be admitted that every usage of the term to express anything but a social and political relation of one man to others involves a metaphor."[33] Green explains that the metaphorical use of the word "freedom" when it applies to any relation other than those which may obtain among men, is the source of a good deal of confusion in the articulation of a theory of freedom. He writes: "Reflecting on their inner life, i.e., their life as viewed from within, men applied to it the terms with which they are familiar as expressing their relations to each other. In virtue of that power of self-distinction and self-objectification, which he expresses whenever he says 'I,' a man can set over against himself his whole nature or any of its elements and apply, to the relation thus established in thought, the term borrowed from relations of outward life."[34]

What Green is saying is that, properly understood, the concept "freedom" applies only to the relations both social and political which tie men together. When the concept is used to denote other kinds of relations it is used in a metaphorical rather than a literal fashion. What are these other sorts of relations in which the concept "freedom" is used in a metaphorical sense? They are those which come about when any individual sets, in thought, a distinction between the I or ego and the various predicates which may denote other parts of his nature, the qualities or properties which may be predicated of him. The point is that a man does not act

[33] Green, *Principles of Political Obligation, op. cit.*, p. 93.

[34] *Ibid.*, p. 3.

upon himself or determine his own behavior in the same way in which one body in space may be acted upon by another body in space. Thus Green writes: "A man in willing is necessarily free since willing constitutes freedom."[35]

As A. J. M. Milne, in his *The Social Philosophy of English Idealism,* interprets Green:

> . . . while it makes sense to talk of a man being unfree in that he is interfered with and restrained by others in his attempts to execute his own decisions, it does not make sense to speak of him as not being free in making his decisions. A decision, by its nature, must be free. A man may make a decision while being exposed to strong inducements one way or the other, but he alone remains responsible for the decision. A decision, as distinct from the attempt to implement it, cannot be restrained or interfered with. Thus rational activity, the activity of self-determination, is necessarily free activity.[36]

The point seems to be that, because there cannot be any restriction in the kinds of mental decisions which a man may make, the concept of freedom does not apply at all, yet decisions are not made in a vacuum. They are made with certain objects in mind which are thought to provide satisfaction. With regard to those objects in terms of which the individual may be trying to develop a satisfying way of living and acting, he may indeed be unfree. He is unfree in the sense that the objects towards which he directs his desires may not be those which, when he actually fulfills them or acquires them, will provide the kind of satisfaction which he anticipates. No one can prevent a man from willing his own satisfaction and therefore no question of freedom may enter into such considerations, but a man may be prevented from reaching the sort of self-satisfaction which he desires if the objects which he desires are not worthy and therefore do not do the job which he expects of them.

The following passage quoted from Milne offers us a fairly concise statement of Green's conception of freedom:

> Rational activity is determined by decision. A decision is a choice between alternatives and every decision is free in the sense that on any given occasion a different choice might have been made from that which was made. Hence rational activity is free. But this is not the end of the matter. There are

---

[35] *Ibid.*, p. 3.

[36] *Ibid.*, p. 121.

different levels of rationality and there is a sense in which these may be regarded as different levels of freedom. The rational agent who moves from a lower to a higher level of rationality is moving from a less to a more adequate way of thinking about human conduct and its situation. He is expanding his horizon and learning to understand and take count of what previously had either been ignored or merely accepted uncomprehendingly. He is putting himself in a position to make better informed decisions than before and so to increase his control over himself and his conduct.

Thus in moving from the level of mere private satisfaction to that of morality, the rational agent is freeing himself from a way of thinking which confines him to the circle of his own private inclinations and for which the responsibilities of social life appear only as alien restraints. He is entering upon a way of thinking which will enable him to criticize, and, where necessary, discipline his private inclinations instead of being subject to them, and which will enable him to see the responsibilities of social living as responsibilities which belong to him. Equally, in moving from morality at the level of rule and custom to morally responsible conduct at the levels of spheres of rational activity, he is freeing himself from the limitations of an uncritical acceptance of established authority, and is entering a way of thinking in terms of which he can understand the nature and ground of rules and customs, and make them his servant rather than his master.[37]

Bernard Bosanquet extends this analysis but one step. And it is this extension which is to some degree reminiscent of the earlier Stoic conception of freedom. For it suggests that the tension which may exist between individuals and agencies of government and society which are at first perceived as restraints upon the individual's freedom are essentially restraints of a trivial order. The restraints of one's own ignorance and caprice of will and weakness of character, restraints which are the result of a less than adequate conception of self and situation are the most damning and irksome. For such restraints come only to those who are not capable of the kind of rational activity which transcends that of mere private self-satisfaction and which enables the individual to perceive the rules and customs of his society not as irksome restraints, but as the conditions for achieving, a personally satisfying way of life. The unreflective man is one who, insufficiently developed rationally, perceives established rules, laws, and customs as arbitrary, restricting, and coercive. He does so because he has not achieved a sufficiently high level

[37] A. J. M. Milne, *The Social Philosophy of English Idealism,* p. 122.

of rationality to understand what the reasons for these laws are and that obeying them provides the path for rational self-realization.

An analogy may help here. Barbarians or savages may perceive nature as hostile, capricious, and unpredictable. Nature is a mystery whose ultimate rationality is beyond human comprehension. Life and nature are in constant opposition and antagonism to each other. Man's bondage to nature is overcome when, gradually, he comes to an understanding of those laws of a physical universe which provide him with explanations for those events which have in the past been perceived as arbitrary and meaningless. To say then that man gains control over nature may well be to say that he comes to an understanding of the principles which govern the forces of nature and that such understanding erodes the antagonism and tension between himself and that nature. In short, his knowledge makes him free. The paradox then between freedom on the one hand and control on the other is overcome with the recognition that the demands which society places upon rational agents must be freely accepted because it is these obligations which membership in society entails.

6

The concept of freedom, II

THOUGH THE CONCEPT of negative freedom is the most closely identified with what might be characterized as the tradition of liberal utilitarianism, its roots run deep in the Western political tradition. Indeed, the historic disputes among the Greek philosophers concerned the question of human institutions, whether, that is, such institutions are arrangements which reflect the natural order of things and are therefore themselves natural or whether they are artifacts or conventions created by men for purposes of convenience. The line of argument with which we are here concerned derives from historical disputes as ancient as the writings of the pre-Socratics.

Among Plato's protagonists, the Sophists, the single most significant expositor of the Sophist doctrine was Protagoras. Protagoras, among his other achievements, is the author of a rather famous aphorism: "Man is the measure of all things; of all that is, that he is; of all that is not, that he is not." This aphorism is subject to a variety of interpretations. For the purposes of this argument, however, it means simply that the world is constructed, both with regard to its physical as well as social and moral elements, in accordance with the way in which men perceive it. Human institutions, moral principles, and criteria of behavior are all contingent upon human opinion. The later Sophists, men like Alcibiades and Critias, as well as Callicles and Thrasymachus were particularly concerned to extend Protagoras' conclusions so that they applied to legal systems as well. If knowledge is not public in the sense that it is not possible to apprehend an ultimate reality, and, moreover, if, as in the past, reality which had been attributed to a creation of the gods can now no longer be so attributed, then it follows that for enlightened men laws are the products of their activities and experiences, that is to say, laws are conventions, rather than proscriptions which follow from nature or from some primary moral postulate issued and sanctified by divine *imprimatur*.

Moreover, the Sophists' argument may be further extended, as it is by Callicles, who argues, in Plato's dialogue, the *Gorgias* the converse of Plato's position concerning what is to be considered conventional and what is to be considered natural. In his argument with Socrates, Callicles argues that all those virtues which Socrates takes to be natural, namely, in accordance with the natural propensities of well-adjusted and integrated individuals, such as promise keeping, fulfilling contracts, telling the truth, paying just debts, living honorably, and so forth, are really only conventions reflected in laws created by the weak, the cowardly, and the ineffectual. Consider, for example, Callicles' reply to Socrates' allegation that "it is wrong to do injustice":

> . . . you, who pretend to be engaged in the pursuit of truth, are appealing now to the popular and vulgar notions of right, which are not natural, but only conventional. Convention and nature are generally at variance with one another. . . . The reason . . . is that the makers of laws are the majority who are weak; and they make laws and distribute praises and censures with a view to themselves and to their own interests; and they terrify the stronger sort of man, and those who are able to get the better of them, in order that they may not get the better of them; and they say, that dishonesty is shameful and unjust; meaning, by the word injustice, the desire of a man to have more than his neighbors; for knowing their own inferiority, I suspect that they are too glad of equality. And therefore the endeavor to have more than the many, is conventionally said to be shameful and unjust, and is called injustice, whereas nature herself intimates that it is just for the better to have more than the worse, the more powerful than the weaker; and in many ways she shows, among men as among animals, and indeed among whole cities and races, that justice consists in the superior ruling over and having more than the inferior.[1]

It is only one step beyond this view to the formulation of the theory of psychological egoism. Callicles, in a succeeding passage, takes the step, commenting as he does, on the platonic ideal of moderation:

[1] *Gorgias*.

On the contrary, I plainly assert, that he who would truly live or to allow his desires to wax to the uttermost, and not to chastise them; but when they have grown to their greatest he should have courage and intelligence to minister to them and to satisfy all his longings. And this I affirm to be natural justice and nobility. To this however the many cannot obtain; and they blame the strong man because they are ashamed of their own weakness, which they desire to conceal, and hence they say intemperance is base. As I have remarked already, they enslave the nobler creatures, and being unable to satisfy their pleasures, they praise temperance and justice out of their own cowardice. For if a man had been originally the son of a king, or had a nature capable of acquiring an empire or a tyranny or sovereignty, what would be more truly base or evil than temperance—to a man like him, I say, who might *freely* be enjoying every good, and has no one to stand in his way, and yet has admitted custom and reason and the opinion of other men to be Lords over him? Must not he be in a miserable plight whom the reputation of justice and temperance hinders from giving more to his friends than to his enemies, even though he be a ruler in his city?[2]

The implication is clear. Were it not for laws, courts, and punishments, in short, were it not for government and the restraint exercised by its agencies, men would be truly free. And being free here means doing whatever one can do, restrained only by his own nature and its limitation and by those who are stronger, more courageous, and superior. This is precisely what Thrasymachus has in mind when he expresses the aphorism "justice means nothing else than what is to the interest of the stronger party."

Callicles and Thrasymachus are expressing a view of freedom which is certainly plausible and, in some respects, commonsensical. They argue simply that apart from social and political organization, men would act in accordance with the same principles which govern beasts in a jungle. Freedom, understood as the absence of restraint and coercion, is possible only in a state of nature.

Hobbes

This is precisely the view expressed by Thomas Hobbes: "Liberty, or Freedom, signifieth (properly) the absence of Opposition; (by Opposition I mean external Impediments of motion;) . . . a Free-Man is he

[2] *Ibid.*, p. 491–92. Italics mine.

that in those things, which by his strength and wit he is able to do, is not hindered to do what he has a will to."[3]

Hobbes, in this argument, is merely elaborating the implications of the views expressed by the Sophists. If it is indeed true that freedom is to be understood simply as the absence of coercion and repression by external agencies, then freedom must be possible only in a state of nature. But if a state of nature is perceived, in the manner of the Sophists, namely, a state of affairs where the powerful subjugate the weak, where the wealthy exploit the poor, where the strong intimidate the cowardly, then freedom is a quality possessed only by those who are powerful, courageous, and strong. Of course, this is at best an insecure kind of life. For, in practice, it means that everyone in this state of nature lives in perpetual fear with constant and reasonable expectations of being done in by his neighbor.

The kind of freedom which exists in the sort of nature described by Hobbes is at best a temporary and insecure freedom possessed by those who have for the moment triumphed over others, and is at worst, to use Hobbes' words, a life which is short, nasty, brutish, and solitary. It is the freedom of terrified, fearful, and insecure individuals who live lives no better than beasts. The creation of society and of the powerful political institution which Hobbes sees as the core of social organization, is a process which enables men to "escape from freedom."

Freedom, according to Hobbes, is freedom from insecurity. Insecurity comes about as a consequence of living under the conditions of a state of nature where the power of the law cannot be exercised to repress those individuals who seek only the satisfaction of their own interests. Indeed, when individuals become the sole criteria of what is best or desirable, whether in a state of nature or in civil society, the result is fear and insecurity. Thus Hobbes writes:

> . . . I observe the *diseases* of a commonwealth, that proceed from the poison of seditious doctrines, whereof one is, that every private man is judge of good and evil *actions*. . . . This is true in the condition of mere nature, where there are no civil laws; and also under civil government, in such cases as are not determined by the law. But otherwise, it is manifest, that the measure of good and evil actions, is the civil law; and the judge the legislator, who is always representative of the commonwealth.[4]

---

[3] *Leviathan,* Everyman's Library, p. 110; cf., p. 66.

[4] *Leviathan,* part 2, chap. 29.

Thus, it is only when men are not permitted the free exercise of their energies in accordance with the single principle which dominates that activity, namely the selfish pursuit of their own ends, is freedom truly possible. For it is this constraint, a constraint composed by law, which provides the sort of security where freedom of any sort is possible.

For Hobbes freedom means two things: first, the natural freedom of beasts in the jungle to do away with each other, and, secondly, true freedom which is the result of the constraints of law. How is this latter freedom possible? In what sense can it be said that a man is free only so far as he submits to the restraints imposed upon him by the laws of civil society? He is "free," according to Hobbes, from the insecurity and fear which are natural consequences of life in a state of nature. And since it is security which men want more than anything else, and indeed it is freedom which has impelled them to join in the creation of civil society, then, it appears, that what is involved here is the question of which sort of restraint men will choose as the more desirable. In other words, the choice is between the informal restraints in the state of nature where the strong exercise control over the weak, and where life is essentially an unpredictable and chaotic affair, and a second sort of restraint which comes about as a result of having a civil society and a legal system where the restraint is orderly and where one may reasonably have the sort of expectations appropriate to a stable community.

What then have we said about freedom? Simply this: if liberty is perceived as the absence of restraint, then liberty and authority are antithetical concepts and ultimately irreconcilable. Yet this sort of liberty is not true freedom at all. It is not because only the very strong and then only at certain moments in time are able to transcend the restraints which others may exercise upon them. This state of nature is of course no different than the natural state of affairs referred to by the Sophists. Yet it cannot be taken as satisfactory for the bulk of mankind. The solution to the problem then must be that all men may be free with regard to some forms of conduct if they are prepared to surrender what would be considered freedom in a state of nature with regard to other forms of conduct. What, then, are those areas of life which are not subject to control by others, whether "others" in this context means the organized agencies of government or simply the superior power of the stronger in a state of nature. All political theorists, with the possible exception of the Sophists, agree that the latter state of affairs, a state of nature, is an altogether inadequate circumstance for the preservation and sustenance of the kind of life men, for the most part, wish to lead. Thus, the question is narrowed to a consideration of the kinds of conduct which are subject to legislation and the kind of conduct which may be said to be free.

Hobbes' reply to this question is simply that men are free on all those matters concerning which the law is silent. What is it then that law protects us from? The law ought at least to protect one from the *arbitrary* constraints characteristic of life in a state of nature. Yet, the law is the creation of a sovereign and the sovereign is obliged to secure for us just those conditions of life which have eluded us in a state of nature and for which we have become organized into a civil society. Since we demand nothing more than security, we receive nothing more than security. Thus the duties of the ruler are contained, as he writes in one sentence: "The safety of the people is the supreme law." The kind of liberty which men secure in civil society is the liberty they bargain for. They are free from capricious and arbitrary rule and to that degree they have obtained security and safety.

Locke

The differences between Hobbes and Locke are legion. Yet, with regard to some crucial concepts in the political theory of each, they are remarkably similar. Let us consider the following passage from Locke's essay *Concerning the True, Original, Extent and End of Civil Government:*

> The natural liberty of man is to be free from any superior power on earth, and not to be under the will of legislative authority of man, but to have only the law of Nature for his rule. The liberty of man in society is to be under no other legislative power but that established by consent in the Commonwealth, nor under the dominion of any will, or restraint of any law, but what that legislative shall enact according to the trust put in it. Freedom, then, is not . . . "a liberty for everyone to do what he lists, to live as he pleases, and not to be tied by any laws"; but freedom of men under government is to have a standing rule to live by, common to every one of that society, and made by the legislative power erected in it. A liberty to follow my own will in all things where that rule prescribes not, not to be subject to the inconstant, uncertain, unknown, arbitrary will of another man, as freedom of nature is to be under no other restraint but the law of nature.

This freedom from absolute, arbitrary power is so necessary to, and closely joined with, a man's preservation, that he cannot part with it but by what forfeits his preservation and life together. For a man, not having the power of his own life, cannot by compact or his own consent enslave himself to anyone, nor put himself under the absolute arbitrary power of another to take away his life when he pleases. Nobody can give more power than he has himself, and he that cannot take away his own life cannot give another power over it.[5]

This critical passage in Locke suggests to us the significant strands of that part of his theory which help us to clarify what he has to say about the concept of freedom. The conventional paradox between liberty and law is not, according to Locke, a paradox at all. For just as man in a state of nature may be said to be free from the exercise of power by agencies of government which restrain or prevent him from doing as he wishes, he is nevertheless subject to the law of nature. What then are the terms of this law of nature? Locke says: "The state of Nature has a law of Nature to govern it, which obliges everyone, and reason, which is that law, teaches all mankind who will but consult it, that being all equal and independent, no one ought to harm another in his life, health, liberty or possessions; . . ."[6]

The state of nature and the law which governs it is a state of perfect freedom. What then are the restraints exercised upon men by the law of nature itself?

If the question is asked in a commonsensical sort of way, then it is apparent that there are certain "laws," as it were, which do in fact restrain us from doing what we wish to do but cannot do. For example, the world being what it is, restricts us from playing havoc with time. We cannot, at will, literally go back in time and relive an earlier part of our life. We cannot, by the same token, speed time up. We cannot find gold where there is no gold, or change the structure of the physical universe in any significant way. Now, under such cirumstances, it makes no sense to recommend that one ought to follow the law of nature, since one is clearly not free to do otherwise. It is not merely a question of the punishments to which one may be subject if he fails to obey the law of nature, for construed in this way, he cannot fail to obey the law.

---

[5] Locke, *Concerning the True, Original, Extent and End of Civil Government,* pp. 127–28.

[6] *Second Treatise,* chap. 2, paragraph 6.

Yet the examples which Locke gives us of the law of nature indicates clearly that what he has in mind is that there are certain kinds of conduct with regard to the social relations which obtain among men which are delineated by the law of nature. The reasons which he gives for believing that the law of nature obliges everyone to avoid harming another in his life, health, liberty or possessions, seems to be that men are the "workmanship of one omnipotent infinitely wise maker." What this amounts to is that men are God's property, the product of his workmanship, and are made to last according to God's pleasure and not one another's. Locke derives from this observation that subordination, destruction, exploitation, and similar sorts of conduct or conditions as they appear among men, are directly contrary to the intention and will of God himself. Thus he writes: "Every one as he is bound to preserve himself, and not to quit his station willfully, so by the like reason, when his own preservation comes not in competition, ought he as much as he can to preserve the rest of mankind, and not unless it be to do justice to an offender, take away or impair the life, or what tends to the preservation of the life, the liberty, health, limb, or goods of another."[7]

Liberty then, is a natural right. It is the product and result of the law of nature. Yet no one can be considered to be obliged to obey a law if that law has not been promulgated to him.[8] It must then, therefore, be reasonable to ask, how is the law of nature promulgated to us? And Locke's answer is that the law of nature is promulgated or made known by reason only; to discover the boundaries of permissible conduct we consult the dictates of reason. But reason speaks with many voices, and an appeal to reason as the final arbiter of right conduct is no more adequate in the context of Locke's arguments than it is in Aristotle's—or anyone else's, for that matter.

It ought to be apparent at this point that Locke's notion of "freedom" comes close to what most of us, in our ordinary discourse mean by order or stability. Natural freedom, for Locke, means living in accordance with the laws of nature. It means, fundamentally, that I may do what I choose to do only so far as my conduct is compatible with what is required of me by the laws of nature and that the conduct in question is compatible with the natural rights of others. I am free, it appears, when I act in accord-

---

[7] *Ibid.*

[8] *Ibid.*, paragraph 57.

ance with the requirements of the law. By the same token, civil liberty means no more than simply acting in accordance with the civil law which, as we have seen, must be, if it is to be valid at all, compatible with the natural law.

Yet this position is somewhat different from the one which Locke is ordinarily assumed to take. The usual interpretation of Locke's theory of freedom alleges that men are free to do as they wish provided they do not act in ways which abrogate or deter other persons from acting in accordance with their own natural rights. The conventional interpretation maintains that the role of law in Locke's civil society is similar to the role of a policeman who directs individual wills in such a way as to prevent them from clashing one with the other. Yet in certain other passages he says that the end of law is not to abolish or restrain, but to preserve and enlarge freedom. What can we make of this apparent inconsistency?

In attempting a clarification, let us recall what is involved in coming to know what the law of nature is. It is not to be discovered except through the exercise of reason. It is reason which leads us to acknowledge the essential rightness and natural character of what are called our "natural rights." If it is in accordance with our natural rights that we are able to discover what our duties and obligations are, then, it is reason which provides us with a vehicle for discovering what the boundaries of our permissible conduct may be. Freedom must be seen as the rational apprehension of those areas of life and conduct which are possible and permissible within the confines of law. And since the civil law, this is to say, the law of the land, is, under the best of conditions, a reflection of the law of nature itself, what we apprehend must be the essential rationality, rightness, fittingness of the law, whether it be civil or natural.

If we look to Locke not for theoretical articulation of the concept of freedom, but rather with a view to determining the application of these principles for the resolution of practical concrete conflicts which may occur within civil society, we find that a good deal of what he has to say is altogether inadequate. Let us consider for example the matter of toleration and freedom of conscience. Since the issue of religious persecution and religious tolerance is a subject about which Locke felt deeply we would have a right to expect that he would make an effort to analyze the problem which comes about when a conflict develops between the government and the society on the one hand, and the consciences of individuals on the other. In his *Letter Concerning Toleration,* he raises the question concerning the possible conflict which may arise between a magistrate when the latter enjoins anyone by his authority to perform or to cease from performing an action which appears unlawful to the conscience of a private person. In characteristic liberal fashion, Locke replies that ". . . if government be faithfully administered, and the counsels of the magistrate be indeed directed to the public good, this will seldom happen."[9]

This reply is of course no reply at all. For Locke is saying nothing more than if the law be faithfully administered, no conflict will arise, the evidence, it must be assumed, that the law is not faithfully administered is that a conflict has indeed arisen. To the question, "How do we resolve such conflicts when they do arise?" Locke gives us no answer. To the extent that he does give an answer in other contexts, he seems to have exercised no tolerance whatever for the conscientious objector. He writes that ". . . the private judgment of any person concerning a law enacted in political matters, for the public good, does not take away the obligation of that law, nor deserve a dispensation." On the basis of this argument, Locke's concern with civil liberties ceases when claims made on behalf of individual civil liberty conflicts with the law of the land. Locke's concept of revolution does not help us here. He is prepared to say that in cases where an irreconcilable conflict develops between the magistrate who believes that laws are for the public good, and the subjects who persist in believing the contrary, God alone can judge between them. He is not so generous, nor apparently is God permitted to enter into the matter, when the issue concerns not only subjects, that is to say, persons in the plural, but a given particular individual person. It may be true that subjects in the collective, have a right and indeed an obligation to revolt when they agree in their collectivity that the law in question is unnecessarily repressive and therefore contrary to natural law and right yet the single conscientious objector has no recourse and no escape.

The Levellers

Locke often writes as though the fundamental right which all men have is to their own property and it is with regard to the disposal thereof

---

[9] Locke, *Letter Concerning Toleration.*

that their freedom is least ambiguous. Yet, even more than Locke, the Levellers emphasize the concept of freedom with regard to property, such that the freedom, construed as proprietorship over one's own person, capacities, and properties, constitutes his human essence. The Levellers deserve our analysis in this discussion insofar as they extend this concept of property, conceived as a necessary condition for freedom and humanity, to include civil and religious liberty as well. For just as property is a prerequisite for freedom and humanity and must therefore be universal, so must civil and religious liberty be for all, for if they are not, they may be for no one. Thus Lilburne writes: ". . . for what is done to anyone, may be done to everyone: besides being all members of one body, that is, the English Commonwealth, one man should not suffer wrongly, but all should be sensible, and endeavor his preservation; otherwise they give way to an inlet of the sea of will and power, upon all their laws and liberties, which are the boundaries to keep out tyranny and oppression. . . ."[10]

The content of the Levellers' argument, its structure or its origin, is less important here than the fact that the claim on behalf of man's right to freedom is made not with regard to references to natural law or natural right, but rather with regard to the practical consequences which come about as a result of denying such laws (and other assurances of liberty). The argument for freedom is made essentially on utilitarian grounds. Civil liberties is a virtue and must be granted to everyone if certain consequences such as arbitrary arrest and imprisonment are to be avoided. (The curious thing about all this is that the Levellers themselves referred to the freedom of every man to own property and to dispose of it as he wishes as a natural right or a birthright, but yet at the same time, they offered nonnatural-right arguments in justifying civil liberties.)

This utilitarian ingredient is, at least on the face of it, incompatible with a natural law justification of liberty. The concept of negative freedom, it may now be seen, is compatible with two distinctly different arguments which may be offered on behalf of the justification of that concept. It is possible to understand negative freedom within the context of classical liberalism where men's freedom or liberty derives from the

---

[10] *The Just Defense of John Lilburne,* Haller and Davies, p. 455.

essential characteristics of their humanity and which therefore requires no further justification. It remains a theory of negative freedom in the sense that the state may in no way abrogate those liberties which men may claim to be derived from natural law. On the other hand, precisely the same liberties may be justified with reference to an entirely different sort of argument. The argument in question historically involves two parts, first, the rejection of natural rights theory as inadequate insofar as it is excessively dependent upon intuition and self-evidence, that is, dependent upon unscientific modes of reasoning and, second, the articulation of a theory of utility which reflects the drift of science and social thought away from rationalist arguments and solutions to empirical modes of reasoning.

Whatever the historical reasons may have been for the transition from natural rights justifications to utilitarian justifications for the concept of liberty, the logical transition is clearly contained within the arguments offered by the Levellers. For it is here in a subtle way that the justification for civil liberty is established at least partly on utilitarian grounds. It is not, however, until the 19th century that the utilitarian logic becames the foundation for the expression of a theory of negative freedom. And it is in this connection that we turn to a consideration of the theory of liberty as it is expressed by the most significant thinker, though perhaps not a representative one, of utilitarianism.

Mill

In the very first passage of Mill's celebrated essay *On Liberty,* he writes: "It is proper to state that I forego any advantage that could be derived to my argument from the idea of abstract right as a theme independent of utility."[11] In other words, whatever else Mill may be saying, what he says or argues will not, presumably under any circumstances be derivable from a theory of natural right or natural law. Ultimately the justification for all arguments, moral and political, will rest upon utility. "I regard utility as the ultimate appeal on all ethical questions; but it must be utility in the largest sense, grounded on the permanent interests of man as a progressive being."[12] What then are the

[11] Mill, *On Liberty,* 11a, p. 14.

[12] *Ibid.*

arguments which are to derive no advantage from the idea of abstract right?

Let us first consider the kind of arguments which Mill offers on behalf of the notion that there ought, in the well-ordered society, to exist the fullest liberty of professing and discussing, of thinking and believing, as a matter of ethical conviction, any doctrine, however immoral it may be considered. The liberty of thinking, speaking, and of writing must, of course, be justified not with reference to a man's natural right, but rather with reference to the private or general utility which is served by such liberty. We must then ask, "What are the consequences of suppressing an opinion?" Mill writes:

> The opinion which it is attempted to suppress by authority may possibly be true. Those who desire to suppress it, of course, deny its truth; but they are not infallible. They have no authority to decide the question for all mankind and to exclude every other person from the means of judging. To refuse a hearing to an opinion because they are sure that it is false is to assume that *their* certainty is the same as *absolute* certainty. All silencing of discussion is an assumption of infallibility. Its condemnation may be allowed to rest on this common argument, not the worst for being common.[13]

It will not do to argue, Mill says, that there is no necessary assumption of infallibility in forbidding the propagation of error on the grounds that it is always necessary if one is ever to act on one's opinions, or care for one's interests and duties, to ultimately come to a decision about what is to be done. Under such circumstances those objections which hinder the implementation of policy which is arrived at through extensive consideration may well warrant suppression. "If we were never to act on our opinions, because those opinions may be wrong, we should leave all our interests uncared for and all our duties unperformed."[14] Thus it may well be that it is: ". . . the duties of governments and of individuals, to form the truest opinions they can; to form them carefully and never impose them upon others unless they are quite sure of being right. But when they are sure (such reasoners may say), it is not conscientiousness but cowardice to shrink from acting on their opinions and allow doctrines which they honestly think dangerous to the welfare of mankind."[15]

---

[13] *Ibid.*, p. 2.
[14] *Ibid.*, p. 23.
[15] *Ibid.*

The essence of Mill's argument appears to be this: An individual or minority which expresses dissident political or social views (or indeed any dissenting views whatever) ought not only be free to do so but is in fact obliged to do so. For in those circumstances where the bulk of mankind has arrived at what they consider to be true opinions, the function of a dissident minority is to offer arguments which will force the majority to sharpen and temper its views. Criticism then becomes a device in terms of which the majority may assure itself that the views to which it subscribes have been tested and found satisfactory. A dissenting minority provides a service which is required for the rational articulation of those policies which the majority wishes to implement. The minority provides the conditions under which the viewpoint of the majority may be tested, confirmed and, perhaps, under certain circumstances, modified. However, if the majority is mistaken in its assumption that it knows what the truth is, the only circumstances under which it can arrive at some apprehension of its own errors and proceed to rectify its mistakes is through the simple device of entertaining hypothesis which are contrary to what it has considered to be the received truth. Indeed, if it may be said that there is among men the possibility of rational opinion and rational conduct it is because of a peculiar quality of the human mind. For, as Mill says, ". . . the source of everything respectable in man either as an intellectual or as a moral being," stems from the fact that men are capable of rectifying their mistakes by discussion and experience. Thus he writes:

There must be discussion to show how experiences are to be interpreted. Wrong opinions and practices gradually yield to facts and arguments; but facts and arguments, to produce any effect on the mind, must be brought before it. Very few facts are able to tell their own story, without comments to bring out their meaning. The whole strength and value, then, of human judgment depends on the one property, *that it can be set right when it is wrong, reliance can be placed on it only when the means of setting it right are kept constantly at hand.*[16]

Moreover, the only way in which man may develop the habit of correcting and completing the opinions which he holds is through the development of habits which allow him to entertain alternative hy-

[16] *Ibid.*, p. 25. Italics mine.

pothesis. Mill puts the point as follows: "The steady habit of correcting and completing his own opinion by collating it with those of others," offers the assurance that no light which can be thrown upon the subject from any quarter has been shut out.

The similarity between the kind of message and, ultimately, the kind of justification which Mill offers on behalf of his concept of liberty, and the scientific method, is apparent. Just as no one would want to deny that any scientist functioning in accordance with what is best in the scientific tradition must take into account the findings and hypotheses of others so must those who make decisions about the plausibility of a public policy, or those (presumably all of us) who must decide matters of morality, constantly check such decisions in the light of the findings of others. Thus it is only when others (as well as ourselves) have been sufficiently free to explore what the conventional orthodoxy may consider to be heresy and to offer such alleged heresies as alternative hypotheses, have the conditions for discovering the truth been established.

It is clear to us then that the ultimate justification for the kind of freedom with which Mill is preoccupied is its ultimate utility. Yet some questions may be raised concerning the precise nature of the concept of freedom as it occurs in Mill. In some respects, the concept of freedom and the concept of security are indistinguishable. Indeed, Bentham was well aware of this and writes: "As to this word *liberty,* it is a word, the import of which is of so loose a texture, that, in studied discourses on political subjects, I am not . . . very fond of employing it, or of seeing it employed: *security* is a word in which, in most cases, I find an advantageous substitute for it: *security* against misdeeds by individuals at large: *security* against misdeeds by public functionaries; *security* against misdeeds by foreign adversaries. . . ."[17]

Thus, the concept of freedom, understood at least in some respects as closely allied to the concept of security, and moreover justified ultimately in accordance with utilitarian arguments must in the final analysis be seen as a response to another issue. The issue in question has to do with the criteria with which Mill provides men in determining what is good and bad, what is correct and incorrect. In the essay *On Utilitarianism,* Mill argues that there are no such things as intrinsically valuable entities. A

---

[17] *Works,* Vol. VIII, p. 509–10.

value system and therefore a system of moral principles rests ultimately upon the indicated desires of men.

His famous proof for the principle of utility, a proof which is the source of a great deal of criticism by Mill's commentators goes as follows: The only proof that a thing is visible is that it is seen; the only proof that a thing is audible is that it is heard; the only proof that a thing is desirable is that it is desired. That men desire that which gives pleasure and happiness, is what is good. And there is no other criterion for the good. Yet our experience clearly indicates to us that the bulk of mankind given a choice between piggery and philosophy, between the herd and Socrates, choose for the most part piggery. Yet Mill insists that given an opportunity to adequately experience both of two possibilities, say the poetry of T. S. Eliot on the one hand, and Edgar Guest on the other, most men would choose the former over the latter. That they do not merely testifies to the fact that they have not had an *adequate experience* of each. Indeed, what makes T. S. Eliot the greater poet is that those who *know,* that is, those who, having sufficient education and insight and having experienced both, choose T. S. Eliot. This is in fact all that is required to make T. S. Eliot the greater poet.

Few philosophers have suffered at the hands of the critics to the degree that Mill has. And a good deal of what has passed for criticism of Mill revolves about his concept of liberty. It is often alleged that Mill's concept of liberty is strictly a negative one, and indeed, that is precisely the view which we have taken in this brief description of Mill's concept of liberty. Thus it is that Mill conceives of freedom as no more than the absence of restraint: man should be free or unrestricted in self-regarding acts; but in the case of acts which are harmful to others, society has the right to intervene. Critics have declared that this concept of liberty is too negative and too narrow, since liberty implies not merely an absence of restraint but an absence from unwise and illegal restraint. Advocates of a positive conception of freedom argue that the concept of liberty must include the idea of societies' positive role in influencing individual conduct. Liberty, these critics have alleged, is not abridged by the state, but is established and created by it, for the state, through its laws, must promote moral freedom, and moral freedom is to be secured even at the expense of personal or civil liberty. In promoting moral freedom, society is preventing crimes, not simply punishing them. Man's doing what he likes is license; his doing what he ought to do is liberty; and Mill and the Utilitarians should realize that the greatest happiness principle requires that individuals must often do things they may not outwardly wish to do.

This is a commonplace dispute. And indeed it may not be a dispute about Mill's doctrine at all, but rather a disagreement as to the proper use of the term "liberty." For Mill is certainly not saying that a situation of complete liberty is desirable. He writes that his problem is the nature and limits of legitimate intervention, and he must offer a principle to serve as a guide in judging which restraints are unwise and which laws are good; and this is precisely what he has in mind when he distinguishes between self-regarding and other-regarding actions.

While it is possible to object to Mill's using the word "liberty" to mean absence of restraint, it would be unreasonable to accuse him of advocating license. In fact, there are passages in the essay *On Liberty* in which Mill indicates ways that society can influence the individual and prevent crime, as, for example, compulsory education and under certain circumstances, restraining an individual who has repeatedly misused his liberty. Furthermore, Mill acknowledges certain positive duties which one owes to one's fellow men, as for example: "When a person, either by express promise or by conduct, has encouraged another to rely upon his continuing to act in a certain way–to build expectations and calculations, and stake part of his plan of life upon that supposition–a new series of moral obligations arise as on his part toward that person."[18]

Such views are not really inconsistent with the greatest happiness principle when taken in the context of Mill's conception of society as an aggregate of individuals.

Another formulation of Mill's definition of liberty which occurs in the last chapter of his essay is expressed positively rather than negatively and defines liberty as doing what one desires: "If either a public officer or anyone else saw a person attempting to cross a bridge which had been ascertained to be unsafe, and there were no time to warn him of his danger, they might seize him and turn him back, without any real infringement on his liberty; for liberty consists in doing what one desires, and he does not desire to fall into the river."[19]

---

[18] Mill, *On Liberty,* p. 126.

[19] *Ibid.,* p. 117.

Even in its positive form, this definition has not escaped criticism, and it has in fact been objected that the passage in question undermines the entire essay. For Mill assumes in the example of the bridge that it is possible to know with complete certainty that the bridge will not hold. Such absolute certainty is impossible, and therefore, Mill's statement contains the suggestion that society has a right to interfere even if the assumptions upon which it acts fall short of complete certainty. Moreover, one cannot escape the conjecture that Mill here must mean that society can determine the real needs and desires of the individual within it. We have only to say that the drunkard really wants happiness and not degradation, and we are presumably justified in prohibiting his drinking. Thus, Mill's definition, the last one cited, is similar to the doctrine of the real will theory, so far as a society may ensure conformity by claiming to fulfill the true desires of the individual whom it wishes to restrain. One commentator writes that if we accept this statement then we must also consider the following action justifiable: X wishes to succeed in business. Y knows that the particular business X has chosen will not succeed. Y may therefore forbid X to exercise his chosen trade.[20]

Of course Mill is aware of the problem of certainty and makes a serious effort of overcoming some of the problems implied by it. So there may be a temptation, such as the one suggested by the example of the bridge, to suppose that Mill sanctions interference even where absolute certainty about the outcome of a particular piece of conduct is less than complete.

> Nevertheless, when there is not a certainty, but only a danger of mischief, no one but the person himself can judge of the sufficiency of the motive which may prompt him to incur the risk; in this case, therefore (unless he is a child or is delirious, or in some state of excitement incompatible with the full use of the reflecting faculty), he ought, I conceive, to be only warned of the danger; not forcibly prevented from exposing himself to it.[21]

Thus, in cases where a person's actions are not certain but likely to oppose his desires, the person ought to be warned of the danger. Yet Mill is quite clear about the inappropriateness of restraint. Even in the bridge

---

[20] D. G. Ritchie, *The Principle of State Interference,* p. 86.
[21] Mill, *On Liberty,* p. 117.

example, the implication is that the public officer may seize the individual only because there has not been time enough to warn him.

Not only is it the case that society must not intervene without the certainty that the result of an action will be counter to the agent's desires, but it is also true that society may not restrain individuals under the guise of fulfilling their true desires. Although in *Utilitarianism* he does speak of happiness as the end of each man's desires, Mill asserts in several places in his essay that each individual *qua* individual has a different standard of happiness. It cannot be left open to society to establish or interpret what one really desires. In the last analysis, ". . . no one but the person himself can judge of the sufficiency of the motive which may prompt him to incur the risk." And on another occasion earlier in the essay he writes: "While with respect to his own feelings and circumstances, the most ordinary man or woman has means or knowledge immeasurably surpassing those that can be possessed by anyone else."[22]

Mill assumes that each individual is in a privileged position with respect to his desires: the individual has special access to the private workings of his mind and to the content of his passions which others cannot have and therefore, others cannot know his desires better than he. Moreover, beyond simply being in a position to adequately comprehend, each man for himself, what his own desires may be, he is, perhaps more importantly, in a position to judge what is best for himself more adequately than any other agency or person. Though we may all agree that a particular individual ought to forbear engaging in some piece of conduct because it would be better for him to do so, there are no circumstances under which he may be rightfully compelled to so forbear, even if it is clear to all of us that it will make him happier.

When Mill comes to a discussion of the problem of individuality he raises another issue which appears on the face of it to be incompatible with his concept of liberty as the absence of restraint. In this discussion he writes: ". . . it is desirable . . . that in things which do not primarily concern others, individuality should assert itself. Where, not the person's own character, but the traditions and customs of other people

---

[22] *Ibid.*, p. 93.

are the ruler of conduct, there is wanting one of the principal ingredients of human happiness, and quite the chief ingredient of individuals and social progress."[23]

It is in the context of this discussion that Mill appears to be offering a normative definition of liberty consisting of, what one critic has called, "acting in accordance with motives which assert and increase originality."[24] In the passage cited, Mill is making a direct attack on conformity. He has argued that unless individuality rather than custom is the basis of action, the agent cannot be happy; progress cannot be made. Critics are disturbed by the fact that while Mill is opposed to conformity on the one hand, he seems to be saying that conformists may nevertheless be people who are doing as they desire: "I do not mean that they [conformists] choose what is customary in preference to what suits their own inclination. It does not occur to them to have any inclination except for what is customary."[25] It would appear that when conformists do as they desire, then according to Mill's definition of liberty, they should be considered to be free. Yet, Mill refers to them as "those who do not desire liberty and would not avail themselves of it."[26] Can we say then that Mill's concept of freedom is not simply a matter of doing what one desires but is rather a question of acting in an original way? If this is indeed so, then Mill may be charged with imposing his own values on individual conduct and therefore stands as culpable as any other person or group which sets itself up as an arbiter of individual desires.

Nonetheless, there are a considerable number of statements in Mill's writings which lead us to believe that when Mill speaks of "desiring" he does so in a far more limited fashion than the critics have supposed. Perhaps what Mill is in fact saying is that liberty is doing what one desires where the expression "doing what one desires" is construed as meaning "doing what one chooses." For it seems clear that Mill uses the word "desire" in his definition of liberty in the active sense of rationally choosing between alternative courses of action, as opposed to the passive and unreflective sense of conforming to the dictates of custom.

---

[23] *Ibid.*, p. 68.

[24] J. P. Scanlan, "J. S. Mill and the Definition of Freedom," *Ethics*, Vol. 68 (April, 1958).

[25] Mill, *op. cit.*, p. 75.

[26] *Ibid.*, p. 78.

It is clear that Mill would censure the man who reflectively chooses to conform, yet there is a sense in which a man can prefer to act according to custom and yet be free. It may be necessary to make a further distinction between the man who conforms unreflectively and the man who conforms accidentally, where, that is, his chosen act happens to coincide with the customary ways. For example, consider a man who lives in a middle-class business oriented, suburban environment and who chooses to live in accordance with the values of that community. Is such a person in all cases a conformist? It may be that he has attempted various occupations and found that the conditions of life in such a community are best suited for the development of his character, that he would be happiest doing what everyone else does and valuing whatever everyone else values in that community and as a result is able by so conforming to both profit from, as well as contribute to, that community. Such a person has exercised his freedom to choose and his conformity to the established orthodoxy of the community in question is the result of calculation and reflection. What Mill objects to is the sort of person who never considers what he is most suited to, who unthinkingly conforms to the expectations of his *milieu.*

Another person with artistic inclinations living in the same bourgeois environment as in the case considered above, if he unthinkingly conforms and becomes bourgeois, will probably contribute nothing to his own happiness or to the community in question; whereas if he were to exercise his freedom to choose a different sort of life, say, the development of his art while living in a loft, he would be fulfilling himself, acting in accordance with what is required for the full development of his character and creativity. It is this latter sort of person to whom Mill refers as a conformist, as one who does not desire liberty. His antipathy to unreflective conformity is in no way inconsistent with his definition of liberty, since the person in question does not choose, does not subject himself to a wide variety of experiences, and for these reasons cannot be said to be doing what he desires.

Liberty, as a positive virtue then, consists in each man's having the right to experience many diverse aspects of life, to hear many conflicting opinions, and to have sufficient opportunity to consider these as alternative guides to action, so that he may exercise his preference for a way of life, a way of life which he thinks best suited to his individual character.

Among the principles to which Mill appears to be committed is the notion that individuality could be preserved only if each person was acknowledged to have possessed an inviolable area of liberty, namely, the area of self-regarding concern. Yet the distinction between acts which affect only the agent and acts which have social consequences does not help in determining exactly what kinds of consequences may be considered harmful to others. It is far from clear that the distinction between self-regarding and other-regarding is self-justified. In 1859, in the *The London Review,* there appeared an early criticism of Mill's essay *On Liberty* arguing that "no moral quality is limited in its action to the sphere of its possessor's own history and doings. . . . Society has an interest, over and above that of mere self-defense, in the conduct of every one of its members." James Stephen once remarked: "It is surely a simple matter of fact that every human creature is deeply interested not only in the conduct, but in the thoughts, feelings, and opinions of millions of persons who stand in no other assignable relation to him than that of being fellow creatures. . . . A man would no more be a man if he were alone in the world than a hand would be a hand without the rest of the body."[27] There are modern day variations of this sort of criticism: "It is quite impossible to distinguish between that part of a person's behavior which affects himself and that part which also affects others; and there is nothing to be gained by attempting to make distinction."[28]

In attempting to reply to some of the traditional and modern criticisms of Mill's distinction between self-regarding and other-regarding actions, we will follow rather closely the arguments presented by Professor Rees, who in an article "A Rereading of Mill on Liberty," argues that traditionally critics have not paid careful enough attention to the form of words used by Mill in statements concerning self- and other-regarding acts.[29] Although Mill in his first formulation of the principle uses the words "merely concerns" and "concerns others," in the statement in which he reviews the two maxims making up his doctrine, he uses the

[27] Sir James Stephen, *Liberty, Equality, Fraternity* (London: Smith, Elder & Co., 1873).

[28] R. P. Anschutz, *The Philosophy of John Stuart Mill* (Oxford: Clarendon Press, 1953).

[29] Rees, "A Rereading of Mill on Liberty," *Political Studies,* Vol. 8 (June, 1960), p. 119.

word "interests." While there are many variations on the first phrase, for example, "what only regards himself," "conduct which affects only himself," "things wherein the individual alone is concerned," there are also many passages in which the word "interest" is used. For example, "concern the interest of others," "affects the interest of others," "damage to the interests of others." It has been the fault of critics to have passed over these different modes of expression without giving a sufficient accounting of what Mill's meaning might have been.

Ideology and freedom

We have given a good deal of attention to sharpening the distinction between positive and negative freedom. Positive liberty, closely identified with holistic theories of the state, means simply that the state, or some agency of the state, recognizes a responsibility and obligation to do more than simply create the conditions under which men may lead certain kinds of lives, generally described as moral, but where the state itself participates actively in creating moral and, therefore, free persons. "Freedom" in this sense is to be understood as an internal, psychological, and moral phenomenon where the best in our character represses the worst and where, therefore, we are made free of those passions which act as bonds upon our development as human beings.

Negative freedom on the other hand has meant for us the drawing of boundaries within the general realm of human conduct and providing criteria which allow us to say that states may intervene in the conduct of human affairs only up to a point, and that beyond that point, whether it be in the area of natural rights, or in the area of what serves utility, the state has no jurisdiction or authority.

Of the various theories of freedom represented by these models, there is in each logical inadequacies and descriptive limitations. The holistic model creates problems for us in several different ways. First, the ordinary acceptance of the word "freedom," that is to say, the way in which we use that word in ordinary discourse, is certainly incompatible with the notion of being forced to be free. Saying that men can be free only within a moral universe where the choices which they make constitute a victory over defective character and enable them to pursue those activities which are thought to be compatible with the development of men's personalities and creative capabilities, is to ignore utterly the commonsensical meaning of the word "freedom."

Secondly, at least part of the notion of positive freedom is indistinguishable from the concept of self-control. It may well be, as the Stoics claimed, that I shall be free of pain when I have learned the habit to refuse to recognize certain stimuli as painful, stimuli, that is, which others who do not subscribe to my moral stoicism, recognize as painful. Yet the stoic imperative itself, in its very articulation, fails to pay obeisance to the way in which the word "pain" is used in ordinary discourse. For the imperative makes no sense, unless it is true that our ordinary inclination is to regard certain stimuli as painful, and thus the dictum is after all only an appeal to respond differently to those stimuli than the way in which most people generally respond. Perhaps another example will clarify what is at issue here. A masochist is one who derives certain pleasure from having inflicted upon him stimuli which are ordinarily thought to be painful by most persons. Though it is not incorrect to say that such a person derives pleasure from pain, it is perhaps more correct to say that the symptom of his illness is that he derives pleasure from what others consider to be pain. We treat him as the odd case simply because he does not respond in the way in which ordinary people respond and therefore does not use the language which describes our responses in the same fashion.

How is this analogous to the problem entailed by conception of positive freedom? When the holist uses the word "freedom," in the sense of positive freedom, he is not using the word in the way in which we ordinarily use the word. For he refers not to the absence of restraint exercised upon an individual by other individuals or by agencies of government, but rather as the product of a process of internalization which makes what would hitherto be counted as an external restraint, an internal antagonism overcome by the suppression of interests which are unmodified by social and political considerations. Thus it is that freedom and "morality" are used in ways which render them indistinguishable one from the other.

It is almost as though the theorist who subscribes to the concept of positive freedom has solved the problem of political theory, namely, the problem of the natural, external, and objective antagonism between individuals on the one hand and the agencies of state on the other, simply by treating the concept of freedom in such a way that the resolution of this antagonism is the product of the introjection of external imperatives. Thus, the antagonism dissolves through the acquiescence of the individual to the forces of authority. And the justification for this surrender, as it were, is simply that the authority of the state becomes the internalized moral authority of the individual. What one is freed from, is the debilitating effects of subscribing to a value system which may be incompatible with the demands made upon one by the state itself.

Conscious of the fact that if the state is described as having these characteristics, properties, and functions, then there appears to be no way in which the quality of authority may be evaluated by those subject to it, those who subscribe to the theory of positive freedom have qualified the theory in such a way as to conceive of the state as the embodiment of a certain conception of life. Thus, T. H. Green argues that even on holistic grounds individuals may be critical of existing institutions. And moreover, their freedom consists in being in a position where they have apprehended the essential rightness, the essential morality, of the state, criticizing the state only with regard to whether or not it embodies a sufficiently adequate conception of life. The goal thus achieved is that criticism takes place not from the point of view of an individual who conceives of himself as having certain rights which may be in opposition to demands made upon him by the state, but rather as an individual who has been freed from being tied to a mere consideration of his own desires and who may now offer criticisms of the body politic at the level of "morality." The major difficulty, of course, rests upon the dangers inherent in supposing that when the state represents or embodies an adequate conception of life, that there is in fact some one conception of life or other which may be adequate for all those living in that particular society. Such a conclusion clearly suggests the possibility of coercive imposition of patterns of life and behavior upon those who reject utterly, not simply the particular conception of life embodied in this or that state, but the very notion that any one conception of life can adequately take into account the vast differences of interest and aspiration which may exist among a variety of people.

Another difficulty encountered in the elaboration of the theory of positive freedom concerns the generous constructions possible in articulating that theory. Green, for example, says that perhaps the task of the state is the removal of obstacles which may stand in the way of the orderly and rational progress of men toward the realization of creative personalities. On the surface, this view appears to us as an attractive one, for so far as ignorance may be treated as a defect of character and therefore an obstacle to the development of one's character, to that degree the state has a responsibility for "removing that obstacle" by requiring a certain level of education for all those living within that society. By the same token, as Green says, alcohol may be prohibited since a man who uses alcohol makes himself a slave to what is base in his character and thus the state has a right to remove that obstacle by the prohibition of alcoholic beverages. Yet, nowhere does Green provide us with criteria enabling us to determine what will constitute a genuine obstacle and, as such, a description of the circumstances under which the state may not legitimately interfere in the lives of its citizens. Theoretically, no area of life would be secure from the intervention of states and their agencies so far as the state may declare a considerable area of conduct to constitute an obstacle to the development of its citizens and therefore it may conceive of the suppression of this vast area of conduct simply as the elimination of such obstacles.

It is important however to see that in a curious way the theory of positive freedom is a response to some misuses of the concept of freedom as it appears in the expression of the theory of negative freedom. The fact that the theory of positive freedom is closely connected with the concept of a moral good provides that theory with a moral foundation which makes it absurd to speak of freedom in cases where freedom does not contribute in some way to a moral purpose. A thinker like T. H. Green is appalled by the absence of a moral content in the theory of negative freedom. Consider for example the following instances where the word "freedom" is used in a way altogether compatible with the negative theory and incompatible with the positive freedom of liberty.

1. A baby who has *freed* himself from the confines of his crib, and is now *free* to plunge headfirst to the floor.
2. A pupil who has willfully absented himself from school, and is now *free* to pass his time in idleness.
3. A patient suffering from acute appendicitis who *frees* himself from the attention of surgeons and physicians.

4. An honest and competent official who is suddenly given permanent *freedom* from all responsible work by an irresponsible administration.
5. A corpse *free* from the cares of life.[30]

It is of course possible to multiply such instances, a picture gallery *free* of light; a deaf person *freed* from hearing aids; a child *free* to eat poisoned candy; a nonswimmer in deep water *free* from all contact with floating objects; a populous city *free* of oxygen; etc.

These examples are, of course, a caricature of the theory of negative freedom, yet, their uses in the language are perfectly compatible with the concept of liberty as the absence of restraint. And it is obvious to us once again, that for the most part, talk about political freedom is talk about a moral quality. In this respect, the theory of positive freedom emphasizes that freedom is a good and to be desired. Under this circumstance, we must recognize that the ordinary acceptance of the word "freedom" is far too broad and general to provide us with the criteria for how that word is to be meaningfully used in our political discourse.

The theory of negative freedom is in the final analysis predicated on the assumption that the moral character of individual persons is either formed prior to his incorporation into any political organization or the product of cultural forces which are essentially nonpolitical, or finally, the result of experimentation of the sort described by Mill. In each case, however, the theory does not give an account of the conditions necessary for political community as such. For political community depends upon the emergence of private interest for the sake of the welfare of the social whole. It must therefore assume that each individual, when left to his own devices, which is after all to say, when left to be free, will exercise sufficient reason, intelligence, and prudence in pursuing those goals which will enable him to fulfill his life best. For even Mill insisted that a necessary condition for liberty was the high degree of sophistication and the level of civilization achieved by the people in question.

Yet the history of the species if it demonstrates anything at all shows us that for the most part men do not know what their best interest is.

---

[30] John Somerville, "Toward a Consistent Definition of Freedom and Its Relation to Value," *Liberty, Nomos IV*, Carl J. Friedich (ed.) (New York: Atherton Press), p. 292.

And that even when they exhibit intelligence, forbearance and restraint, they nonetheless make tragic errors. One recalls in this connection the words of Paul Tillich: "If ever in history there was a time when human objectives supported by an infinite amount of good will heaped disaster upon disaster on mankind, it is the twentieth century."[31]

---

[31] Quoted by Michael Polanyi, "On the Modern Mind," *Encounter*, May, 1965, p. 12.

7

On social and political inquiry

THE POINT OF this chapter is to examine the various ingredients of a rather elaborate and continuing argument about the character of social science and the ways in which the social sciences have manifested characteristics and properties which are different from those of the physical sciences. Our purpose will be to ask simply whether or not it is the case that the nature of the subject matter which is the proper object of investigation in the social sciences requires, either on logical or on empirical grounds that certain central alterations be made in the methodology appropriate to the subject matter in question. Is there, in other words, a methodological difference between those disciplines which have sometimes been called the "historical and social inquiries," and the physical sciences.

Answers to this question have historically fallen into two groups: those which have alleged that the methodology, techniques, and instruments of analysis appropriate to discovering the nature of the physical world are the only techniques for arriving at objectively true statements, explanations, theories, and laws which, taken together constitute proper objects of knowledge. On the other hand, there are those who allege that human beings, their institutions, and the sorts of relations which obtain among them are clearly different in character, complexity, and structure and cannot be treated and understood through the application of methods which provide explanations of the way in which inanimate particles in motion behave. Those who subscribe to the latter orientation have taken the position that special cognitive procedures appropriate to the uniqueness of the subject matter in question are required in the social sciences. The distinction may very well be expressed in the terms in which it has been made historically by the late 19th century German sociological thinkers, among them, Richert, Dilthey, Windleband, Simmel, and Weber. This tradition has also been supported by the English thinker Robin Collingwood, and in Italy by Benedeto Croce.

The distinction in question rests upon the allegation that there are two distinctly different ways of doing things: inquiry may be nomothetic or idiographic. A nomothetic inquiry refers to one in which it is possible to formulate abstract general laws for indefinitely repeated processes. An idiographic inquiry is one which involves the understanding of unique and nonrecurring events. The school which subscribes to the view that the social sciences are disciplines which require for the most part idiographic kinds of explanation and which, in turn, rejects the argument that the methods and instruments of analysis appropriate to the physical sciences may be, without alteration, applied to the social sciences, is called, on some occasions, the "idealistic" school, and its views are identified with historicism. What are these views?

Historicism and the problem of objectivity

Some idealists have argued that generalization as a methodological procedure in the natural sciences is necessarily useless in the social sciences and that experimental methods in the former cannot be the model for the latter.

The problem, as formulated, is not: "Can there be generalization and experiments in the social sciences?" to which one could reply, "There can be because there are," but the question concerns the usefulness of such general statements and experiments; not, that is to say, their pragmatic utility, but the logical possibility of their utility. Hence, the allegation that such generalizations are necessarily useless may be refuted by either giving one case in which it is not contradictory to utilize general statements in the social sciences, or, to describe those conditions under which it would not be contradictory, or, to show that the reasons which the idealist brings to support his contention are not sufficient to demonstrate the logical impossibility of utilizing general statements and experiments.

The idealist supports his views concerning generalizations by noting the following characteristics which relate to societal facts, but which do not, presumably relate to facts about the physical world, or to the way in which they are to be gathered: their less-repeatable character; their less-direct observability; their greater variability and lesser conformity; and the greater difficulty in isolating one factor at a time.

If it is granted, then, that all these reasons which the historicist gives for his rejection of the possibility of general statements or experiments in the social sciences are sufficient, the question may nevertheless be asked: "Can we demonstrate one instance in which the historicist argument lacks sufficient logical force to maintain the point?"

If the historicist is concerned with demonstrating the difference between physics on the one hand, and social science on the other, in terms of the limited and narrow scope of possible general statements of social science and the universal character of such statements in physics, then the difference is expressed in quantitative rather than qualitative terms. One may be prepared to admit that the general statements in the social sciences which have in the past been, and are now being, offered may indeed be limited and narrow, without granting the historicist's point that they are altogether inappropriate. Indeed, within the physical sciences themselves, the generality of laws varies from one discipline to another. The historicist's claim merely indicates that the degree of success achieved in the social sciences does not approach that of physics. Yet one can also claim that the degree of generality approached in a physical science like geology is not comparable to that of physics. Merely indicating the limited or narrow scope of the general statements expressed in the discipline does not serve as a criterion for distinguishing between physical and social science.

The historicist may rest his argument on the view that societal or historical laws are necessarily limited to the cultural environment in which these are formulated. Unfortunately, the point is unconvincing since it is equally possible to demonstrate the role of the physical environment on the formulation of laws and physics. Yet the point in question goes somewhat more deeply than this. The tradition of thought representing this position, sometimes called the "sociology of knowledge," argues that all thought in a given era is determined, at least in part by the times and circumstances which comprise the cultural *ambience* of the theorists in question. In short, it is argued, theories are essentially ideologies.

We have discussed this concept of the sociology of knowledge in connection with Marx. The view consists of a justification for the relativity of values in the sense that values and ideas are the product of certain times and cultures, and must therefore be judged within the context of the origin of the idea itself. Under these circumstances it is thought that generalizations and experiments are impossible.

There are several difficulties with the view expressed by those who subscribe to the doctrines implicit in the sociology of knowledge. The first and most obvious is that the very articulation of the principles of the sociology of knowledge, the chief ingredient of that theory being cultural relativism, is that it acts against the sociology of knowledge itself. In other words, if it is true that every idea must be judged in accordance with the cultural and social environment in which it is produced, then that statement itself must be examined as a product of a given environment and the credence possible to produce for it must be limited to the circumstances under which it is expressed. Secondly, this historicist argument rests upon a confusion between two different sorts of questions which may be asked about any theory or idea or concept. It is possible to ask, on the one hand, questions about the truth or falsity of a theory, such that these questions are entirely independent of questions about its origins. There is after all in logic an elementary principle known as the genetic fallacy. This fallacy applies to the confusion between questions about origin, and questions about truth. It is easy to see how this confusion may work in a very concrete sort of situation.

Consider, for example, a position one takes with regard to the overall benefits which may be derived from federal support to education. A protagonist may reply that the position taken is a result of self-interest, self-seeking, or simply perhaps that it is uncritically adopted as a result of the pressures of cultural orthodoxy. The protagonist may suppose that such arguments are sufficient to explain the reasons why one takes the position which he does. And, of course, in this respect, the protagonist may be correct. Yet, what he has failed to do is to examine the logical validity or empirical adequacy of the arguments offered on behalf of federal aid to education. In short, one has not offered an adequate explanation or analysis of the truth value of a statement when one has offered nothing more than an explanation of what one's motives may have been for adopting the proposition, or a policy implied by a set of propositions.

It ought also to be kept in mind that there are no good reasons why general statements in the social sciences cannot be formulated with respect to all people at all times (a suggestion the historicist rejects). It may be true that such formulations would be excessively general and thus perhaps trivial, but not necessarily.

Moreover, if the historicist argues that universal laws in the social sciences are impossible because these can never be validated beyond the period or periods in which they have been observed to hold, then the same can be said of physics as well, since it can never be known that a law in physics will hold universally and for all time—and it is possible to suggest under what conditions a given law would not hold.

Granting the difficulties in drawing a sharp parallel between methodologies of the physical sciences on the one hand, and social sciences on the other, two points can be made: There are no qualitative differences in the two procedures, but merely a difference in the complexity involved in the one as compared with the other and, secondly, the best the historicist can do is to point to these differences.

Consider an example offered by Professor M. Cohen, in his *Reason in the Social Sciences:* "A man says to a woman, 'My Dear.' Physical stimulus is here a very definite set of sound waves, and we have reason to believe that the physical effects of these waves is always determinate. But what the lady will in all cases say or do in response depends upon so many factors that only an astonishing complacency about our limited knowledge of human affairs would prompt a confident answer."[1] The point, of course, that Cohen is making is that if social phenomena depend upon more factors than we can readily manipulate, even the doctrine of universal determinism will not guarantee an attainable expression of laws governing the specific phenomena of social life.

Yet if we examine the example which he offers to substantiate this last

---

[1] M. Cohen, *Reason in the Social Sciences,* p. 668.

allegation, one may reply: "Perhaps not a confident answer." The best the historicist can do is to argue that there is no guarantee in the limited time open to us there must be a complete repetition of social patterns. But, of course, the physicist has no guarantee either.

We turn now to a second major historicist principle: the notion that prediction in the social sciences is very difficult or impossible because of what has been called the "Oedipus effect," that is, that the prediction influences the predicted event, and hence objectivity in the social science is impossible since the social scientist would recognize that predictions have a social efficacy over and above their truth value. This is the view which leads to Mannheimian thesis that sociological doctrine and schools can be explained by referring to their connection with the predilections and interests prevailing in a particular historical period.

Without repeating our analysis of this view, it may nonetheless be possible to suggest an alternative explanation. The difference between prediction and explanation is of a pragmatic character. . . . Whatever can be said concerning the logical characteristics of explanation or prediction will be applicable to either. If, then, what can be said of the logic of explanation can also be said of the logic of prediction, the denial of the possibility of prediction in the social sciences by the historicist entails a denial of the possibility of explanation. Of course, in arguing this way one is open to the charge of question begging, since the historicist could argue that if *explanation* is taken as having the following characteristics (an explanandum, i.e. a description of the empirical phenomenon to be explained, and an explanans, i.e. initial conditions and general laws), then explanation is *in fact* impossible, since for the historicist general laws of sort required are unacceptable. This historicistic objection can, I think, be countered by (1) showing that every explanation either tacitly or explicitly assumes general laws of one sort or another (certain behavioral maxims, for example) or (2) that without explanations of one sort or another, it is impossible to go beyond a mere description of the subject matter.

Another argument concerning the historicistic notion of *relativism* warrants a brief remark. The historicist argues that there can be no criterion of truth in historical, sociological, or political investigations since the biases and prejudices which are the result of the enculturation of the social scientist renders all such investigations relative. There are two ways, at least, which point up the difficulties with this rather common view: First, there is a form of naïve relativism which comes about because one fails to distinguish between the psychology of historical interpretation and the logic of historical and sociological interpretation. That is, between history or politics as *thought,* and history or politics as *knowledge*. In the case of the former, it is no doubt true that values, prejudices, biases, etc., influence the historical and sociological thought of the investigator, but it does not follow that the proposition he asserts cannot be shown to be true or false and hence objective. Relativism results from a failure to distinguish between the two. Secondly, it would appear that the charge of bias must itself always be made from a point of view which assumes that objectivity is at least a theoretical possibility. It is an empirical fact that we distinguish more and less biased political and historical accounts, and that we judge the less-biased accounts to be more adequate than the more biased. To make such judgments requires certain standards of objectivity. The very formulation of bias as the characterization of the limitations of social science is self-refuting. To whatever degree historicist principles require the denial of the possibility of establishing standards in terms of which propositions in the social sciences may be judged and their claims to objectivity in offering descriptions and explanations of social events confirmed, to that degree the historicist is alleging a false proposition.

Let us consider with regard to the aforegoing point an example. Suppose we are dealing with an argument like the following: a Southern sociologist offers an account of what he describes as the *War between the States* in which he argues that slavery is morally justified because of the natural inferiority of black people and the consequent natural superiority of whites. Does the historicist mean to claim that the best we can do in offering a judgment of a description of this sort or of an analysis of historical events which rely upon assumptions of this sort, is to shrug our shoulders and say that it is clear that his judgment is the result of his having been brought up in this particular community, in a particular culture, and a particular time, etc. and, simply to acknowledge the fact that it is perfectly natural that he should have reached a conclusion of this sort? It is clear that we, as well as the historicist, would want to go further and to say that there may be no disputing about matters of taste, there is considerable area for disputing matters of belief which rest upon what is thought to be a fact. The investigator who makes the allegations considered in the example above may be judged to be saying, or at least assuming, something to be true which is known objectively to be, on other grounds, false. The history which he writes of the Civil War will be clearly inferior to one written by an investigator whose beliefs, and therefore whose judgments, are based on factual grounds and who can offer superior reasons for the position which he takes. There is a wide difference, in other words, between offering a judgment based upon questions of taste, and offering a judgment based upon a belief which must be secured by the accumulation of convincing factual evidence and data.

In passing, consider a similar kind of argument in which it is sometimes suggested that the very selection of what will count as a proper object of inquiry is itself biased by the value system of the culture in which the investigator lives. It is a commonplace that historians are not particularly interested in 17th century Greek literature, but are rather interested in the literature of the Golden Age. No one, except perhaps Ph.D. candidates, evinces any special interest in the political life of the people of Sardinia, though many, many volumes have been written concerning the events of the French Revolution. In other words, what is of interest to an investigator is at least partly determined by the needs and values of his culture and of his age. And, it is alleged that the role of the value system which plays a large part in consideration of what will constitute a legitimate problem in the social sciences plays no role, or at least not a comparable one, in what will be considered to be an important problem in the physical sciences.

Here again, we are offered an argument about the motive which may impel men to find some problems interesting and others not. Yet, it ought to be pointed out, that one does not ordinarily take into account the motives of the physical scientist in evaluating the conclusions which he reaches as a result of his exercises in a laboratory. Whatever his motives may be for his decision to study cancer cells, for example, they do not in any way affect the legitimacy or illegitimacy of the kind of conclusions which he reaches.

A completely fair account of the matter, however, must after all take into perspective that the investigator may himself face a problem when he seeks to avoid the inclusion of his own social interests and points of view and the work which he does as a social scientist. Consider the following, well-reasoned passage, from Quentin Gibson:

> Whether in the study or in the market place, no one lives in a social vacuum, and no one can afford to ignore the adverse influences on his beliefs. This is why it may be said that the true remedy is rather to make one's self conscious of these influences. To take seriously the investigation of the origin of social theories has value precisely because it helps people to do this. To show that one's theories are socially conditioned does not of course in itself stop those theories from being socially conditioned. But it may help to alter them, for the simple reason that neither prejudice nor bias nor the influence of custom survive detection. The value of this remedy should not be overestimated. For it does not help to overcome distortions which are due simply to the limitation of one's social situation. And even in the case of the other influences, though it is true that these do not survive detection, we must remember that they are often extremely difficult to detect. For these reasons it may well be necessary to fall back on a remedy of a different kind, namely, controversy. If all who had the same evidence at their disposal took perfect account of it, all would arrive at the same conclusions and there would be no disputes between them. But this, as we know, does not happen, and one of the reasons for this is that different people are subject to the influence of different motives, customs and situations. The best way to eliminate these influences, it may be suggested, is to bring the holders of the different theories together and insure that they are able to engage in open criticism of one another without fear of consequences. Left to ourselves we are an easy prey to influences adverse to objectivity. We do not easily become aware of our own bias, our own unreflective presuppositions, or the limitations of our own point of view—we need to have them pointed out to us by others. Ensuring that social inquiry is a competitive collective enterprise is thus the best guarantee of such objectivity as is within our reach.[2]

The prescription offered by Gibson to the social scientist, that it is incumbent upon him to make an effort to become aware of the kinds of prejudices and cultural and environmental distortions which may find their way into his work, holds as well for the physical scientist. In both cases, the scientist is in effect acknowledging that there exists universal and objective criteria, principally methodological in nature, to which his empirical conclusion must be made subject.

---

[2] Quentin Gibson, *The Logic of Social Inquiry* (London: Routledge & Kegan, Paul), p. 87. See Also Karl Popper, *The Open Society and Its Enemies,* Vol. 2 (Routledge, 1945), chap. 23, pp. 206–211.

We shall return to the problem of values and indeed the entire issue of morality and politics, in a succeeding discussion. Meanwhile, let us turn to another principle of historicism which requires extensive examination.

Historicism and the problem of explanation

Historicist and idealist thinkers subscribe to the view that special cognitive procedures must be invoked in the social sciences in order to understand the behavior of human beings. What, precisely, do persons who have argued in this way have in mind? Let us turn first to an examination of some of the assumptions underlying this view.

Suppose one were to argue that the material of social, political, and historical knowledge is human experience; only human occurrences are historical in the sense that psychological, or human experiences are historical. Historical accounts are concrete descriptions and explanations of nothing but human feelings, thoughts, and acts of will. The only external events which appear in the field of history appear as they are reflected in the inner experiences of the individuals or groups who participate in them. "All outer occurrences, political and social, economic and religious, legal and technical, would be neither interesting or intelligible to us if they did not result from or give rise to psychical reactions."[3] The external events in man's life are only bridges between the impulses and feelings between men. How does one go about acquiring such psychological or psychical knowledge? The historian must gain the material which his mind is to form into an historical narrative by virtue of an awareness of the physical data of others (a transsubjective awareness). This awareness is brought about by a combination of sympathetic understanding and a direct feeling of transsubjectivity: "He who has never loved will never understand the lover, a choleric temperament will never understand a phlegmatic one . . . and conversely, we will more readily understand the movements, expressions and actions of others the more often we ourselves have experiences whose affections for which these are the symbols."[4]

Thus, on the basis of our own experiences we apprehend the elements

---

[3] George Simmel, *The Problems of the Philosophy of History* (1892), 1907.
[4] *Ibid.*

in the psychic life of others. The social scientist must also see how these elements of the psychic life of others are fitted together into a whole which is the true personality of the subject. This synthesis leads to a direct feeling of transsubjectivity which rests on the typical nature of the sympathetic identification.

The material of history is the apprehension of the psychical experience in its concreteness and its individuality. In short, Simmel's argument is that no historical work is able to reproduce actual experience without radically transforming it. Such a transformation proceeds according to a priori categories, and that these categories provide a guarantee that the knowledge that results from their employment is not limited by the personality and period of the historian. This guarantee is expressed in the form of a direct *feeling* of transsubjectivity. The feeling is a product of the category, and is, at the same time, the test by means of which the historian or social scientist measures subjectivity.

A similar view is expressed by Wilhelm Dilthey (1833–1911) who also establishes the possibility of historical objectivity on the presence of spiritual forms in history. The purpose of the historical scientist is to understand life in terms of itself. Life cannot be brought before the judgment seat of reason. The fundamental reality of life is immediately experienced by us. This immediate experience gives us our only direct contact with reality. Moreover, immediate experience gives the *whole* of reality since reality is a continuum. No portion of immediate experience can be grasped or reproduced in isolation. Memory *selects* according to meaningfulness and it is through this meaningfulness that portions of immediate experience can be grasped as a whole. But what is meaningful? Dilthey replies that it is those portions of experience which *relate* to one's own condition, that is, to one's own desires, goals, will, etc., which constitutes the conditions of meaning. Thus, it is that our primary knowledge of reality is related to our values, and value is subjectively conceived.

The meaning of *Verstehen* is to enable us to grasp an inner event through those signs which come from the outside, that is to say, those signs which are strictly behavioral. These are the signs which constitute the materials of social inquiry. We *reexperience* the experiences of historical figures on the basis of an analogy. The analogy is based on the relationship between the way in which we behave and the thoughts which go on in our minds, on the one hand, and the kind of behavior we observe with regard to historical figures, and what we assume to be what goes on in their minds, that is to say, in the minds of others. Propositions asserted about the psychical states of others is the result of an inference on the basis of the behavior in which we observe them to be engaged. Yet, it must be seen, that since *erlebnis* and *verstehen* are both related to the values we now attach to symbolic or external behavior and since these are themselves relative, Dilthey has hardly escaped from the dilemma of the relativist.

It would be a mistake to suppose that the concept of *Verstehn* is somehow an exceptional one and the result merely of the characteristic excesses and pretentions of German metaphysicians. Consider for example the following passages from some contemporary sociological thinkers: "We can understand the behavior of human beings by being able to share their 'state of mind.' This ability to share other people's minds is a special *knowledge*. Statistical knowledge without 'empathetic' knowledge is superficial and unintelligent."[5]

Again: "Vicarious experience enables the student of human behavior to gain a specific kind of information which the natural experimenter . . . ignores altogether."[6]

P. Sorokin writes that: ". . . the social sciences must employ the *logico-meaningful* method which enables us to perceive connections which are much more intimately comprehensible, more readily perceived, than are causal functional unities."[7]

Finally, MacIver speaks of a *special method* which must be used whenever we study causal causation. He calls this process *"imagination reconstruction."*[8]

It is Abel's intention to describe the character of the method of *Verstehen*. He writes that: ". . . it is surprising to find that, while many social scientists have eloquently discoursed on the existence of a special

[5] H. E. Cooley, *Sociological Theory and Social Research* (New York: Scribner's, 1932), p. 290.

[6] F. Znaniecki, *The Method of Sociology* (New York: Farrar & Rinehart, 1934), p. 167.

[7] Sorokin, *Social and Cultural Dynamics* (New York: American Book Co., 1937), p. 26.

[8] MacIver, *Social Causation* (Boston: Ginn & Co., 1942), p. 263.

method in the study of human behavior, none has taken the trouble to describe the nature of this method."[9]

Let us consider for our analysis one of Abel's illustrations of the operation of *Verstehen*. He writes: "Last April 15th a freezing spell suddenly set in, causing a temperature drop from 60 to 34 degrees. I saw my neighbor arise from his desk by the window, walk to the woodshed, pick up an ax, and chop some wood. I then observed him carrying the wood into the house and placing it in the fireplace. After he had lighted the wood, he sat down at his desk and resumed his daily task of writing."[10]

It is possible, argues Abel, that his neighbor, who, feeling chilly, builds a fire to get warm. This conclusion is warranted by the observer's ability to recognize a relative connection between the stimulus "drop in temperature" and the response "making a fire." One may then claim that he not only "understands" the behavior of his neighbor, but that he is certain of it "provided I note carefully to what this certainty refers." One cannot be certain that this is the correct or true explanation of his conduct, argues Abel, but one can be certain that his interpretation *could* be correct.

But to observe a relevant connection between the stimulus and a response involves a process of internalization. The arbitrary procedure employed to internalize the stimulus consists of imagining what emotions may have been aroused by the impact of a given situation or event. We then generally *infer* the motive of an act from a known or observed modification it produces. We find then, continues Abel, "that in all its essential features the operation of *Verstehen* is based on the application of personal experience to observe behavior. We 'understand' an observed or assumed connection if we were able to parallel either one, with something we know through self-observation does happen."[11]

To demonstrate the logic of the process involved, Abel quotes the following passage from the psychiatrist Franz Alexander:

---

[9] Abel, "The Operation Called *Verstehen*," from Feigle and Brodbeck (eds.), *Readings in the Philosophy of Science* (New York: Appleton-Century-Crofts, 1953), p. 678.

[10] *Ibid.*, p. 679.

[11] *Ibid.*, p. 684.

Our understanding of psychological connections is based on the tacit recognition of certain causal relationships which we know from everyday experience and the validity of which we accept as self-evident. We understand anger and aggressive behavior as an action to an attack; fear and guilt as results of aggressiveness; envy as an outgrowth of the feeling of weakness and inadequacy. Such self-evident connections as "I hate him because he attacks me" I should call emotive emotional syllogisms. The feeling of the self-evident validity of these emotional connections is derived from daily introspective experience as we witness the emotional sequence in ourselves. . . . Just as the logic of intellectual thinking is based on repeated and accumulated experiences of relations in the external world, the logic of emotions is based on the accumulated experiences of our own emotional reactions.[12]

To analyze those arguments on behalf of the theory of *Verstehen,* let us consider a counterargument of this theory which is in fact a counterargument generalizable against all efforts at establishing a bifurcation between behavior on the one hand and mind on the other.

A considerable literature has appeared during the past three decades principally in philosophical journals, and primarily through the good offices of Professors John Wisdom, John Austin, and Gilbert Ryle, concerning the problem of other minds. Mr. Wisdom takes the problem to be brought on by such questions as "How do we know that another man is angry?" or "How can we know the thoughts, feelings, sensations, emotions, etc., of another person?" The question, we shall ask, is analogously, "How do we know that our neighbor builds a fire in his hearth because he is chilly?" Consider the following discussion which may cast some light on our problem. I assert that I see a red patch. I point in a given direction, you look, and report seeing a red patch. We both speak the same language, have normal eyesight, have the same object as our referent, and assert the same word. Are we both having the same sensation? A barbarous question, one may reply. Indeed, it remains an open question as to whether such inquiry can be said to be meaningful. Consider another bizarre situation. I see my friend Sam. Sam is grimacing, limping on one foot, leaving a trail of blood, moaning, and passing out at my feet. I revive him, and ask, "Are you in pain?" He replies affirmatively and I sympathize. But what do *I know* when I know that

---

[12] Franz Alexander, "The Logic of Emotions and Its Dynamic Background," *International Journal of Psychoanalysis,* Vol. 16 (October, 1935), p. 399. Quoted in Feigle and Brodbeck, *op. cit.,* p. 684.

Sam is in pain? Do I myself feel pain? Do I introspect my friend's pain? Hardly. Granting that I am not one of those fortunate individuals who had never experienced pain, do I remember what pain was like when I experienced it and hence am now capable of "understanding" what another is experiencing? The latter sounds more reasonable, but no less improbable. While my friend lies at my feet I do not conjure up memories of past pains. Is the knowledge that I have of Sam's pain any different than the knowledge that I have of his spilled blood, his moans, and his grimaces? Is it necessary to postulate a new cognitive category, a new way of getting to know, to account for my knowledge of Sam's pain? Do words which are ordinarily used to indicate psychical states, like "pain," have a privileged status? Probably not. My evidence for believing that Sam is in pain is, at least partly, that he says that he is in pain. The point, I think, is clear. The way in which I know that another is in pain is logically the way in which I know that he is bleeding or moaning. I see the blood and I hear him moan and say that he is in pain.

To return now to Professor Abel's neighbor, it may be true, that if I were a pre-Promethian man, I would be quite confused by my neighbor's gyrations. My knowledge of another's actions would depend, in part, upon my previous experience. I see the temperature gauge drop. I see the neighbor leave his home, gather wood, return to build a fire in his fireplace. Of course, many things are possible; that for example he is trying to collect fire insurance and is intentionally committing an illegal incendiary act. But granting that Abel's neighbor is innocent of such trivialities, it is at least possible that the man is chilly and seeks warmth. Of course, it would also be necessary to grant that I have not only acted as Abel's neighbor is acting, but that I have neither fire insurance nor perhaps a fire-God fixation, and that I too have on occasion built fires in my fireplace to keep warm. I could then infer that the observable actions on the part of the neighbor is a causal sequence, the stimulus to which is the "falling thermometer" and the response "building a fire." The inference would be justified once I internalized the stimulus and response by categorizing the given situation, in this case, causal sequence, and evoking a personal experience which fits into that category. Abel is quite aware of all that must be granted, and hence he asserts the following: "I am certain that my interpretation could be correct." Secondly, "we can recognize that the connection asserted by the generalization is relevant; that is, we 'understand it,' and so consider it *possible.*" And thirdly, "The arbitrary procedure we employ to internalize a stimulus consists of imagining what emotions *may* be aroused by the impact of a given situation."[13]

Yet the point is again clear. Like Sam's blood, I have the overt behavioral manifestations of Abel's neighbor as objects of knowledge and nothing more. But the neighbor performs actions *p* and *q* and that I have, at some time past, also acted in a way very much like my neighbor is now acting does not permit me to make any inference regarding his psychical state. Nor, if I were to make the inference, would it be possible for me to hold that it is one which yields knowledge. To assert that "I am or can be certain that my interpretation could be correct" seems to me to be unsatisfactory, since it is possible even in the simple-minded illustration about Abel's neighbor to postulate *ad hoc* innumerable interpretations, any one of which *could* be correct, but the one which is in fact correct, could never be known with the certainty which I may know the overt actions he performs.

August Comte, who is said to be the first to establish what may be termed the postulate of *Verstehen,* asserted that no sociological demonstration is complete until the conclusions of historical and statistical analysis are in harmony with the laws of nature. A. J. Ayer in his *Language, Truth and Logic,* says essentially the same thing with respect to all methodologies, the methodology of the physical sciences as well. What then render social science in need of further, perhaps more rigid and more demanding procedures? Ayer argues that statistical or quantitative data must yield conclusions which are both consistent with previous hypothesis, as well as satisfy the demands of common sense.

However, those who defend *Verstehen* do so on the assumption that the operation of *understanding* yields knowledge which the natural scientist ignores altogether. The question we must ask is not about the nature of the contents of such privileged knowledge, but rather, about the sense it makes to say that the knowledge which I have when I know "*x*," is qualitatively different from the knowledge which I have when I understand "*x*"?

Consider the following passage:

---

[13] Abel, *op. cit.*

Faced by the insecurity of a changing and hostile world, we seek security by creating "eternal verity" in our thoughts. The more inadequate we feel, the more we indulge in this type of wishful thinking. Conversely, the clergy has always complained, in times of prosperity and security, man tends to neglect his Gods. It has been suggested that the Platonic preference for the changeless may be due to the fact that the Greeks did not have a mathematical technique such as the calculus for dealing with modes and rates of change.[14]

Lundberg appears to be alleging that certain relevant relations obtain between events or conditions occurring in the external world (a changing and hostile world) and events or conditions which are indications about one's disposition toward a "hostile and changing world" i.e. a verbal response expressing a belief in eternal verities. If one had no statistical examples, on what basis can one assume definite relations of concomitance between such states as those cited? Obviously, it is possible to establish a statistical basis and thereby accumulate evidence to substantiate the validity of an hypothesis which asserts a disposition of men to become idealist philosophers in times of insecurity and change. In the first instance, where sufficient evidence is lacking and the validity of a proposition stating the relation between external events cannot be substantiated in a fashion analogous to the way in which we ordinarily substantiate propositions in science, the *Verstehen* theorist does not *know* that such relations do in fact obtain, but he allegedly *understands* the connection asserted by the generalization. To the question, why understand on insufficient grounds, where statistical concomitance is lacking, what can be *known,* with some degree of certainty once the process of controlled inference is introduced and utilized, the *Verstehen* theorist replies, that social phenomenon must be understood in terms of "meaningful" categories of human experience where the causal-functional approach of physical science is not applicable. Thus, the external connection between events (between a chaotic world and idealist philosophies) is "meaningfully" explained when each is interpreted as an expression of certain *psychical* or *motivational* states. To do so involves an intimate process of internalization of the events to be considered and a referral of these events to relevance within one's own experience. If the investigator cannot empathize, imagine, or identify elements in his own

[14] Lundberg, "Thought Ways of Contemporary Knowledge," *American Sociological Review,* Vol. I (1936), p. 703.

experience with the data to be *understood* he is incapable of adequately explaining the phenomena. The assumptions which underlie the hypothesis of *Verstehen,* which are not themselves self-certifying assumptions assert that agents participating in some social phenomena are in some psychological state; and that there obtain certain relevant relations between such states and certain overt behaviors. The question which remains is simply, "Do we understand social phenomena with greater certitude and adequacy than we understand or know physical phenomena?"

Professor Ernst Nagel puts the question this way: "Do we understand more clearly and know with greater certainty why an insult tends to produce anger, than why a rainbow is produced when the sun's rays strike raindrops at a certain angle?" The question for him is rhetorical, for the obvious answer is, "No!" He argues that the technique for arriving at generalizations regarding the behavior of individuals is the same one utilized in arriving at similar conclusions in the physical sciences. Attitudes are, thus, according to Nagel, merely a descriptive name for propensities on the part of individuals and communities to exhibit determinate behavioral forms in the presence of an appropriate stimulus. The *Verstehen* theorist conceives of attitudes as a psychical state, a condition of the consciousness which must be elicited through the implementation of a certain method. The knowledge derived from this method is thought to be qualitatively superior than that possible through statistical analysis. It is sufficient to say that when we characterize people by mental predicates we clearly go beyond what we see them do and hear them say, but this "going beyond" is not going beyond in the sense of making inferences to occult causes.

Professor Gilbert Ryle asked the question in a slightly different way: "What is the difference between merely witnessing a performance and understanding what is witnessed?" Our question is, "Does the natural scientist merely witness a performance in contrast to the social scientist who understands a performance?" Is the difference between the two procedures one of hearing what a person says and the other of making sense of what he says? Is the function of the *behaviorist psychologist,* for example, merely to note what he has heard, that is, register a verbal report, as compared to the social scientist whose object is to *understand,* in the sense of making sense of a verbal report?

But the *Verstehen* theorist wishes to go beyond the mere event. What is involved is (1) the hearing of noise, a response, (2) determining the origin of the noise, stimulus, and, when this is possible, introjecting both the stimulus and the response. (The noise must admittedly be intimately associated with social behavior, the roar of a crowd, a cry of pain.) The social scientist has (1) been a member of a roaring crowd, (2) been in pain and cried out; or (1) can imagine what it can be like to be a member of a roaring crowd, (2) can imagine what it would be like to be in pain and cry out. He is then capable of *understanding* the event of "hearing noise." How does this differ in the first instance from the physical scientist? The answer is of course that it does not differ at all.

The assumption underlying the aforegoing argument appears to come about as a result of thinking that what one can participate in is subject to a greater understanding than that which can only be an independent object of perception. The assumption is that we live through our own experiences, and in doing so become aware of them. But we also participate, along with others in social processes, and in doing this are able to grasp the situation, not only from our own point of view, but from theirs. By identifying ourselves with them, we come to feel what they feel, or at any rate, to think their thoughts. And this applies not only for present social situations in which we are actually participating, but also for the past which we can, as historians, relive or re-enact for ourselves, thereby achieving a vicarious participation. Since it is by participation in the social process that we are said to gain this knowledge, it may be quite properly spoken of as internal knowledge, to contrast with the knowledge that could be gained by a spectator looking on it from outside.[15]

This passage makes clear the difficulties involved in this assumption.

Let us start with the simple idea that we gain knowledge of things by participating in them. The anthropologist, for example, who goes to live with a primitive tribe is said to understand its customs in a way that would be impossible if he merely paid a visit and took notes. Someone who lives in a country is said to understand its political institutions in a way which is closed to the foreigner.

There is no doubt that in many ways it makes perfectly good sense to say things like this. The man to ask is the man who has the inside knowledge. But when we say it, we do not mean to suggest that the man with the inside knowledge has evidence for his conclusions which are different in kind from that of others. What we mean is that he is in a peculiarly favourable position

[15] Gibson, *op. cit.*, p. 50.

to accumulate evidence. Unless the anthropologist becomes accepted by the members of the tribe, there are many things he will not hear about. Unless he is in a position to observe the daily round of inconspicuous activities he will not have the material from which to infer beliefs and attitudes. In this respect he is like the pilot, who has an understanding of the shoals and channels in an estuary which is not possessed by the visiting ship's captain. The pilot would not be said to be participating in the currents and the tides, simply because we do not speak of participation unless the contact is a social one. But while we recognize that there is a difference between social contact and contact with inanimate objects, it does not follow from this that knowledge gained through making social contacts is knowledge gained in a peculiar way.

We may bring this out further by pointing to the fact that closeness of social contact is sometimes considered a disadvantage for a social enquirer. It puts him in a peculiarly favourable position to accumulate evidence, but it also puts him into a position in which his conclusions are more likely to be affected by his interests and emotions. Again it may prevent him from taking the broader view—that is, from making use of evidence derived from various other sources. This weighing of advantages and disadvantages would seem quite unreasonable if man on the inside had a separate special kind of evidence available to him which was inaccessible to others.[16]

Another dimension of the *Verstehen* argument is the claim that the kind of participation described by the *Verstehen* theorists is a requirement, in the sense of being a necessary condition for understanding the meaning of human actions. Consider Gibson's counterargument:

What is said about "participation" may be said also about the idea of people's observed movements having meaning. In all kinds of diagnosis, we speak of an observed condition having meaning if it indicates the presence . . . of something else. Spots on the skin have a meaning—they mean measles. Shells dug up in an inland desert have a meaning—they mean the earlier existence of an inland sea. Similarly, your smile has a meaning—it means that you are feeling pleased. In this last case the something else is a state of mind, and that is the difference. Talking about the meaning of people's movements does not suggest that the way of ascertaining its presence is not the same as the way of ascertaining the meaning of anything else.[17]

Moreover, the notion of imagination identification with the historical figure as a condition of understanding the psychic contents of the figure in question runs into certain other difficulties. It is clear that we cannot

---

[16] *Ibid.*, pp. 51–52.

[17] *Ibid.*, p. 52.

use our imagination in any way we like. In the final analysis the requirement that we put ourselves in someone else's position in order to find out what they are feeling assumes the availability of certain kinds of empirical data. If it is at all a reliable guide, it must be one despite the fact that we are encouraged, naïvely, to overlook the differences between ourselves and others and to make an assumption which may well be unwarranted to the effect that everyone reacts to a given situation in the same way in which one particular individual might. Consider for example:

> If I were simply to put myself into Napoleon's place, I would imagine myself reacting in ways very different from those in which I know he did. In order to correct this I would have to draw on my already acquired knowledge of Napoleon's character. . . . The thing is not merely to imagine myself in another's *situation,* but to imagine myself being another *person.* This requires that evidence is not merely information about how he has acted in a great variety of other circumstances. Identification, therefore, is an ideal which it will be difficult to achieve. In attempting it we will certainly not gain that complete and immediate knowledge which was demanded by the critic of abstractions.[18]

There is a further assumption which the *Verstehen* theorists must make and which cannot always be granted with ease, namely, that the people with whom we are supposed to identify are in fact acting rationally. Acting rationally may mean nothing more than being the sort of person who changes his mind in the face of evidence which does not support his beliefs, and who will in the final analysis choose means to ends which are the best under the circumstances. Such a procedure does not provide us with a special way of making contact with the thoughts of others. For we cannot escape the responsibility of producing empirical evidence to support our belief that the act in which the actor is engaged is rational and secondly that he recognizes it as such and is not merely acting from ignorance or prejudice.

The lesson of this discussion is that the social scientist so far as he is concerned with the formulation of propositions which may function as proper objects of knowledge must adhere, and does in fact adhere, to the traditional and conventional canons of any science, namely, that propositions must ultimately depend upon observable data, that they must

---

[18] *Ibid.,* p. 53.

conform to that data, and that propositions or allegations asserted independent of supporting data are not sufficient as such to warrant our assent.

The problem of values

To this point in our discussion, we have been interested principally in those respects in which the social sciences, and by implication political science itself, are comprised of disciplines whose object is knowledge. We have concentrated on a demonstration of the proposition that the scientific method appropriate to social inquiry is not significantly different on logical grounds from the methodology appropriate to the physical sciences. The grounds on which people have on occasion argued that the social sciences are in fact significantly different usually fall into two groupings. First, the views of those who claim that the social sciences must be concerned with the unique and particular and that such concern saves them from the distortion of a science which depends heavily upon the formulation of general statements, has been examined at some length. The second sort of argument revolves around the fact that social inquiry appears to be concerned almost wholly with the facts of social life whereas those who are generally interested in social problems are concerned not so much with facts as with values. That social science ought to be as much concerned with what people ought to do as they are with what people in fact do, is after all a claim which most people are likely to make and not without some justification.

It is worthwhile recalling that the conventional orthodoxy current in political science is that there is, in theory, a distinct bifurcation between matters of fact and matters of value, and that any argument consisting of premises which are matters of fact cannot yield a conclusion which asserts a matter of value and, conversely, that any argument consisting of premises which are statements of value cannot yield a conclusion which is a statement of fact. This hard-headed view is clearly expressed in the following passage:

> Positivists see no way of establishing what ought to be by asserting what is. They see no way of verifying normative statements by empirical methods. They see no logical way of proceeding from the realm of fact to the realm of value. From their point of view, values or conceptions of the desirable stem,

openly at least, from will and emotion, and they are thus volitional rather than being dictated by empiricism or logic. Thus, . . . values must be regarded as self-justifying; they are simply postulated.[19]

It goes without saying that this is the simpler approach to the matter, since it simply asserts the logical heterogeneity of statements of fact on the one hand and statements of value on the other. The distinction in question comes about when we take into account what it is that we are after. Social science, like science in general, must have as proper objects of knowledge certain propositions which can be confirmed with reference to experience. Propositions then, which are neither logical in character (analytic) nor empirical, that is to say verifiable with reference to experience, must be excluded from the class of statements which can count as being true or false. The problem of the social scientist is that if one of the conditions of his being a scientist is that he excludes such statements, it would appear that part of the task of social inquiry in general is closed to him.

When the distinction between facts and values is made as the positivists make it, then the precise sort of analysis offered of ethical statements doesn't matter very much. We are told only that such statements are *ipso facto* without sense, and therefore have no place in any inquiry which purports to be scientific. Part of the positivists' task however is to justify the distinction.

Consider the analysis of judgments of value offered by A. J. Ayer:

We shall set ourselves to show that insofar as statements of value are significant, they are ordinary "scientific" statements; and that insofar as they are not scientific, they are not in a literal sense significant, but are simply expressions of emotion which can be neither true nor false.

We begin by admitting that the fundamental ethical concepts are unanalyzable, inasmuch as there is no criterion by which one can test the validity of the judgments in which they occur. So far we are in agreement with the absolutists. But, unlike the absolutists, we are able to give an explanation of this fact about ethical concepts. We say that the reason why they are unanalyzable is that they are mere pseudo-concepts. The presence of an ethical symbol in a proposition adds nothing to its factual content. Thus if I say to someone, "you acted wrongly in stealing that money," I am not stating anything more than if I had simply said, "you stole that money." In adding

---

[19] Vernon VanDyke, *Political Science: A Philosophical Analysis* (Stanford University Press, 1960), p. 9.

that this action is wrong, I am not making any further statement about it. I am simply evincing my moral disapproval of it. It is as if I said, "You stole that money" in a peculiar tone of horror, or written of it with the addition of some special exclamation mark. The tone, or the exclamation mark, adds nothing to the literal meaning of the sentence. It merely serves to show that the expression of it is attended by certain feelings in the speaker.

If now I generalize my previous statement and say, "Stealing money is wrong," I produce a sentence which has no factual meaning—that is, expresses no proposition which can be either true or false. It is as if I had written "Stealing money!!"—where the shape and thickness of the exclamation marks show, by a suitable convention, that a special sort of moral disapproval is the feeling which is being expressed. It is clear that there is nothing said here which can be true or false. Another man may disagree with me about the wrongness of stealing, in the sense that he may not have the same feelings about stealing as I have, and he may quarrel with me on account of my moral sentiments. But he cannot, strictly speaking, contradict me. For in saying that a certain type of action is right or wrong, I am not making any factual statement, not even a statement about my own state of mind. I am merely expressing certain moral sentiments. And the man who is ostensibly contradicting me is merely expressing his moral sentiments. So that there is plainly no sense in asking which of us is in the right, when neither of us is asserting a genuine proposition.[20]

It is plain to see that though this view may be acceptable in the physical sciences, it does in fact present problems in social inquiry. As Professor Morris R. Cohen observes: "We cannot disregard all questions of what is socially desirable without missing the significance of many social facts."[21]

Before we turn to an examination of those theories which are clearly incompatible with the strict distinction drawn by the logical positivist between statements which assert matters of fact and statements which assert matters of value, let us pay some attention to those theories which, though they may be compatible with the positivist assertion about the heterogeneity of such statements, may nonetheless offer a different analysis of value judgments, such that some role or other is provided for them within the class of meaningful statements.

---

[20] Ayer, *Language, Truth and Logic* (New York: Dover Publications, Inc., 1936), pp. 102–3.

[21] Cohen, *Reason and Nature* (Kegan, Paul, Trench, Trubner & Co., 1931), Bk. 3, chap. 1, section 1, p. 343.

To begin with, there is the simple observation that moral beliefs, no matter what sort of analysis is thought to be appropriate to them, affect action and behavior. It is a simple fact that when people believe that some state of affairs is good or that there is some value to be achieved in some goal or other, any explanation of their conduct would have to take such beliefs into account in precisely the same way that factual beliefs are taken into account. Indeed, it may be argued, that such moral beliefs are to be treated in the same way that facts are treated since it is simply a fact that some people have acted in accordance with moral beliefs. Thus, explanations in the social sciences often take into account, if they are to offer adequate explanations of social behavior, what has been called "value-laden" goals, in terms of which sense may be made out of behavior. Yet it ought to be clear that taking such values into account as facts of social life and social behavior does in no way imply that these provide the occasion on which the social scientist may provide value judgments of his own. Consider Max Weber's statements on just this issue:

> The fact that one investigates the influence of certain ethical or religious convictions on an economic life and estimates it to be large under certain circumstances does not, for instance, imply the necessity of sharing or even esteeming those casually very significant convictions. On the contrary, I am most emphatically opposed to the view that a realistic "science of ethics," i.e., the analysis of the influence which the ethical evaluations of a group of people have on their other conditions of life and of the influence which the latter, in their turn, exert on the former, can produce an "ethic" which will be able to say anything about what *should* happen.[22]

Weber's position is simply that a complete account of human affairs must take value-oriented goals as part of that account and treat these in the same way in which any other facts may be treated. By the same token, though this position is wholly compatible with positivism, it does not meet the requirements of those who would argue that the social scientist must in some way be prepared to treat certain words like "good" and "right" as referring to empirically discoverable features of social life. Moreover, it differs somewhat from emotivism in the sense that it does not treat the assertions made by persons in a social or political context

---

[22] Max Weber, "The Meaning of 'Ethical Neutrality,'" *The Methodology of the Social Sciences* (Glencoe, Ill.: Free Press, 1949), p. 13.

where these assertions ascribe values merely as utterances which denote the actor's attitude and nothing more. As Gibson puts the point: "There is a persistent feeling that when we use these words the expressing of attitudes and the stating of empirical facts of certain kind does not exhaust our meaning. When people say, for example, that liberty is a good thing, or that men ought all to be treated equally, it seems that they usually claim to be saying something about liberty and equality, not merely approving of them or recommending them."[23]

Secondly, it is possible to juxtapose another view of how we are to deal with the problem of values with the positivists' position. Consider for example an ethics which construes straightforward value judgments as abbreviations for statements which are in fact verifiable in the way in which a prediction may be said to be verifiable. Thus the expression "X is good" or, "You ought to do X," may be construed as meaning "I predict that *X* will be found good for the purpose of obtaining end *Y* under conditions Z." This prediction can be tested in the same way as any other prediction; we are simply advised to try *X* as a policy and see what will happen. The point of course is that when one says "*X* is good," or "You ought to do *X*," what one is saying is that if you wish to attain *Y* then the means to that goal may well be policy *X* and it is therefore good for some purpose. Obviously, *X* as a policy has an instrumental rather than an intrinsic value. Consequently, though we may see how the social scientist is entirely justified in making recommendations of this sort, and may be in a better position to do so than the layman when confronted with circumstances which involve his own expertise *qua* social scientist, the "ought" which occurs in the statements which prescribe policies is used in a way which is clearly different than the "ought" in the statement which prescribes the ends to be sought. Perhaps the following will clarify the problem somewhat:

Suppose the proposition is made that the independence of a state should be preserved. Obviously, the statement could designate either an end or a means. If it designates a means, however, there must be an assumption that the preservation of the independence of the state would serve an end, e.g. the welfare of the inhabitants. Thus, the full thought requires two statements. The first would be that the welfare of the people is the end to be postulated. The second would be that the welfare of the people will more probably be

[23] Gibson, *op. cit.*, pp. 62–63.

promoted by preserving the independence of the state than by abandoning it in favor of any available alternative status. Now the first of these statements is obviously normative, and the second asserts a finding of fact—a descriptive finding.[24]

Certainly no one would want to deny that prescriptive statements of the instrumental sort have a place in the vocabulary of the social scientist. The difficulty with the argument of course is that these are not strictly speaking prescriptions of moral value. They are predictions which may be treated as any other sort of prediction.

A third analysis is less of an argument than it is a matter of calling to the attention of the positivist a rather important fact about the way in which the descriptive language works, or, about some of the assumptions which the positivist is forced to make about a descriptive language which may not be altogether tenable. One of the characteristics of the language of physical science is that it is a specialized one in which terms are defined in such a way as to remove the ambiguities generally encountered in ordinary discourse. And although the social scientist, particularly is sociology, has made considerable progress towards the development of highly specialized languages, the fact of the matter is that in most of the descriptions of social life encountered in political science, for example, the language used is generally encrusted with the rich and undifferentiated fabric of meanings encountered in our ordinary language. We have already noted, in previous discussions, that words like "democracy," "freedom," and "equality," are, in fact, value laden, and despite the fact that they may appear to denote a state of affairs and function therefore in a purely descriptive way, such an impression is clearly incompatible with the facts of the case. For if it is true that there is a value content to these concepts, then their use as descriptive words is limited.

Though this charge appears to be, on the face of it, a serious one and suggests a variety of problems for the social scientist who wishes to adhere to the canons of objectivity and evidence demanded by the logical positivist, it is in fact a relatively minor issue. It can be dealt with by pointing out that the very allegation that such value-laden concepts, appear to be inextricably part of the fabric of our ordinary discourse, rests

---

[24] VanDyke, *op. cit.*, p. 11.

upon the acknowledged possibility that one can discern those contexts in which the word is used descriptively and those contexts in which it is used either tacitly or explicitly to convery a sentiment or induce an attitude or influence conduct through moral persuasion. Thus, though there may be many concepts which may function descriptively as well as prescriptively (though in an implicit way) the fact that we can often determine the way in which the concept is being used in a particular context is a fact which merely serves to warn the social scientist that he must exercise considerable caution in the use of the such concepts.

A fourth view, a somewhat more sophisticated one than the preceding, stands in direct contrast to the logical positivists position. It maintains that the distinction between fact and value assumed by the positivist is untenable when purposive human behavior is being analyzed, since in this context value judgments enter inextricably into what appear to be factual statements. Accordingly, those who subscribe to the thesis claim that an ethically neutral social science is in principle impossible, and not simply that it is difficult to attain.

The view in question is forcefully expressed by Professor Leo Strauss who writes as follows:

> Would one not laugh out of court a man who claimed to have written a sociology of art but who actually had written a sociology of trash? The sociologist of religion must distinguish between phenomena which have a religious character and phenomena which are irreligious. To be able to do this, he must understand what religion is. . . . Such understanding enables and forces him to distinguish between genuine and spurious religion, between higher and lower religions; those religions are higher in which the specifically religious motivations are effective to a higher degree. . . . The sociologist of religion cannot help noting the difference between those who try to gain it by a change of heart. Can he see this difference without seeing at the same time the difference between a mercenary and non-mercenary attitude?
>
> The prohibition against value judgment in social science would lead to the consequence that we are permitted to give a strictly factual description of the overt act that can be observed in concentration camps, and perhaps an equally factual analysis of the motivations of the actors concerned: we would not be permitted to speak of cruelty. Every reader of such a description who is not completely stupid would, of course, see that the actions described are cruel. The factual description would, in truth, be a better satire. What claimed to be a straightforward report would be an unusually circumlocutory report. . . . Can one say anything relevant on public opinion polls . . . without realizing

the fact that many answers to the questionnaires are given by unintelligent, uninformed, deceitful and irrational people, and that not a few questions are formulated by people of the same caliber—can one say anything relevant about public opinion polls without committing one value judgment after another?[25]

Professor Strauss' critique is directed against Max Weber's effort to provide the foundations for what he calls a value-free social science: "What is really at issue is the intrinsically simple demand that the investigator and teacher should keep unconditionally separate the establishment of empirical facts (including the 'value oriented' conduct of the empirical individual whom he is investigating) and his own practical evaluation, i.e. his evaluations of these facts as satisfactory or unsatisfactory (including among these facts evaluations made by the empirical persons who are the objects of the investigation)."[26]

What Weber means by "empirical facts" refers to that which is ordinarily taken to be the object of any given science, whether the science is sociologically or physically oriented. The "value oriented" conduct of those individuals who comprise the object of social science is an empirical fact only so far as an analysis of their conduct is an empirical procedure. These empirical facts are logically different than statements about these facts which are themselves not statements of facts. But statements are taken to be judgments about facts and as such include that class of statements which assert judgments about judgments. Hence, just as it is scientifically correct to assert that "*X* is the case" or "*X* has the property *P* and *Q*," it is equally correct to say "*X* consistent with certain cultural values strives to acquire *Y*." It is not, however, scientifically legitimate to assert e.g., that "*X* is good" or that, "It is desirable that *X* drives to acquire *Y*" or that "It is desirable that *X* thinks that it is good to strive for *Y*." Thus, it is within the province of the social scientist to examine the behavior of empirical individuals where that behavior has a "relevance to values"; that is, behavior which is directed toward the acquisition of certain values, or behavior which occurs with reference to certain values.

Moreover, the phenomena which comprise the objects of social in-

[25] Leo Strauss, "The Social Science of Max Weber," *Measure,* Vol. 2 (1951), pp. 211–14; cf. Nagel, *op. cit.,* p. 491.

[26] Weber, *op. cit.,* p. 11.

quiry and which serve to distinguish a social science from other scientific disciplines, are further defined in terms of value relevance. The facts of social existence are to be selected in accordance with certain values through which the social scientist may emerge from a brawling confusion of undifferentiated empirical data. As we have already indicated, the historian, e.g. is generally concerned with 5th century rather than 15th century Greece and analogously, the chemist is concerned with the chemical constituents of soya bean and the potentialities of soya bean and breadmaking rather than the chemical properties of a bagel.

Weber writes, "It should only be recalled, that the expression 'relevance to value' refers simply to the philosophical interpretation of the specifically scientific 'interest' which determines the selection of the given subject matter and the problem of an empirical analysis."[27] Clearly, the reference to value which serves to characterize the social sciences does not logically require value judgments or valuations of the subject matter selected. Weber is quite unambiguous on this point: the causal relations or statistical concomitance which comprise the data of a social science, contingent, as it were on the demands of a hypothesis which is itself a reflection of given cultural values, are not themselves subject to value judgments.

Secondly, Weber emphasizes a point which we have discussed in connection with policy making and prescriptive judgments which may be illuminated if we consider a familiar discussion in Plato's *Republic* which may serve to enlighten this issue. Plato argues, in his analogy of a ship of state, that the art of politics is analogous to the skill of the navigator of a vessel. The parable presupposes a distinction between knowledge and skill or between knowing *that* and knowing *how*.[28] The knowledge of navigation and the knowledge of routes by which particular destinations can most quickly and safely be reached together form an indispensable part of the equipment of the navigator, but he must also know how to make use of the knowledge at his disposal. Analogously the statesman's qualifications will consist of both science and skill, of theoretical knowledge and the ability to apply it in practice. There is, however, what may be perceived as being a fatal limitation to this analogy; a

[27] *Ibid.*, p. 2.

[28] On the distinction between knowing *that* and knowing *how* see Gilbert Ryle, *Concept of Mind* (New York: Barnes and Noble, 1955), p. 28.

limitation which will clarify one of Weber's points. Plato errs when he draws a parallel between a governor's choice of a policy and a navigator's setting of a course. The true analogy is between the choices of a policy by a politician and the choice of a destination by the owner or passengers of a ship. The point is one of the relations which obtain between ends and means. Plato represents a question about what is to be done (as an end) as if it were like a question about what is to be done (as a means) in order to achieve some given or agreed end. It is precisely this obscurity on the part of Plato, which points up Weber's lucidity on a similar concept. Commonly postulated practical goals are, for Weber, not facts in the ordinary sense, but rather "a priori ends." So far as the social sciences are concerned with means for given ends, to that extent are they responsible for understanding those ends. But understanding clearly does not mean acceptance or rejection. The central problem revolves around the choice of ends, rather than of means. In what sense can the evaluation (i.e., the ends), which the individual asserts be treated not as a fact but as the object of scientific criticism?

In Weber's view it is not sufficient merely to assert that an evaluation is uttered. The utterance is meaningful only if the conditions under which the evaluation is made can be specified. So far as the evaluation is susceptible to empirical analysis with respect to the individual social conditions of their emergence and continued existence, these conditions can never, under any circumstances, lead to anything other than an "understanding explanation." The understanding of these ends, however, serve to demonstrate that the real "significance of a discussion of evaluation lies in its contribution to the understanding of what one's opponent or one's self really means, i.e., in understanding the evaluations which really and not merely allegedly separate the discussants and consequently in enabling one to take up a position with reference to this value."[29] But the position which is thus taken up is no more nor less legitimate than another. The object of the social scientist is to clarify the conflict and to elicit implications; but more to the point, to investigate the procedures initiated by empirical individuals directed toward the acquisition of cultural, as opposed to individual, goals, and the behavior manifested in certain determinate ways in accordance with these values.

---

[29] Weber, *op. cit.*, p. 14.

The values may and do change, and to the extent that they change, so do the sciences (so far as the scientist is himself an empirical individual) but *the factual content* which is comprised of the behavior of individuals in accordance with the system of culturally accepted values, does not change, at least insofar as men have consistently held certain values in all cultures and in all epochs. It does not follow, however, from the recognition that some values appear to be universal that all are, nor is it possible to conclude that those which may have been universally maintained are in fact valid. "Genuine" values, so far as universally valid values are concerned, are not merely practically unfeasible but theoretically impossible.

Now it is against this view, expressed by Weber, that Strauss' arguments are directed. Strauss believes that to accept the Weberian thesis necessarily leads to nihilism, "or to the view that every preference, however evil, base or insane has to be judged before the tribunal of reason to be as legitimate as any other preference."[30] The object of the following discussion is to evaluate Strauss' charge that a value-free social science is neither a science nor even a possible enterprise.

Weber, argues Strauss, in considering the prospects of Western civilization saw the following alternatives: either a spiritual renewal or else "mechanized petrifaction," i.e., the extinction of every human possibility except that of "specialists without spirit or vision and voluptuaries without heart." Weber concluded: "But by making this statement we enter the province of judgments of value and faith with which this truly historical presentation shall not be burdened." It is absurd, writes Strauss, to conclude that it is not proper for the historian or social scientist "that he truthfully describe a certain type of life as spiritually empty or describe specialists without vision and voluptuaries without heart as what they are."

In the first place it is perfectly clear that Weber is certainly not *describing* anything of the sort when he speculates about the future of civilization. Similarly, such speculations are logically different from predictions. For the most part, we are inclined to use the word "speculate" or "prophesize" for situations where a prediction cannot be made.

Strauss asks, "Is it not the plain duty of the social scientist truthfully

---

[30] Strauss, *Natural Right and History* (University of Chicago Press), p. 42.

and faithfully to present social phenomena?" Indeed, truthfulness and a faithful rendering of social phenomena is at least one of the functions of the social scientist. But what would Strauss have us describe truthfully and faithfully? Surely not a social condition which does not exist. But suppose, for a moment, the question were one of considering the truth of the proposition "there are specialists without spirit or vision and voluptuaries without heart." So far as the truth of the statement is determined by its manner of verification, through what procedures would Strauss have us verify the statement? It is clear that there is no method in any science which can come to terms with phrases of the sort which occur in the example. This is not, however, to say that Weber is a bad scientist and can do no more than phrase predictions in a poetic or metaphoric mood; which brings us to the second point. Strauss asks, "Do we not know petrifraction or spiritual emptiness when we see it? And if someone is incapable of seeing phenomena of this kind, is he not disqualified by this very fact from being the social scientist, just as much as a blind man is disqualified from being an analyst of paintings?"[31]

Precisely what sort of phenomenon "spiritual emptiness" would be is difficult to say. The issue in question however concerned the legitimacy of considering such questions, that is to say, loosely formulated judgments, as proper objects of theoretical concern. Weber, in reflecting on matters of future contingency is clearly not offering a prediction and thus not operating at the level of a scientist. Yet it appears to be that Strauss is at fault in failing to distinguish between Weber as social scientist and Weber as social commentator.

Yet if we return to the paragraph first quoted from Strauss' critique of Weber, it is clear that it is Strauss' contention that one cannot function as a social scientist without indeed functioning as a social commentator. And this is so, he thinks, because without such valuations the complete picture of social and political arrangements cannot be offered, and therefore, the social scientist cannot give a complete description of whatever it is he is trying to describe. If we examine more closely the allegation that Weber, or any social scientist, who fails to make judgments cannot in fact distinguish between genuine and spurious religion, for example, the question which interests us in this connection is this: to what extent are

---

[31] *Ibid.*, p. 50.

such issues matters of fact and to what extent matters of evaluation? It is, of course, a truism to say that the sociologist of religion must distinguish between religious and nonreligious phenomenon. But is it the case that to do so he must know what *religion* is? To know what religion is implies knowing the essence of religion, or knowing what is common to all religions; i.e., knowing a standard or criterion by virtue of which a religious experience may be differentiated from other varieties of experiences. But this may be the very problem the solution to which the social scientist directs his observations. The distinction which Strauss passes over is one between knowing what religion is and knowing what a religion is. This is however saying little more than some forms of knowledge are contingent upon prior experiences and this, it would appear, is merely a truism. Furthermore, arguing, as Strauss does, that understanding what religion is enables and forces the social scientist to distinguish between genuine and spurious religion is a *non sequitur*. For in knowing what a religion is, there is no logical force calling for a decision between genuine and spurious religions; in knowing what religion is in the sense of knowing the essence of religious experience or phenomena, it is possible to make such a judgment, but it is not logically necessary to do so. Moreover, although it may not be logically compelling to make such a judgment, it may be psychologically compelling to distinguish between more or less desirable religious manifestations, but to draw such normative distinctions is to be making a value judgment rather than offering a description, and it is difficult to see how when such judgments are made the description is in any way enriched or, in fact, even altered.

We must, nevertheless, be prepared to grant that there are situations in which the social scientist does in fact make judgments even in terms of such amorphous matters as higher and lower forms of religious experience. For example, Strauss does speak of "sublime religious thought" and "pure sorcery." When he does so, the distinctions are at least subject to empirical verification. It is not an empirically empty question as to the level of cultural attainment of a society which cannot distinguish between sexual orgies and prayer. But even in such a case, a judgment is not warranted unless it can be demonstrated that the sexual content of religious manifestation is an impurity; it is far from clear how one would go about demonstrating the legitimacy of the claim since religion by its very character does not admit to demonstrations of that sort. It is nevertheless both legitimate and correct for the social scientist to note the fundamental incongruity between what men divine when they speak of their gods and what they actually practice; further, it is possible to distinguish between levels of consistency in the verbal behavior of performances. It is not correct, nor acceptable to judge such acts as good or bad.

Recall for a moment the passage quoted from Strauss which reads as follows:

> The prohibition against value judgments in social science would lead to the consequence that we are permitted to give a strictly factual description of the overt acts that can be observed in the concentration camps and perhaps an equally factual analysis of the motivation of the actors concerned: we would not be permitted to speak of cruelty. Every reader of such a description who is not completely stupid would, of course, see that the actions described are cruel. The factual description would, in truth, be a bitter satire. . . . The whole procedure reminds one of a childish game in which you lose if you pronounce certain words, to the use of which you are constantly incited by your playmates.[32]

The whole procedure is of course a game, at least in the sense that there are rules which govern the use of the language games of the social scientist. Yet it is a game with considerably greater significance than the games of children. In the way in which the physicist who talks a "physical object" language when his playmates talk in "energy" language, is talking technical nonsense, to that extent does the social scientist make a mistake when he confuses levels of language. A description of events occurring under certain determinate conditions is assuredly not prevented from including among these descriptions statements which testify to cruel actions. First, although such a characterization may not be warranted by the facts, the statement makes perfectly good sense if asserted in the mood of the social scientist as socially sensitive observer. Yet, secondly, the statement of that sort could be asserted within the framework of the science. A report statement, for example, by a former inmate, to the effect that certain treatment afforded prisoners was cruel, is an empirical fact which warrants the same treatment of any other fact. In some cases it is possible to describe objectively the state of affairs about

[32] *Ibid.*

which a judgment of sorts is admissible. So far as it is admissible it is no longer a judgment in Weber's usage since "judgment" is stipulatively rather than lexically defined. It can be an empirical fact whether people behave intelligently or stupidly, honestly or deceitfully, rationally or irrationally, once a determinate usage, i.e., meaning, is given to those terms. Without such definitional determinations, the levels of language, i.e., the concepts of each language game, become confused and vague and no longer serve scientific purposes.

Strauss offers another argument which is in some way similar to the argument which we have been considering. He writes as follows:

> The rejection of value judgments endangers historical objectivity. In the first place, it prevents one from calling a spade a spade. In the second place, it endangers that kind of objectivity which legitimately requires the objectivity of interpretation. The historian who takes for granted that objective value judgments are impossible cannot take very seriously that thought of the past which was based on the assumption that objective value judgments are possible, i.e., particularly all thought of earlier generations.[33]

This observation on the part of Strauss is not, on the face of it, a condemnation of history which denies the validity of objective value judgment, but rather a commentary on the alleged limitations of all histories. For if the historian "who takes for granted that objective value judgments are impossible cannot take very seriously" past thought which is based on a contrary assumption, then it follows that historians who assert that value judgments are objective will not take seriously past thought which was based on the assumption that only subjective value judgments are possible. Since every history presupposes either an objective or subjective position with respect to value judgments, every history is faced with the same paradox, thus the criticism carries no more weight against Weber's position than it does against Strauss' or anyone else's for that matter.

Moreover, if Strauss is correct in alleging that the historian who takes for granted the impossibility of value judgments cannot take seriously past thought which is based on the assumption that value judgments are possible, then one is entitled to ask for clarification of the grounds on which Strauss makes this statement. Obviously, in making the distinc-

---

[33] *Ibid.*, p. 62.

tion between objective and subjective judgments of value, one can himself not be committed to both. Yet it is clear to us that if one is committed to the view that there are objective judgments of value possible in history, then, according to Strauss, one can say nothing about subjective value judgments and conversely, if one is committed to the view that there are subjective value judgments possible in history and that these are the only judgments possible, then he can say nothing of objective value judgments. Thus, Professor Strauss is either asserting a specious judgment about the possibility of subjective value judgment or, if he is seriously maintaining the distinction, he is asserting a self-contradictory statement.

There remains one further argument put forward by Professor Strauss against Max Weber, the clarification of which is instructive to us. Professor Strauss tacitly implies that the methodological scheme proposed by Weber does not itself satisfy the requirements of the scheme. That is to say, the prescriptive language which is used in the articulation of the scientific method, according to Weber, is itself not warranted by the method. This is a common sort of criticism and the student has often encountered it if only at a rather trivial level, as for example, in the expression "all general statements are false." The statement in question is of course a general statement. Perhaps the point in question may be more adequately demonstrated with reference to another context. One estimates a statement of fact with reference to the conditions under which it was formed, then one's own statement must be estimated with reference to its own conditioning factors, and this entails a further statement which must also be thus estimated. If it is true, the argument goes, that whatever is said is the product of certain social and political circumstances then having said this must itself be the product of certain social and political circumstances and so, for any clarifactory statement. Analogously, the statements which describe a method of analyzing social phenomena must either themselves fulfill the conditions prescribed by the method or appeal to another statement of method the terms of which must be understood in that methodology. If that is not possible an infinite regress ensues.

Some years ago, Bertrand Russell introduced to the philosophical world a proposed solution widely accepted and known as the *Theory of Types*. The *Theory of Types* holds that the truth value of a class of statements which are not themselves a member of that class is determined by a criterion other than the criterion in terms of which the truth value of the statements within that class is determined. Hence, the statements which Weber asserts about the nature of method are not of the same logical class-type as those which the method delimits, and thus Strauss' criticism about the prescriptive character of Weber's statement of the method is itself a violation of that method, is not to the point.

VALUE AND REASON

We have been engaged in a lengthy and perhaps tedious discussion of the possibility of establishing social science upon the same broad firm foundations upon which the physical sciences appear to be established. It has not been an easy matter to perceive why it should be necessary to do so, or, indeed, why there have been outspoken protagonists for the view that a social science which emulates the methods and assumptions of the physical sciences is bound to be sterile and perhaps even brutalizing. The dispute is obviously one which goes deep into the intellectual roots of the Western tradition. It is not our purpose to offer an intellectual history of the West in order to answer such questions. There are really in a sense two quite different issues here. On the one hand, there are those who are determined to argue that we can do no less than try to understand human behavior and social conduct in precisely the same way that we have come to understand, to whatever degree we have been successful, the physical universe. Yet there is an inescapable part of our experience in history which shows us clearly that we have been far more successful in understanding the movements of bodies in space or the chemical constituents of organic entities than we have in understanding human behavior, motivation, and value.

For after all there is a sense in which we would like to agree with both Strauss and Nagel. On the one hand, we feel it encumbent upon ourselves as human beings to assert that some forms of human and social behavior are contemptible or admirable, and yet on the other, we recognize the necessity of separating such judgments from the purely descriptive language which we are inclined to think is a necessary prerequisite to scientific inquiry.

In the final analysis, we may simply be forced to acknowledge that both tasks are necessary if we are to understand human behavior on the one hand and human aspiration on the other. But we may also be forced to acknowledge that what is required to answer these two questions are two different sorts of disciplines. The social scientist so far as he is a scientist must adhere to the canons of his discipline. Yet such adherence must not be construed as moral or ethical neutrality with regard to all aspects of life. A scientist is also a father, a husband, a citizen, a member of the Elks club, a lover, a voter, and a tennis player. He is obliged, as we are all obliged, to follow the rules of whatever activity or role in which he finds himself engaged. No man is a scientist all of the time. The real issue is not simply the role which a value system plays in the life of individuals, or indeed that there are certain areas of human activity where appraisal statements are inappropriate, but rather it is a question of what we think values are and of how they come about.

If it could be shown to be true that what is right and good are objects of knowledge in the same way in which propositions about the hardness of diamonds or mathematical statements may be shown to be proper objects of knowledge, the difficulties we have encountered would not be difficulties at all. If for example Plato were correct in supposing that there are eternal verities which could be known to us with the same precision and with comparable degrees of certainty in the moral sciences as they may be known in the physical sciences, the problem of values would not be a problem. Regrettable as it may seem, whatever else values may be they are far more elusive than the facts discoverable by the physical scientist. What we *ought* to do, therefore, what kinds of lives we ought to lead, what sort of men we ought to be, what kinds of institutions we ought to have, in short, what is the good life, are questions which cannot be answered simply on the basis of what we know to be true about the physical or social world; though, they cannot be answered without reference to what we know to be true about the social and physical world. The point is that though we cannot have secure confidence in answers to questions about values, it does not necessarily follow, as some have supposed, that we can have no answers at all.

If we are not prepared to assert that values are somehow built into the nature of things, or derivable from sacred texts or the commands of God, neither are we prepared to assert that values are no different than prejudices and preferences. Can we discover a middle way, a middle ground between complete relativism and subjectivism on the one hand, and the objectivity about moral issues which issue from doctrines which are metaphysical or theological in character?

The answer of course is that we must. We cannot rest content, either psychologically or on logical grounds, with the alternatives offered to us. What might the character of this middle ground be?

Though we have learned to be skeptical about the aphorism often repeated in the history of political thought to the effect that man is a rational animal, and though it is exceedingly difficult to understand the meaning of the aphorism, it is nonetheless the principle upon which our commitment to the possibility of meaningful value statements must rest. Whatever else may be involved in saying that men are rational (and, indeed, that they ought to be so), part of what is involved is the notion that it is possible to give reasons for, or to justify the beliefs, attitudes, and ideals, in accordance with which they organize their lives. It is of course not to say that men are always rational or even that they ought always to be rational, but merely that they are capable of acting rationally and that they do on occasion act rationally. Surely no one would want to deny the characterization. But what has this to do with matters of value?

Let us recall for a moment the writings of those who deny that there are such things as ethical judgments or value judgments, or at least deny that such judgments may be made meaningfully. They argue that such judgments are mere expressions of approbation or disapprobation, that they express nothing more than an exclamation point which functions in an autobiographical way. That is to say it informs one that the speaker or writer when he uses the word "good" is telling us about his own feelings. It is the positivists' contention that those occasions when two protagonists disagree about the facts the argument may be resolved with reference to those facts. This is presumably the way in which rationality manifests itself. Thus, if you and I disagree about the name of the city which serves as the capital of northern Nigeria the disagreement may be resolved by checking out the answer in our geography book. Once I have shown you that the map indicates that Kaduna and not Kano is the correct response the matter is presumably settled if you are a rational person. Should you however continue to insist that you are correct and that both I and the geographer are wrong we would look for further evidence to prove or disprove either contention. Should you insist in the face of overwhelming evidence that your position is the correct one and continue to do so, then it would be correct to say that you are not behaving rationally about the matter.

But in matters of value, where an ethical judgment is the source of contention, there is no geography book or map or specialist to whom we may turn in an effort to settle the matter. And it is precisely this point that the positivists' analysis appears to be unsatisfactory. We may indeed find that there is no further room for argument when we have reached a premise or axiom which one person denies and the other affirms. The argument can go no further. Yet, the difference of opinion has not vanished. If the argument ceases, it is not because, or need not be because the argument is resolved. A difference of opinion remains and if the arguing continues, it is not clear what one is trying to prove. Clearly, I am not arguing to prove that I approve of the given act nor are you arguing to prove that you dislike the act. For I do not doubt that I like the act nor do you doubt that you dislike it. What we are attempting to do in this process is to convince each other that in the final analysis my approval of the act is justified and your disapproval of it is not and of course vice versa. We are in fact saying that the act in question has a character, and we are educing reasons on behalf of that allegation, such that it deserves to be done or liked or approved of.

It is when ethical disputes are construed in this way that we may understand how the question of rationality arises. For it is after all possible to provide reasons for an act being good or desirable and to justify the position one takes in matters of that sort in a rational way.[34]

Perhaps we may consider two extreme possibilities which come about as the result of the later development of ethics when we enter upon the stage of moral obligation entailed by living in society.

The second course is to encourage criticism, and to modify the code in institutions: to assert their absolute authority, to legislate for every possibility, to isolate the community from outside influences, to discourage independent speculation in the airing of grievances, and to provide a communal aim which the citizens must like—or lump.

---

[34] Sir David Ross, *The Foundations of Ethics* (Clarendon Press, 1939), pp. 38–41.

The second course is to encourage criticism, and to modify the code in institutions, wherever it is reasonable to believe that, by a possible change, unnecessary strains could be removed and new opportunities created or exploited; in fact, so to organize the institutions of the society that they develop naturally in this way taking into account every citizen's aims and grievances.[35]

Given these two types of development, admittedly extreme possibilities, how is it possible to say that one is more rational than another? How, that is, is it possible to justify by an appeal to reason, an open vis-à-vis a closed society.

The first type of development cannot be justified by any appeal to reason, for it is the outcome of mutually contradictory desires in the rulers. They want to insist on the citizen's fulfilling absolutely a set of "moral obligations" towards them, which, at the same time, they want to be excused from respecting towards the citizens—thus presenting in the guise of "morality" a collection of privileges without foundation in ethics.

The second course, on the other hand, is in line with the natural development of ethics. It is in the nature of ethics that changes in the moral code should have as their goal a self-developing, "open" society—a society in which individuals are free, and encouraged, to make their own moral decisions—rather than the tribal, tyrannical and collectivist, "closed" society.[36]

At least part of the point in this discussion is that a belief about what is best may be justified by an appeal to reason and found satisfactory if it is in accordance with facts and if it is not at variance with the rules of logic. Thus an inconsistent demand on the part of rulers and their consequent insistence about a policy or a set of moral principles which reflect those inconsistencies are in effect irrational and therefore beyond justification. Can we apply this criterion of rationality to an historical event?

Suppose we consider the events in Nazi Germany, particularly with regard to the racial policies pursued by the Nazi government. Those who wish to say that it is natural and desirable to condemn the Nazis on account of their behavior toward people whom they considered to be racially inferior do so on the grounds that the systematic annihilation of millions of people is incompatible with all those values which men have

---

[35] Stephen Toulman, *Reason in Ethics* (Cambridge University Press, 1960), p. 171.

[36] *Ibid.*, p. 171.

in the past prescribed for themselves. Or, perhaps, that such barbaric conduct is a violation of the law of nature and the dictates of right reason. Yet, no matter how we may sympathize with these sentiments, they constitute a rhetorical rather than a rational set of locutions.

The contemptible and irrational dimension of the Third Reich's racial doctrines stemmed from the fact that racial superiority is a false proposition, that it was known to be false by those who propounded it, and that it was used to justify conduct which could not be justified were it not for the false principles in question. Indeed, if it were in fact true that Jews, Gypsies, Slavs, and Mediterranean peoples generally were of an inferior racial type, if it could be demonstrated that they were in fact less than human, then the reprehensible character of the conduct of the Nazis toward these people would have to be modified. If non-Arians could be shown on empirical grounds to be no different than rabbits or mice in a laboratory, would we not then judge the Nazis' conduct towards these people differently?

The moral judgments which we make and which we attempt to justify on rational grounds must be entirely compatible with the facts of the matter. To intentionally propagate a doctrine which is completely at variance with what we know to be true, to intentionally mislead, distort, to defeat reason altogether, is to commit the most grotesque of atrocities.

Index

This book has been set in 11 point Fairfield, leaded 3 points, and 10 point Fairfield, leaded 2 points. Chapter numbers and chapter titles are in 24 point Spartan Medium. The size of the type page is 27 x 44½ picas.